A Quiet Peace

*Keep
coming
Back = STAY!*
5/31/17
P.C - 905-242-7606

Daily Meditations
from the Fellowship of
Cocaine Anonymous

385-826-5175

Gisele Bella Duval
Face Book:
613-741-9385

i

Copyright © 2014 All rights reserved.
Cocaine Anonymous World Services, Inc.
Second Edition 2015

Printed in the United States of America.

Library of Congress Cataloging-in-Publication (CIP) Data
A Quiet Peace
Daily Meditations from the Fellowship of Cocaine Anonymous

Library of Congress Catalog No. 2014906525

ISBN 978-0-578-13315-7

Cocaine Anonymous, C.A. and "We're Here and We're Free"
are registered trademarks of Cocaine Anonymous World
Services, Inc.

Twelve Steps and Twelve Traditions reprinted with adaptation
by permission of A.A. World Services, Inc.

Cocaine Anonymous World Services, Inc.
P. O. Box 492000
Los Angeles, CA 90049-8000 USA
www.ca.org
e-mail: cawso@ca.org

A Quiet Peace

**Daily Meditations
from the Fellowship of
Cocaine Anonymous**

**Cocaine Anonymous World Services, Inc.
Long Beach, California USA
2014**

To the addict who still suffers and to those seeking to improve their conscious contact with God *as they understand Him.*

PREFACE

Cocaine Anonymous was formed in November of 1982, when several recovering addicts met and established the first C.A. Group. At the spiritual center of Cocaine Anonymous is a message of hope, faith, and courage. C.A. is a spiritual program, not a religious one. With its all-inclusive Third Tradition and First Step, Cocaine Anonymous welcomes anyone with a drug or alcohol problem and offers a solution.

During 2001-2002, Cocaine Anonymous conducted a book survey, resulting in an overwhelming request for a daily meditation book. In 2003, the process began, and members were asked to submit their original compositions for a brand-new C.A. publication.

Submissions were received from the worldwide Fellowship of Cocaine Anonymous over the next several years. Additional materials were harvested from C.A.'s previous publications and service archives. Each element was carefully reviewed, edited, and ultimately compiled into the book you hold in your hands: *A Quiet Peace, Daily Meditations from the Fellowship of Cocaine Anonymous.*

Over the course of assembling this book, those involved were humbled by a sudden realization. With God's help, encouraging words were taking shape to help recovering addicts, *some of whom haven't even been born yet!*

We hope every reader will find solace and comfort from these meditations. May you know serenity and experience a quiet peace.

TABLE OF CONTENTS

x

INTRODUCTION

We invite you to peruse the first meditation book from the Fellowship of Cocaine Anonymous. This book consists of 366 inspirational readings about living free from cocaine and all other mind-altering substances. It offers daily thoughts, insights, prayers, and personal meditations for sustaining a clean and sober life, one day at a time. Each reading begins with a quote, followed by a meditative narrative, closing with a contemplative thought or prayer. The narratives were written by both men and women, members from around the world of varying ages and lengths of sobriety. Their voices and experiences are vastly different except that they are all addicts who have found a solution in recovery. Wherever you may be in your journey, we encourage you to relate to the feelings and spiritual principles being shared.

For easy reference, a title index (Appendix A) alphabetically lists all 366 page headings. We have also identified the subject matter within each daily meditation, assembling these into a detailed master topic index (Appendix B). Appendices C, D & E list C.A.'s Twelve Steps, Twelve Traditions, and Twelve Concepts.

This book may be used any number of different ways. Possibilities include:

- As a daily practice, by reading the applicable page for today's date, meditating on its meaning, and then seeking to bring that meaning into your life;
- As a basis for reflection, meditation, or journaling on a specific topic;
- As a starting point for discussion in a meeting, other group setting, or between sponsor and sponsee;
- As inspiration for a wider reading of other C.A. literature (please see Appendix F for additional information about Cocaine Anonymous).

In whatever manner you wish to use *A Quiet Peace*, we hope you will find its contents relevant and enlightening. Welcome the Higher Power of your understanding into the experience, and you may be astounded at the revelations you receive.

JANUARY

WHAT BROUGHT ME HERE

Ultimately, in despair, I called the Cocaine Anonymous hotline. I was sure it wouldn't work for me, but I had no one else to call.
Hope, Faith & Courage, *page 36*

When I found Cocaine Anonymous, I learned that addiction is a progressive illness, one that is chronic and potentially fatal. I was relieved to be told that addiction is not simply a moral problem, but rather a true illness over which the will alone is usually powerless. All the same, I must take responsibility for my own recovery. There is no secret, no magic. I have to quit and stay sober, but I don't have to do it alone.

Newcomers are welcomed to C.A. with more genuine warmth and acceptance than you can imagine—for newcomers are the lifeblood of the program. In great part, it is by carrying the message of recovery to others like myself that I keep my own sobriety. I help myself by helping others.

~~~~~

I pray that I will be able to join the Fellowship and not attempt recovery alone. May I continually be empowered to take responsibility for my actions, helping myself by reaching out to others.

PHYSICAL ALLERGY - MENTAL OBSESSION

> *. . . the body of the alcoholic is quite as abnormal as his mind.*
> Alcoholics Anonymous, 4th Edition, *page xxvi*

In Step One, I learned what an addict and/or alcoholic really is. I learned about the physical allergy—I looked back over my life and realized that normal people don't drink/use so much that they pass out in parking lots or in people's bathrooms on a regular basis. When I drank/used, it was for the effect it gave me. Whenever I picked up, I could never successfully predict when I would stop. I could intend to only have one drink or one line, but that rarely ever happened. I usually drank and used until it was gone! I learned also about the mental obsession—how I would promise myself and anyone who would listen that I wasn't going to drink or use again, and then someone would offer me a line or something similar, and I would be off and running. For the longest time I had doubts that I was really an addict/alcoholic. I kept hearing the war stories in meetings and could not relate. I did not go to prison; I didn't lose my home, job, or my kids.

However, when I looked back over my life and saw my own clear experiences with both the physical allergy and the mental obsession, I could finally admit to my innermost self that I was an addict and an alcoholic. It didn't matter how or what I used or drank, or what my bottom was or wasn't. My desire to stop using cocaine and all other mind-altering substances earned me a seat in C.A.

~~~~~

I pray I remain aware of both facets of my disease, the physical allergy and the mental obsession. May I remember, without fail, the cunning, baffling, and powerful nature of addiction.

GOD IS EVERYTHING

> *. . . we had to fearlessly face the proposition that*
> *either God is everything or else He is nothing.*
> Alcoholics Anonymous, *page 53*

My sobriety is dependent on my recognition that God is everything. Each day, I talk to God (pray) and listen to God (meditate) in order to keep my life on track.

I can pray in the car, at the gym, before a meeting, or any time during the day when I feel uncertain or disturbed. Especially important for me is praying on my knees in the morning to start my day off right. There I discover humility.

I can meditate anytime I have a second to pause. All I have to do is ask, "God, what would you have me do?" Then I stop and listen to that small voice in my heart. Taking more time (half an hour works well), closing my eyes, calming my body, and *really* listening to God—this is where I find true direction.

God is always present, always willing to assist with simple guidance. God is everywhere, in everything. This knowledge leads to continuous sobriety, comfort, gratitude, and love.

~~~~~

I know my sobriety is contingent on my connection with my Higher Power. I now understand, "What seemed at first a flimsy reed, has proved to be the loving and powerful hand of God." (*Alcoholics Anonymous,* page 28.)

ILLUSION OF CONTROL

*. . . we who now freely admit that we are cocaine addicts thought
that we could control cocaine when in fact it was controlling us.*
To the Newcomer (C.A. Pamphlet)

It took me years of futile attempts to use successfully, to control the amount I
used, and finally, to try to stop on my own willpower—each time failing miserably.
I was so relieved when someone finally explained to me that I have an abnormal
reaction to all mind-altering substances. This allowed me to stop fighting and
surrender fully to the program of Cocaine Anonymous. This, to me, is the heart of
Step One. I no longer had the insane idea that I could control the amount of drugs
I used, freeing me to work the next eleven Steps. As the result of a thorough
effort, I have recovered from the hopeless state of mind and body that is addiction.
I no longer need using to change the way I feel because I actually *like* the way I feel
today!

~~~~

Do I fully understand that I cannot stop using of my own accord—that any attempt
to "manage" my usage is pointless? The Twelve Steps are the hammer I need to
shatter my old illusions of control.

SURRENDER

And we have ceased fighting anything or anyone—even alcohol.
Alcoholics Anonymous, *page 84*

After my third relapse, things changed in a big way. When I read the above quote, I was actually able to *digest* what I read . . . and finally got it! The meaning was so much broader than the struggle with alcohol and drugs. My real battle was, and had always been, with my "self": self-knowledge, self-perception, self-indulgence, self-will, self-reliance, self-control. I realized that I had to totally let go of "self" in every form it had manifested in the past.

Before C.A., my "self-everything" was how I had managed to survive and succeed throughout my life. I had drawn from this reservoir successfully—up to a certain point. When I became willing enough to stop clashing with God, He blessed me with the awareness of how my old instincts/survival methods were no longer beneficial. The progression of my disease had rendered self-propulsion useless.

I began to feel God's grace in my life and embraced total surrender, recognizing, acknowledging, and accepting all the ways in which I was still fighting God and my powerlessness. Many of the slogans abruptly became meaningful, facilitating a turning point in my recovery. I was finally able to pause and ask for direction instead of succumbing to old thinking/behavior patterns. I was now ready to follow God's dictates.

~~~~~

I will remember that I no longer have to fight to survive. I can pray for the knowledge of God's will and then wait for His direction. I will stop fighting and start following.

WHAT HAPPENED?

> *When I came crawling back it was because I knew that if I didn't stop, I would die—plain and simple. The members of C.A. welcomed me home with hugs and understanding.*
> Hope, Faith & Courage, *page 56*

My first sponsor relapsed at eight years sober. Although I was terribly upset when I heard the news, I knew immediately what had happened. She quit going to meetings. Starting her own business took a lot of time—sobriety lost its priority. To this day, I don't know if she ever made it back.

Of all the relapsers I ever encountered who managed to return to tell their tale (sadly, not all made it back), the answer to the question, "What happened?" was always the same: with some variation, their sobriety lost its priority.

Recovery brings dramatic life changes. It's easy to start slacking off. As we begin to feel healthier emotionally, physically and spiritually, our memories of the bloody-awful existence of an active drug addict can and often do fade. My sponsor's experience scared me *closer* to C.A. than ever. Well into my third decade of sobriety, I *still* attend five meetings a week on a regular basis as a result of this early lesson.

Please latch on to this chance to recover and do not relapse. Cling to the program. Work the Steps. Be of service. Surround yourself with our Fellowship. Give away what was given to you so freely. And don't ever get so spiritual that you can't be real. It just might kill you if you do.

~~~~~

Our disease wants to hypnotize us into believing we can safely walk over the cliff lying up ahead. The Twelve-Step way of life is our anti-hypnosis shield of armor. I pray that I will always remember my early lessons found in recovery, that I can rely on those lessons in making choices to enhance and ensure my continued sobriety.

USING THE BASICS

If you want to be clean and sober, you can be. If you want what we have, you can have it. No matter how much cocaine you have used or how low you have sunk, you can get away and stay away from cocaine, by doing what we have done.

Tools of Recovery (C.A. Pamphlet)

Enjoying life without the use of drugs, I have a personal relationship with my Higher Power that I choose to call God. I begin my morning with Him, humbly giving thanks for all the good *and* bad He allows me to experience. I try to give Him my *all* each day, whether things are going well or not. At night, I again express gratitude for my life, no matter how the day transpired.

My sponsor helps me apply the Steps to every circumstance. By attending at least four meetings a week, I stay very close to people in recovery. Between meetings, I use the phone to say connected.

I am doing better than I've *ever* done before, and I do what I've been taught by sharing all of this with someone just like me. That's how it's supposed be!

I never have to use again as long as I follow these basics. Today, I have peace of mind and serenity—doing the right thing feels good.

It works *only* if I work it. This program is not for the ones who *need* it, but for the ones who *do* the work. That's me! And I hope to stay on this journey for the rest of my life—one day at a time!

~~~~

The basics have taken me far, and I am nothing but grateful for the insights and solutions I have received as a result.

I CAN

> *It can be tempting to focus on our differences rather than our similarities, but this can blind us to potential sources of support in our recovery. As we hear other members' stories, the most important question to ask ourselves is not, "Would I have partied with these people?" but rather, "Do these people have a solution that can help me stay sober?" We encourage you to stick around and listen with an open mind.*
> Who is a C.A. Member? (C.A. Meeting Format Reading)

When I first entered treatment and encountered a Cocaine Anonymous meeting, I thought it wasn't for me. I didn't like cocaine and certainly didn't consider myself a cocaine addict.

As I gained some experience in recovery and my clean time started adding up, I quickly discovered that no matter what drug or drugs I did, or whether I even drank alcohol, it was all the same. The disease we have is not curable, nor will our minds ever be free from the obsession without practicing a program of recovery. My sobriety is based on abstinence from ALL mind-altering substances, which C.A.'s First Step so beautifully covers. C.A.'s warm and welcoming principle of 'non-exclusivity' is a shining example of acceptance, tolerance, and love.

The people I meet in meetings and their shared stories carry the message to me. They are the reason why I am alive today.

~~~~~

When we say we *can't,* we undermine our sobriety. Believing that we *can* helps keep us clean. I pray that all who have a desire to stop using cocaine and all other mind-altering substances have the opportunity to find C.A. May I remain active in the Fellowship in order to share the Twelve-Step gifts with others still suffering who have not yet found these rooms.

WHO'S AN ADDICT? I AM!

> *But eventually we had to face facts. We had to admit that cocaine was a serious problem in our lives, that we were addicts.*
> To the Newcomer (C.A. Pamphlet)

I found myself sitting in a Cocaine Anonymous meeting for the first time. I had nine months of sobriety. It was a small meeting. As the only newcomer that night, I was asked to read a portion of the pamphlet *To the Newcomer*, entitled *Who is a Cocaine Addict?* By the time I had finished reading, a few things happened. The first was a feeling of uneasiness. The reading took me back to a time when I had experienced most of what is described in the text. The next feeling was an awesome sense of relief. Finally, I experienced a feeling of safety in knowing I was in the right place and that the others in the room shared a common history with me. Even more importantly, these people offered a solution.

Every newcomer is a constant reminder of the experience, strength, and hope I've found in Cocaine Anonymous. Today I believe God led me into that meeting that night. He has continued to guide me through each day as I trudge the road of happy destiny.

~~~~

Knowing a solution is available and that I belong in a group of other addicts searching for similar relief is a very special, humbling feeling.

...AND ALL OTHER MIND-ALTERING SUBSTANCES

Cocaine Anonymous' First Step is viewed by our Fellowship as a 'blanket' First Step because all types of drug users are welcome as long as they have the desire to stop using.
Hope, Faith & Courage, *page 193*

I am an active and passionate member of Cocaine Anonymous—a member who hardly ever used cocaine. Other mind-altering substances brought me to my knees. Yet after years of hopeless addiction, I found the solution to both my drug and life problems in C.A. I love that the C.A. message of recovery is inclusive, not exclusive. The First Step tells me that we are powerless over cocaine *and all other mind-altering substances.* Coupled with the Third Tradition ("The only requirement for C.A. membership is a desire to stop using . . ."), I understand that *everyone* is welcome in this Fellowship. I believe the Fifth Tradition's primary purpose of carrying the message includes ensuring that all who seek recovery are greeted with open arms.

~~~~~

Do I carry C.A.'s complete message? Am I free from judgment about whatever brought you here? No matter how differently our diseases manifest, the solution is always the same.

HOPE, FAITH AND COURAGE

> It occurred to me that when many of us walk through the
> doors of Cocaine Anonymous for the first time, we do so
> without hope, without faith, but with an ounce of courage.
> Hope, Faith & Courage, pages xxviii-xxix

These three words are so descriptive for the process of recovery. Hope is all I had to hold onto in the first thirty days. I just hoped you all were telling me the truth—that I could live without cocaine and all other mind-altering substances just as you were doing. My faith in God and the program hadn't started to develop yet. As time went on, my faith began to build through hindsight. I'd make it through various experiences, and things were just falling into place. I was able to recognize God's hand in all of it, which led to new circumstances not being so scary. I could see God had helped me up until that point; why would He drop me thereafter? There were also times when the C.A. message of hope carried me through later Step work and beyond.

I've heard it said in the rooms that you can't have fear and faith at the same time. To me, that just simply isn't true. In the space between fear and faith, I believe, lies the definition of courage. Courage is the ability to face your fear in times of uncertainty. We can be scared about an outcome, but courage lets us face it and then walk through it anyway. Even though we're afraid, we have faith that God will see us through.

~~~~~

Do I see where the hand of God has carried me through? Will I continue to face the tough situations in my life with hope and courage, knowing that God will always be there? Do I believe that if I do so, great events will come to me and I will receive exactly the lessons God intends for me at that moment?

A NEW SENSE OF HOPE

> . . . people at this meeting said that they had been as helpless and
> hopeless as I was, and that it was okay to admit that I needed help.
> Even better, these people said that if I asked for help, they could
> share with me the same solution that had worked for them. When I
> heard this message, a glimmer of hope was kindled inside of me.
>
> C.A. NewsGram, 2nd Quarter 1999

I still remember my first C.A. meeting. I went because my best friend needed help,
even though I was pretty sure no Twelve-Step program could help me. Spiritually, I
felt dead inside. It had been such a long time since I had felt any sense of hope. On
the rare occasions that I allowed my mind to dwell on my situation, I was
convinced that I would drink and use until I died a miserable death.

What I remember most about that first meeting was I heard people talking about
surrender. You see, for so long I had been putting every ounce of energy left in my
body into trying to convince everyone (including myself) that I was just fine, thank
you. The truth was that I hadn't been anywhere near fine in a long, long time. As I
continued to go to meetings and to take direction, this flicker of hope was fanned
into a full-blown flame. Thanks to Cocaine Anonymous, I have now been clean and
sober for many years. I have truly been transformed from a Hopeless Dope Fiend
into a Dopeless Hope Fiend!

~~~~~

Hope eventually permeated my entire program, given enough time, work, and
attendance at meetings. I have so much hope for the future, and with that hope
comes faith.

LEARNING AND GROWING

As long as you are willing, your belief will grow. You will learn through your own experience and the experiences of others . . .
A Higher Power (C.A. Pamphlet)

Having been around these rooms for a few 24 hours, I sometimes wonder why the material never gets old. I've seen large rooms and small rooms, full and empty, here and there—and everyone is talking about the same things.

Today, I am beginning to understand it doesn't become tiresome because with each lesson learned, I realize even more growth lies ahead. By opening my eyes, I see all that is yet to be explored. Like my image in a room full of mirrors, the further I look, the more I behold my infinite journey. Today, walking that path is exciting—forks in the road are common, and it matters little that no end is in sight. I feel comfortably guided by my Higher Power, taking time to breathe the air and enjoy the scenery. The expedition is filled with peace and serenity.

~~~~~

God, as I travel life's path, many chances to stray from my lessons occur. Please continue to show me the way, little by little, as I can understand it. I may need You to repeat Yourself a few times, but I suppose You are used to that!

WE CAN RECOVER TOGETHER

The best way to reach someone is to speak to them on a common level. The members of C.A. are all recovering addicts who maintain their individual sobriety by working with others. We come from various social, ethnic, economic and religious backgrounds, but what we have in common is addiction.

What is C.A.? (C.A. Pamphlet)

We are all here for the same reason—our inability to stop using cocaine and all other mind-altering substances. The first step towards solving any problem is admitting that there *is* a problem.

The problem, as we see it, consists of an obsession of the mind and an allergy of the body. The obsession is a continued and irresistible thought of cocaine and the next high. The allergy creates an absolute inability to stop using once we begin.

We wish to assure you that there *is* a solution and that recovery *is* possible. It begins with abstinence and continues with practicing the Twelve Steps of recovery, one day at a time. Our program, the Twelve Steps of Cocaine Anonymous, is the means by which we move from the problem of drug addiction to the solution of recovery.

~~~~~

I pray that I can readily and continually admit I have a problem with cocaine and all other mind-altering substances. I pray that on my path of recovery, I seek to understand both the obsession of the mind and the allergy of the body. May I seek and find the solution of recovery on an ongoing basis.

ENTIRE PSYCHIC CHANGE

> . . . and unless this person can experience an entire
> psychic change there is very little hope of his recovery.
> Alcoholics Anonymous, 4th Edition, page xxix

When I read Dr. Silkworth's letter, this sentence jumped out and grabbed me. What exactly, I wondered, constituted an "entire psychic change"? Perhaps it meant I had to change everything about myself, such as the music, books, and movies I liked—even the clothes I wore.

Thankfully, I was way off. My sponsor shared with me that a psychic change was simply a transformation in my thinking; but I was still at a loss about how to get started. If the disease was centered in the mind, I was certain my thought process was defective beyond repair. "Hold on," my sponsor continued, "You can't *think* your way into a psychic change, you have to *live* your way into one." I soon discovered the only thing needing to change was my perception, and that the world doesn't actually change—just my view of it!

~~~~~

Though I can't always control what pops into my head, I can take action to counter those thoughts. If I am angry or intolerant, I practice understanding. By responding to old thinking with a conscious *alternative* viewpoint, my brain begins to learn new habits.

SIMPLICITY

> *. . . there was nothing left for us but to pick up*
> *the simple kit of spiritual tools laid at our feet.*
> Alcoholics Anonymous, *page 25*

Soon after I made it into the rooms of Cocaine Anonymous, I began the process of discovering what was needed to recover from my drug addiction. I spotted the Steps and Traditions on the wall and straight away started dissecting them into a long, complicated list of tasks I would need to complete in order to survive.

Thank God sober people were there who understood the clouded thought process running through my brain. I listened to what they were saying and to their suggestions—things like "get a sponsor," "go to meetings," and "help others."

Soon I found myself sitting down with another addict who was willing to show me what had worked for him. He explained to me that the Twelve Steps we use in C.A. were written for people who were dying on the streets every day. He went on to say that the Steps had to be simple—so simple that we couldn't miss the solution.

This was truly a revelation for me. I found it hard to grasp the simplicity of the Steps, but as soon as I did, my life changed, and I've never looked back.

~~~~~

As an addict, it's very easy for me to complicate everything I do with a lot of unnecessary worry and fuss. Learning to keep it simple—one of our primary slogans—is the most essential key to fully understanding the one-day-at-a-time concept.

PARANOIA

> *As I sat and listened to the readings, I heard what I had experienced in the last months of my using. The paranoia, the carpet picking, and the sense that "they" were out there. Everything seemed to fall into place.*
> Hope, Faith & Courage Volume II, *page 134*

One of the greatest discoveries Cocaine Anonymous afforded me was how others understood the paranoia manifested by this disease. Who else but addicts share that common ground so seemingly unique to addiction?

As a newcomer, even though the drugs were gone, remnants of paranoia still remained. How could I possibly trust these strangers? Surely their friendly overtures masked some suspicious ulterior motives. I couldn't imagine ever being completely rid of the obsessive terror that someone or something was out to get me—that "they" could return at any moment in many new, horrible ways.

As I kept returning to the rooms of C.A., however, I heard lots of stories just like mine—only these people were *laughing* about their paranoid experiences. At first, I didn't understand how this could be. Then, one day, I found myself laughing, too! I suddenly realized not being alone had helped me turn the corner and begin to heal. My paranoia had slowly faded away and was placed into healthy, proper perspective. I was truly on the road to recovery.

~~~~~

Sharing a common bond with someone draws us ever closer—not just to each other, but to understanding ourselves. It also draws us closer to our Higher Power. Who'd have ever thought I would learn more about *me* by listening to others? Hearing how others found true solutions for their deepest fears has freed me from my own paranoia.

PERSONAL RECOVERY DEPENDS ON UNITY

Our common welfare should come first; personal recovery depends upon C.A. unity.
C.A. Tradition One

Having recovered from a baffling malady by virtue of a spiritual experience combined with a loving and understanding Fellowship, I discovered that I had been given a precious gift. That gift has been the ability to connect deeply with other addicts, both those who are still suffering from the despair of active addiction and those who have also recovered. I sense a deep calling to be part of their lives. Recovery in this sense means a freedom from the bondage of self. Any two people gathered together for the purpose of sobriety with no other affiliations can call themselves a C.A. group. Each sacred meeting of one addict with another addict constitutes a group; the very nature of "relationship" implies consideration of the relationship's "common welfare." I've discovered that my continued recovery from the soul-sickness at the root of my addiction requires not only that I be in relationship with others, but that I consciously take actions to convey something meaningful to these relationships.

~~~~

Am I aware today that my very life depends on the unity of C.A.? How can I best be joined in brotherly and harmonious action with my fellow C.A. members? Let me remember I am a small part of the larger whole; simply put, I am another one of God's children.

_____

SERENITY = GOD'S GRACE

> _I see all around me the peace of mind and_
> _serenity of heart that surpasses all understanding._
> Hope, Faith & Courage, _page 31_

Our Fellowship is about more than recovering from addiction. It offers a way of life which, for me, is enjoying serenity when I can and holding onto my seat with both hands when I can't.

When I stay present in the moment without expectations pulling me toward the future or regrets keeping me stuck in the past, I can enjoy sobriety. I experience acceptance when I am able to differentiate between those situations I can change and those I cannot.

The greatest reward of all is in being grateful for having moments of real serenity. I call this God's grace. For too many years I pursued a phantom called pleasure, never realizing what I really wanted was not at all what I was chasing.

Recently, I was sitting in a meeting among friends who have helped me in my recovery. As I looked around the room at faces I've come to know so well, it suddenly occurred to me, I _love_ these folks. In that riveting moment of clarity, I recognized God acting in my life, and understood that I need only remain present to experience it.

~~~~~

Being present in this moment with awareness of my Higher Power is my best safeguard against the inertia of past addiction and the mania of craving awaiting in an uncertain future. Can there be any wonder why our fellows stress that recovery exists in this day, in this hour and in this moment? Where else could it be?

PASSION FOR THE PROGRAM

> . . . *the tools that I have now, the changes, the growth, and my new attitude toward life have continued to amaze me.*
> Hope, Faith & Courage, *page 79*

What are you passionate about? If recovery wasn't the first word that came to your mind, perhaps your program could use a tune-up.

Into my third decade of sobriety, I am just as excited to be clean and sober today as I was when I collected my first sobriety milestone chip at one month. In many ways, I'm even *more* zealous; because today I know how fabulous life can be, if I choose to make it that way. Today I know how having an evolving spiritual connection fills my life with wonder. Today I know how working with a newcomer creates an incomparable warm glow inside my spirit. Today I recognize peace and serenity to be my most valuable assets.

Do I have a life outside of recovery? Absolutely. My other passions include many things—mostly having to do with utilizing my creative energy, but sometimes just as simple as enjoying coffee with a dear friend. The key is my ability to stay in the moment and appreciate whatever is happening around me right at this very second.

~~~~~

Five meetings a week, sponsoring people, and plenty of service work all keep me in the middle of the recovery boat. Continuously seeking improvement of my conscious contact with God fosters ongoing amazement at the daily miracles placed in my path.

I'LL NEVER FORGET

Throughout the years of my recovery, I have continued to be blessed by being able to be of service. This has brought great spiritual rewards and has allowed me to learn and grow as a human being.
Hope, Faith & Courage Volume II, *page 44*

I'll never forget what it felt like to be a newcomer. Perhaps that is because I was a newcomer so many times. I felt so lonely. I didn't know anyone; I just wanted someone to hug me so I could be a part of this happy, new group of people. At the next meeting I attended, I heard someone share about getting out of self and being of service. After the meeting, I stacked chairs, wiped ashtrays, and did that spiritual act of cleaning out the coffeepot. Something strange happened to me! People kept interrupting me to introduce themselves, and they were all hugging me. At this point in my life I needed lots of love; C.A. was there to love me, and for that, I will always remain grateful.

~~~~~

I never know how my service might reach someone, even when I don't know that it has. If I keep carrying the message consistently, others can hear it when they most need it. Service has been a key facet of my recovery, and I hope to always stay involved so as to keep what I have by giving it away.

MY ADDICTIVE BEHAVIOR

My addictive behavior started at a very early age. It didn't seem to matter what it was; if I thought I liked it, I wanted more.
Hope, Faith & Courage Volume II, *page 115*

I had always wondered when I crossed that magical line that separated me from people who did not use or simply could stop using of their own volition. I was always troubled by not knowing why I struggled so much to get recovery—long after I was drug-free in the rooms and working the Steps.

Several years into the program, I heard my behavior characterized in such a way that I marveled at its simplicity and clarity. It was explained to me that my addictive behavior began long before my first drink or drug and ended long after. This has been a huge insight on the two parts of the equation. My addictive behavior was well in place early on, perhaps as a function of my environment, family, parents who needed the rooms, schooling, religious and/or spiritual upbringing, or any combination of this list. The point is that it was already well-embedded in me when I began my tortured spiral of active dependence. Between the established behavior and my ongoing using, I had no chance to escape full-blown addiction.

In a like manner, the behavior didn't cease the day I stopped using. I had a long period of figuring out how to live in my skin, work a program, and function in a seemingly strange, new, very scary world. Further, I had to juggle being in a relationship, being a parent to my kids, and dealing with my family of origin. It was quite hard. Having an awareness that addictive behavior was part of my make-up proved helpful, especially after I stopped using. I had to refocus my recovery and Step work to overcome those behaviors, in addition to simply recovering from my drug abuse.

~~~~~

God, I thank you for the insight of knowing more about my addictive behavior, so that this might help me in my recovery and perhaps assist some still-suffering addict get relief as well. Please help me place my behavior, both before and after I found the rooms, in as healthy a perspective as possible now that I understand how this fits into the equation of my disease.

COME ON IN

The only requirement for C.A. membership is a desire to stop using cocaine and all other mind-altering substances.
C.A. Tradition Three

Before coming to C.A. and while I still suffered the ravages of addiction, I had set up emotional barriers against pretty much everybody and everything in my life. I had been evaluated, classified and categorized by most of the institutions and communities with which I came in contact. Tradition Three allowed C.A. to be a welcoming place for me. I was there because I said I needed to be there. The Fellowship didn't erect complicated entry procedures and requirements for me to cross. Instead, right on the wall, Tradition Three clearly stated the only requirement for membership was simply my own desire to stop using cocaine and all other mind-altering substances.

There are some groups which add additional requirements. These might be men or women-only meetings and others. With these and all kinds of groups, the members acknowledge that they are C.A. members first and remain dedicated to the C.A. primary purpose.

~~~~~

I pray that today I recognize another's desire for membership is not up to my judgment. May I remember to always do my best to make newcomers feel welcome. Help me to be loving and tolerant towards those whose opinions differ from mine. I am grateful that I was welcomed into a Fellowship of people joined together in brotherly and harmonious action.

A SIMPLE SUGGESTION: PRAY

We asked His protection and care with complete abandon.
Alcoholics Anonymous, page 59

I relapsed many times before recovery finally stuck. As much as I desperately wanted to be done using, I couldn't stay stopped. Another member of the Fellowship suggested that prayer might be the way to prevent another relapse.

A simple suggestion. The problem was I truly didn't know how to pray, nor had I been introduced yet to the Third- or Seventh-Step Prayers. The only prayer that came to mind was from the preamble to the Steps from the *Big Book*. It was a prayer I had heard at every meeting.

I got onto my knees and, for the first time in my life, prayed to a God unknown to me and asked for His protection and care. I did this with complete abandon.

That day was the first of many thousands that have followed in which I have been given the grace to live free from the bondage of my addiction. Maybe it was finally bottoming and becoming teachable, or the realization that I had no one else to even remotely help me, nowhere else to go to even try to get sober and clean. Maybe it was my time, my moment of clarity where the grace of my God finally was there for me to see. Whatever it was, I remain humbled by the experience, its power and the hope I have felt ever since that moment.

~~~~~

Today, I will remember to acknowledge God's grace in my life. Once again, I will abandon myself to this Power that I may do His will.

_____

DON'T EVER FORGET

> . . . experience has taught us that a recovering addict will almost
> certainly relapse without the ongoing support of fellow addicts.
> To the Newcomer (C.A. Pamphlet)

Sitting in a meeting that was 90% newcomers, the topic of love and tolerance quickly turned into a newcomer pity party. Many started sharing stories of being victimized by their current living arrangements. My initial thought was that these members desperately need to get some gratitude, and *I* would straighten them out when it was my turn to share.

While waiting, I found myself reminiscing about my first year in C.A. Back then, I was quite lonely. I was slow to come out of my steel shell and terrified to speak up at a meeting. I was working two lousy jobs to pay off probation, riding a bicycle because I had no license, and seeing my children only once a week. I also recalled my loving and patient sponsor, who endured my whiny, stubborn attitude and the painful years it took for me to turn my will and my life over to the care of God. An old adage from back in the day came to mind, as it had before in similar situations: "If you are not a part of the solution, you are part of the problem."

In a moment of clarity, I realized that my intolerance of these newcomers' stories was the direct result of my false pride and desire to feel superior. Today, I want to be part of the solution, and to do so, I must allow God to work through the Fellowship while I continue to practice love and tolerance.

~~~~~

May I never forget what it was like to be a newcomer. Help me to always be a source of support for those who are new to the program. Let me always lovingly share my experience, strength, and hope with them.

BEGINNING MY RECOVERY

*Many of our friends encourage us by saying that this is but
a beginning, only the augury of a much larger future ahead.*
Alcoholics Anonymous, 4th Edition, *page xv*

As the *Big Book* says in Step Nine, and as I truly relate to it from the bottom of my heart, I had 'roared like a tornado' through the lives of those who loved and cared about me, not caring whom I stepped on or whom I hurt, physically, mentally and emotionally. Thank God for the Steps. Today, I am free from the clanking of the prison gates, free from the bondage of self, and free from the abuse. Through baby steps, one amends at a time, I learned how to take responsibility and grow up. I learned to change my thinking and behaviors on a daily basis. Contingent upon my spiritual maintenance, I am able to know who I am and what I am doing here and now. God has me in the palm of His hand, carrying me, one step at a time, giving me what I need instead of what I want. It was time to grow up and take responsibility. One of the things I learned was to sit down, shut up and listen because I was going to die if I didn't. So I did! Every decision in early sobriety was made with my sponsor's help.

I heard in meetings that faith without works is dead, and that I had to work for everything I got! That included change. Nothing was easy, but it was simple, I was told. If I got out of the way and followed some clear-cut directions as outlined in *the Big Book*, I could accomplish whatever goals I set my heart on. One day at a time, keep on, keeping on!

Today I carry the message of hope. That is one of my favorite program principles. The simple words, "God, please help me," started a personal relationship with a Higher Power that I never dreamed possible. Today I am so grateful to C.A. for loving me until I learned how to love myself again. Thank you for carrying the message of hope through the rehabs, detoxes, and prisons I landed in. Thank you for giving me a chance to get my life back! Thank you for allowing me to be of service on the Hospitals & Institutions Committee.

~~~~~

I pray I may always see clearly the nature of my disease and remember the truth about its hopelessness. I have been, and remain, exceedingly grateful to belong to a Fellowship that provides everything I need, when I need it, with love, kindness, and grace. I will continue to do my part to make our Fellowship thrive so we will all continue to have the comfort of calling C.A. our "home."

HEARTFELT ADMISSION

I learned I had to face the truth and admit to myself that I could not use because the allergy I have to mind-altering chemicals does not let me stop once I get started. I also learned I had a mental obsession that never lets me stay stopped whenever I try to stop. If I can't use because of my body and I can't not use because of my mind, then I know I am truly powerless over cocaine and all other mind-altering substances.

Hope, Faith & Courage Volume II, *page 149*

Sometimes in meetings we hear that "I did my Step One work while I was out there using." Our personal drugalog is invaluable when it comes to looking at ourselves and answering some of the initial recovery/addiction-based questions. However, such history falls way short of a *heartfelt* admission of powerlessness and acceptance of an unmanageable life—whether using or clean. *Alcoholics Anonymous* states, when discussing the alcoholic, ". . . the idea that somehow, someday, he will control and enjoy his drinking is the great obsession of every abnormal drinker. The persistence of this illusion is astonishing. Many pursue it into the gates of insanity or death" (page 30). It continues, ". . . we learned that we must fully concede to our innermost selves that we were alcoholics."

When working Step One with my sponsor, I was asked to share my written life story. Afterwards, I was asked to make a list of twenty-five reasons I belonged in the program. Powerlessness and unmanageability were pretty hard to deny when they were staring up at me in black and white on the paper. This Step was vital to learning the deep truths about the effects my addictive behavior had on my life. In this way, I was able to understand Step One.

~~~~

Understanding the obsession of addiction and the need to fully concede the nature of our disease are perhaps the two most important steps of recovery. "The delusion that we are like other people, or presently may be, has to be smashed." (*Alcoholics Anonymous*, page 30.) The *Big Book* provides us with questions to help us determine if we have a problem. The answers are left to us and only us, as no one can determine for another if he/she is an addict.

HARD WORK PAYS OFF

I learned to work the Twelve Steps. This was, and continues to be, hard work.
Hope, Faith & Courage, *page 92*

I never said, "When I grow up, I wanna be a junkie." But that's exactly where I ended up. After years trying unsuccessfully to "fit in," I entered treatment. In love with dope when I started, I soon fell in love with the founders of our program and others on this path.

I learned about a solution to this chaos. I learned about the Twelve Steps, and that I couldn't do it alone. I made a commitment to the recovery program and to God and resolved to claw my way to the top. My faith grew, and I made it through all Twelve Steps. I visualized myself climbing as I worked. And I just keep going up.

I've heard it said: "Stick around until the miracle happens." Well, I did! Even though it wasn't always rainbows and kittens. Even though it took hard work, I just kept coming back. One day, I looked around, and it all made sense (well most of it anyway)!

I would say I'm living a dream, but I've never had dreams as incredible as my life is today. I'm happier than I have ever been. I finally found my miracle.

~~~~~

All the years of misery through which I trudged, God was leading me to this moment. He was showing me my purpose. I am ever grateful for this fact, knowing many, many people never discover what the program can be in their lives.

ALL~INCLUSIVE STEP ONE

At some point we finally realize that we cannot control our use of any mind-altering substances. The problem isn't the drug of choice; the problem is the disease of addiction. With its Third Tradition and all-inclusive First Step, Cocaine Anonymous welcomes anyone with a drug or alcohol problem and offers a solution.
. . . And All Other Mind-Altering Substances (C.A. Pamphlet)

People come to C.A. thinking one of two things: "I rarely (or never) even used cocaine. I don't think I belong here." or "What exactly does the 'and all other mind-altering substances' part mean? I came to C.A. because *cocaine* is a problem in my life."

C.A. members who have been around for a while have heard questions and statements like this before—perhaps these words were even my own. Over time, I realized that my real problem is not cocaine or any specific drug—it is the disease of addiction. Some C.A. members never even used cocaine. Some used a variety of drugs and others combined cocaine with alcohol and/or other drugs which made for miserable lives. Others rode drug roller coasters—drugs to come down with, drugs to boost the lows, drugs to mellow out, and drugs to take the edge off. The list goes on and on.

During those times of attempting to regain control, any substitution or new combination invariably created the same horrible result. It was easy to get started and hard to stop. Experience after experience revealed substitution was no cure. Our bodies had to be absolutely free of drugs and alcohol, as the obsession to use more of something was always lurking. As I reminisce on my using days, I often would substitute any variety of drugs and pills interchangeably. It really did not matter. The point is, an addict is unable to stop using without help.

Once I finally admitted that I had a problem, a spiritual solution became the answer. I finally realized that drugs were never my problem—I had been mistakenly trying to use them for my solution. I finally was able to put aside the old solution and open myself up to God.

~~~~~

The problem is not how or what I used—the problem is that I thought using was the solution. In C.A., I learn about the real solution—a spiritual program of action.

MOMENT OF CLARITY

Step One is the foundation of the entire Twelve-Step process. Without a full understanding of what this Step means to us personally, we can't expect to make much progress on the other eleven Steps.
A Guide to the 12 Steps (C.A. Pamphlet)

In a moment of clarity, I was slapped with a sudden realization of who I had become! In that instant, the gut-wrenching truth lifted the burden of denial, and the fight was over. It wasn't about losing everything all around me yet again, but discovering that my unmanageability came from within.

Finally accepting myself as an addict and fully acknowledging my disease, I was able to set eyes on and understand the pathway to freedom. Nothing short of complete surrender enables me to continually work the remaining eleven Steps.

~~~~

What a blessed relief to uncover and believe the broad truth about my powerlessness. When in contact with newcomers, I find it vitally important to share my First Step experience, that they may also discover the truth about themselves.

I BEGAN TO HAVE HOPE

It was a brief moment of clarity, followed by an opportunity. A public service announcement came on TV stating, "If you have a problem with cocaine, call Cocaine Anonymous. We can help." I wrote down the number. I believe that moment was necessary for me to take that first step into the rooms of recovery. From what I've observed, the window of opportunity and willingness is often brief, and if I had not acted upon it immediately, it may have snapped shut. I went to my first C.A. meeting the next day.

Hope, Faith & Courage Volume II, *page 79*

When I entered treatment, I met a counselor. One day, he came, sat with me, quietly at first, and then just started talking to me. I was scared and had built impenetrable walls around myself, but hearing his stories helped me to start opening up. I wanted to hear more. I had major trust issues. This man was well-dressed and obviously educated—just the sort of person I usually classified as a "phony"—but somehow I believed he wanted to help me and was speaking the truth, even when he said he'd been clean and sober in recovery consecutively for the past fifteen years. I could feel myself smiling involuntarily.

That very moment, my own recovery changed. I began to feel something I had been searching for in pipes and bottles before I found sobriety. For the first time, I began to have hope. I haven't had a drink or a drug since then. Having recovered from a hopeless state of mind and body, I love myself and am proud of the person I've become. After I got out of treatment, my counselor became a mentor and a good friend. We continued to meet once a month for several years, discussing how things were going for me and how my recovery was progressing. I still see him, occasionally, at the same treatment center when I go back to speak to new patients just getting sober.

After all that I have learned from C.A., meeting with my sponsor, and working the Twelve Steps of recovery, I find doing Hospitals & Institutions work, one-on-one with another addict or alcoholic, is definitely the most rewarding part of my program. I have now sat on the other side of my recovery-changing conversation many, many times. Watching someone get that amazing glint of hope in their eyes, perhaps for the first time in their life, is the most precious gift I could possibly receive.

~~~~~

My wish is for every addict to have such an experience, understanding recovery is possible. I pray that I will welcome the message of hope when I first hear it, always remaining mindful of that key C.A. message. May I then share the message of hope with others still suffering so they might find recovery. I will always welcome the chance to work one-on-one with another addict or alcoholic.

FEBRUARY

LIVING THE PROGRAM

I have learned how to work the Steps in my life every day. I have learned how to apply the Twelve Traditions to my personal life and my relationships. I have learned to stay teachable.

Hope, Faith & Courage Volume II, *page 113*

When I first came around, it seemed natural to think of recovery as only one particular part of my life, separate from my other day-to-day affairs. My recovery seemed to be confined to the meetings I attended, the Step work I was completing with my sponsor, and the service I might contribute to the Fellowship. By viewing recovery within this limited scope, I failed to benefit from the full impact which the Twelve Steps could have on my existence and on the lives of those around me.

As my recovery has progressed, my thinking has changed. I have found myself using the tools in a much broader range of life skills, fully understanding the benefits of a Twelve-Step perspective in my overall existence.

~~~~~

I will do my best to apply the valuable program principles to *all* areas of my life, not just at meetings. I will remember that God is forever with me, even outside the rooms. I will share the love the Fellowship has shown to me in all situations and with everyone I encounter.

SOBRIETY VERSUS RECOVERY

I stayed out of the booze and drugs, and I was definitely dry. My attitude and outlook on life didn't change a bit, though, and I still blamed everyone else for my woes.
Hope, Faith & Courage Volume II, *page 132*

When still an active addict, I'd frequently try to stop using of my own accord. Here and there, I'd even accumulate days, weeks, or months of abstinence. This "sobriety," however, merely consisted of being miserable and not using. I couldn't understand how other people were able to just stop and not touch drugs again. No matter how hard I tried, I'd eventually break down and go back to using.

Once I finally came into the program, I got a sponsor, found a home group, and started to work the Steps immediately. Coincidently (I think not!), since then, I haven't had the need to pick up any mind-altering substances. I now understand the difference between sobriety and recovery. Living in recovery means I enjoy life and all it has to offer. It means embracing the God of my understanding, and getting and remaining excited about spiritual growth. It means being comfortable with myself and those around me—so very much more than just not using!

~~~~~

Simply being abstinent never kept me sober! Today, I will work the Steps to the best of my ability so I can continue to have a purposeful life based in recovery.

GOD IS AN INSIDE JOB

Sometimes we had to search fearlessly, but He was there. He was as much a fact as we were. We found the Great Reality deep down within us.
Alcoholics Anonymous, *page 55*

My whole life, I was always searching for something: raised in a conservative religion; turned to a very culturally different movement; learned to meditate with healing stones; and, at one point, flew to a far-away country to study spirituality while in the depths of a terrible addiction. I was always seeking better ways of life. Cocaine, however, kept the bars locked on my self-constructed prison. Just as *Alcoholics Anonymous* describes on page 62, I was filled with "moral and philosophical convictions galore" that I wanted to live up to, but couldn't.

After getting sober, I started searching again—this time for something to fill the hole cocaine had left inside me. I went on numerous sprees with shopping, relationships, exercise, and food—still looking *outside* myself for the Great Reality. At a year and a half sober, even though I'd worked the Steps to the best of my ability, my life crashed.

Starting over at Step One, I embarked on a fearless effort to face the things that had been blocking me. It was only then I discovered the Great Reality that had been inside me all along. Today I am free. I try to walk hand-in-hand daily with my Creator and my fellow man alike.

~~~~~

When I find myself unsuccessfully focusing on external stimulation for fulfillment, I stop, center myself, and feel God's ever-presence in my heart.

EXPECT A MIRACLE

*I felt lifted up, as though the great clean wind of a mountain
top blew through and through. God comes to most men
gradually, but His impact on me was sudden and profound.*
Alcoholics Anonymous, page 14

A couple of days prior to being released from a three-month, live-in recovery
home, I decided to go outside to meditate and chat with my Higher Power. My
impending "return to society" had me scared to death.

As I was talking to God and looking up at the clear night sky, I made a casual
remark to myself out loud, saying, "It sure would be nice to see a shooting star."
Not one millisecond after the word "star" left my lips, and in the exact spot where
I happened to be gazing, a *huge* blue and white explosion erupted, and a shooting
star rocketed to the left.

I was in shock—unable to talk or move. Just then, my counselor came outside. He
could see I was shaken, and with great concern, he asked what had happened.
When I explained, he broke out in a smile from ear to ear. "Enjoy it," he said,
"God will always let you know, in His own way, that He is constantly with you.
When He shows you through miracles, it's *incredible!*"

To this day, I still cry when I talk about the experience. The tears are an
expression of wonder, awe, gratitude, and feelings I still don't fully understand
even now. I don't ever want to forget how God touched my heart that night, and
how He continues to bless me each and every day in my recovery.

~~~~

May I forever be alert to God's miracles—both large and small! May I learn to
expect, embrace and be humbled by these moments of grace each and every time
they occur.

_____

GIVING IT ALL TO GOD

> *We were having trouble with personal relationships, we couldn't control our emotional natures, we were a prey to misery and depression, we couldn't make a living, we had a feeling of uselessness, we were full of fear, we were unhappy, we couldn't seem to be of real help to other people. . . .*
> Alcoholics Anonymous, *page 52*

When I first got sober, I didn't see my life as being unmanageable. I was clear on the meaning of powerlessness over my addiction, but I had just graduated from college, and things were pretty good. I was teaching preschool and most of the bills were getting paid. In our meeting rooms, I heard people talk about things they lost that I never had. My first thought was, "I can manage my life, just not cocaine."

When someone introduced me to the "bedevilments" from page 52 of *Alcoholics Anonymous*, I was floored. I began to recognize the unmanageability of my life. After being sober for over a year, I had stopped working the Steps and was hitting an emotional bottom. Each day, I woke up wanting to die, feeling completely worthless. I was an agnostic in every sense and had only given God my addiction. Going back through the Steps, I was forced to look at my agnosticism (everything I thought I could control) in my emotions, relationships, and finances. I finally realized I had to give *all* of it to God.

~~~~~

Today I ask myself, "Do I believe God can take me further in *all* areas of my life?" Has my program become stagnant? Perhaps it's time to revisit the work I've already done to see if I can start to grow some more, as well as to continue forward on the path the Steps provide.

NO LONGER ALONE

Our own concept of a Higher Power will come in time as we work the Twelve Steps. Until then, it is good to have the power of the group with us.
The Home Group (C.A. Pamphlet)

I always believed a Higher Power existed. I just could never understand why any such Higher Power would waste time on me. Once I began working the Steps, I slowly started recognizing God's presence in the rooms of C.A. I began noticing the way He was working quite positively in people's lives. Gradually it dawned on me that He was benefiting my life as well. It seemed uncanny how I would be experiencing some problem, go to a meeting, and someone would seemingly out of the blue share how they'd handled the exact same issue. This has happened numerous times to me and many others I know in our Fellowship.

I have finally begun to accept that I am no longer alone, nor do I ever have to be again, that my God is and will always be nearby. I am blessed to be a part of this C.A. Fellowship—to be among *such* incredible, spiritual people. My Higher Power, the Steps, and my fellow C.A. members have been teaching me how to live, how to face life and all its struggles, how to walk through the rough times with grace and dignity, and how to embrace the joys and lessons which are also such a cornerstone of the program. Each day, my faith, gratitude and understanding continue to grow.

~~~~~

The path through the darkness has been slow and hard but has been eased by my relationship with my Higher Power, by my continued Step work and by being part of the C.A. Fellowship. I can never begin to repay what this Fellowship and my Higher Power have given me, but I hope to spend a lifetime trying.

CHAMELEON GOD

> *I can't say upon what occasion or upon what day I came to believe in a Power greater than myself, but I certainly have that belief now. . . . If you don't care for the one I've suggested, you'll be sure to discover one that suits if only you look and listen.*
>
> Twelve Steps and Twelve Traditions, *page 27*

God "as I understand Him" is like a chameleon who expresses Himself to me in many different forms, all important for my recovery.

God "the conversationalist" is sometimes male, sometimes female, sometimes neither and sometimes both. This God helps with the ever-present committee in my head and guides me to try to do the next right thing always.

My "be kind to myself" God is an invisible friend who tells me not to be afraid and gently nudges me along. He helps me not beat myself up about the nature of my disease or when times get tough.

My "awareness" God aids in my daily acceptance of life on life's terms. He reminds me to be diligent when I am hungry, angry, lonely and tired as I trudge the path of recovery. This God also helps me recognize the spiritual gifts which are so plentiful in the program on a daily basis.

Whatever image works for a particular life situation, my faith in God carries me through.

~~~~~

God, to me, will never be a "cookie-cutter" likeness, but will adapt to my spiritual needs, ever-changing as I grow and evolve in my recovery. For this insight, I am eternally grateful.

THE POWER INSIDE

. . . deep down in every man, woman, and child, is the fundamental idea of God.
Alcoholics Anonymous, *page 55*

In the early days of my sobriety, I would hear again and again that I needed to find a Power greater than myself to stay clean. Some people even called this Power "God." This kind of talk made me uncomfortable. Religion had not ever been a part of my life, and I mistakenly thought I'd need to have some sort of formal religious-based affiliation to cultivate this aspect of my recovery.

At first, I just ignored the topic of God completely. Eventually, I knew I could no longer survive on my own, so I started to be open to some notion of God in my life. Thank goodness for the patience of my new program friends. They gently suggested that all I needed to start with was a willingness to believe that *they* believed. The group itself worked quite well as my initial Higher Power, which allowed me to proceed with the Steps.

I guess I was expecting that the clouds might part, or maybe the seas. A clap of thunder, perhaps, would bring salvation rushing in! As I worked the Twelve Steps of Cocaine Anonymous to the best of my ability under my sponsor's direction, gradually, my truth came to light. I found that Power greater than myself deep down inside my being, the *last* place I would ever have thought to look. Now I embrace this Power and seek further understanding of Its nuances and how It affects so many parts of my life and my recovery.

~~~~~

Can I feel a spiritual Power *within myself* today? God, please help me tap into that connection and open a permanent channel linking my human heart to the Divine.

UNCONVENTIONAL FAITH

In just a few weeks I went from being an atheist to having a working faith in a Higher Power, although my path to that faith was somewhat unconventional.
Hope, Faith & Courage Volume II, *page 92*

I used to think that faith and belief were the same thing. I have since learned I can believe in something and not have faith. But I can't have faith if I don't believe.

I asked someone early in my recovery, what is faith? If I can't see faith and don't understand faith, how could it ever work for me? I was told to take some food from the freezer and put it in the microwave. Then I was asked, "Do you believe the microwave will heat your food?" I said, of course it would. All I have to do is press the right buttons, wait a little while, and it will be heated. I pressed "start," and my program friend said, "Look through the glass and tell me what you see." I saw nothing but my food going around and around. Next question was, "How do the microwaves in the oven heat the food?" I thought about this for a minute, and then confessed I really didn't know. I was told, "You believe the microwaves will heat your food. You can't see the microwaves, and you don't understand how they work, but you can still get the benefit of a cooked meal."

I learned that day that if I believe and take the corresponding action, I don't have to understand faith to receive the benefits. I have faith in the program of Cocaine Anonymous because I believe the program works, and I take the corresponding action by working the program every day to the best of my ability. I have faith in the God of my understanding because I believe in Him, and I make a decision to turn my will and my life over to His care every day.

~~~~

To sum this up: Belief + Corresponding Action = Faith.

A GOD BY ANY NAME

> . . . *all you really need is a truly open mind.*
> Twelve Steps and Twelve Traditions, *page 26*

I remember my first meeting of Cocaine Anonymous and hearing the word "God." I wanted to get up and walk out of the room, because I thought that it was a religious program. Then they said, "as we understood Him." I stayed through the meeting, later asking what that meant. I was told that I could have any conception of God, and it was not a religious program. I soon saw that everyone's perception of God was uniquely different, even if they used the same name.

Many of us come into C.A. and get spooked by the words God and prayer. Although these words scared me, I learned that believing in a Higher Power and praying take practice. I discovered that the more I practiced, the more I developed my own insight and understanding of God.

My desire to stay sober kept me in the rooms even when others tried to get me to embrace their notions of God. I have since made many friends of varied faiths, and we are all on the same journey together, even though we all believe in our own personal evolving perception of God.

~~~~~

I will live the spiritual program of action and practice its spiritual principles in my life. I will allow others the freedom to believe as they see fit without prejudice or judgment. I will continue to embrace the evolution and understanding of my own perception of who God is in my life.

_____

A COUNTERFEIT GOD?

Had we not variously worshipped people, sentiment, things, money, and ourselves?
Alcoholics Anonymous, *page 54*

When I used cocaine, it created what I now see was a counterfeit spiritual experience. I have come to believe that when I used drugs, I was committing spiritual adultery. I could not differentiate true from false. What I *thought* was true was, in reality, false. I had faith in a counterfeit god. Lack of Power was my dilemma. I vainly sought that Power when I used.

Once I got to the program, the Twelve Steps revealed the truth. An *authentic* spiritual experience occurred for me. No human power could relieve my addiction, and true Power manifested in my life as I worked the Steps and began living a spiritual life. Every day I must *seek* conscious contact with God as I understand God by practicing these principles in *all* of my affairs.

~~~~~

I was willing to go to any lengths for my drug of choice; I must match that effort in my recovery. As I seek, so shall I find.

MAKING SENSE OUT OF MADNESS

We saw them meet and transcend their other pains and trials. We saw them calmly accept impossible situations, seeking neither to run nor to recriminate.
Twelve Steps and Twelve Traditions, *page 31*

Admitting powerlessness over cocaine and alcohol was easy for me. My big hurdle was finding a Power greater than myself.

Early in recovery, the person I lived with got really angry at me for resigning from "the game"—the sick dance we did so well when we were both using. This person destroyed all my possessions, taking a knife to my clothes and the furniture. Everything in our apartment was ruined beyond repair.

I went to meetings looking for a way to get past this horrible situation, to learn from it, and perhaps place it in some understandable perspective Others talked again and again about believing and relying on a Higher Power and how that helped them through their trying times. Slowly, but clearly, I started to understand that a Higher Power was working in my life even though I did not yet have a definitive understanding. I started to believe that this Higher Power I was just beginning to acknowledge had a plan for me that didn't include living with someone in active addiction. I learned it was not necessary to use. With the strength of my Higher Power and the support of the C.A. Fellowship, I learned that I could cope with whatever happened in my life.

~~~~~

Today I will not just believe in, but I will *rely on* my Higher Power. When I stay connected, both spiritually and to the Fellowship, I don't have to run away from the wreckage of my past or my poor actions and decisions prior to recovery. Making sense out of madness comes naturally when I include my Higher Power in the equation.

NO TIME LIKE THE PRESENT

Who cares to admit complete defeat? Practically no one, of course. Every natural instinct cries out against the idea of personal powerlessness.
Twelve Steps and Twelve Traditions, *page 21*

The very best use of my personal power got me into the rooms of Cocaine Anonymous. Admissions of utter defeat and powerlessness, although truly the solid foundation upon which joyous and purposeful lives are built, are difficult to face, much less accept.

I learned that my disease centers in the mind. My self-obsessed, *unaided* thoughts will not admit any defeat, much less relinquish that false sense of power.

Fortunately, a Power greater than the warped capacity I brought here could remove my self-centered, destructive thoughts. This Power, manifested through the Fellowship and as a result of working the Twelve Steps, enabled me "to become happily and usefully whole." (*Twelve Steps and Twelve Traditions*, page 15.) All I had to do was *consistently* ask this Power to be with me and to direct the course of my day.

When will this Power be with me?

Now.

All I have to do is ask.

~~~~

God, please afford me the strength to stay defeated. I need to use Your guidance *now* in order to recognize Your will. My way of living does not work without Your able assistance.

COURAGE AND FEAR

I learned to identify, accept, and face my fears, and a Power greater than myself has been there to help me walk through it every time.
Hope, Faith & Courage Volume II, *page 25*

Courage is not quaint, nor overly optimistic. It is what we use to get through the day. It takes courage to go shopping or do a Fourth Step, and it takes courage to shower on Monday morning. Courage is the super-ego to fear's id. Courage is the only rational response with which to confront the world. Fear stops us. Courage sets us moving again. If we gave fear free reign, nothing would get done.

We also often forget that courage and fear are not mutually exclusive. We can have both. Indeed, we *must* have both in many situations in our recovery. Fear is not the opposite of courage; it is the very essence of courage. Nor is courage the absence of fear; it is the ability to act in spite of fear. The more debilitating the fear, the more heroic is the courage. Feel the fear, and keep moving. Sometimes all we need to know is that we carry our courage in the same place we carry our fear—in our hearts.

Courage doesn't have to be flashy or dramatic. In fact, it manifests when we least expect it, as when we have a project we've been putting off because of some irrational fear. Then courage comes creeping in. Don't think you have to be a big hero every time some little fear raises its head. That's not the end of the world. And you don't have to find the courage because it is located at all times in your heart. Go ahead and feel the fear. Even enjoy it for a moment or two. And then keep moving.

~~~~~

I pray to acknowledge those times when I am in fear and to affirm those times when I have courage. I pray to remember that my courage is, at all times, located inside of me—in my heart.

ONE OF A LARGER WHOLE

For our group purpose there is but one ultimate authority—a loving God as He may express Himself in our group conscience. Our leaders are but trusted servants; they do not govern.

C.A. Tradition Two

Addicts who have experienced the miracle of recovery have, at some time in the progression of their transformation, come to rely upon a Power greater than themselves. In the course of that contact, life takes on a new form. No longer self-reliant, the spiritual tool of God-reliance becomes readily available. As I rely on my Higher Power, the events of my life become joyous, useful, and meaningful.

The same concept occurs for a group. Each group is different from the others. Members of the group have different life experiences and different cultural views. Yet each group has to come to the same realization—in order for it to survive, the ultimate authority must be a Power greater than the group. Simply stated, this Power expresses itself through the group conscience. An effective group conscience is one that has been informed by its members' collective experience and wisdom. Over time, a group will find that the group conscience is far more reliable than the direction of an individual member. The group will come to rely on it.

~~~~

Today, let me trust the group process, including group conscience, sharing, voting, etc. Let me come to support decisions by the group which differ from my own opinions. Let me realize that I am just one of a larger whole. Help me to remember that my thoughts and experiences are important. With God's help, I will find the courage to express them openly, honestly, and appropriately.

JUST ONE MORE TIME

> *In C.A., I was given help and direction. I was told that I could use my intellect to think about the importance of each Step. I was told to look around the rooms and find all the sober people who were working the Steps, and then stick with the winners. In going to the business meetings, doing H&I panels, and being of service, I had unconsciously surrounded myself with winners, people who were serious about the program and who were actively involved in working the Steps. I watched and emulated these people who had the sobriety that I wanted. I got sober and grew with these people.*
> Hope, Faith & Courage Volume II, page 66

It's crazy to think that I could do just one.

I remember someone at a meeting talking about insanity (repeating the same actions, expecting different results) and about thinking through the high before I actually got high again. I knew in that moment that things hadn't changed in my addiction, and there was no way I could have "just one" of anything, even then. If I wanted to remain sober, I had to surround myself with people, places, and things that helped me stay clean and sober.

I began to use the tools I learned in the rooms to resist the temptation to pick up again. It meant sticking with the winners. I had a real chance at a new life then. Life on life's terms still happens, and there will always be temptations of all sorts in sobriety, especially when I least expect them. That's life. If I continue to do the next right thing, as suggested, that cunning, baffling, powerful and patient broken thought of "just one more time" will fade. The thought may come and go, but I don't have to face it alone. I have a God, the Fellowship, the Steps, and the legacy of C.A.

~~~~~

My disease is strong; it will wait and tempt me when I am at my weakest. If I stick with the winners and continue to do the work, my disease is kept at bay. I need to remain open to suggestions I receive at meetings, from Fellowship friends, and especially from my sponsor.

February 17

HOPE FOUND

*Hopelessness was written large on the man's face as he replied,
"Oh, but that's no use. Nothing would fix me. I'm a goner."*
Alcoholics Anonymous, *page 157*

I did not know much about hope until I made it into the program of C.A. For me, hope was when you wished for something you wanted and got it. The only thing on *my* mind was hope that the dealer was not out of dope when I got there. I knew what hopeless was because that is where my first blast of the pipe took me. The only thing emptier than my body was my state of mind, and I had felt that way for years. I was alone in my own brain even when people were around. I was on the outside looking in—isolated through shame and fear.

I heard the C.A. message in prison when the H&I Committee brought in a meeting. They gave me an introduction to recovery, and I understood for the first time that sobriety was, in fact, possible. I didn't want to accept my addiction immediately; it took some time to want to do something about it. Eventually, I surrendered and was finally able to comprehend what a Higher Power was all about. I came to believe the God of my understanding could keep me sober if I took the Twelve Steps.

I have not used now for many years. Since I stopped, I have gained enormous hope through the Twelve Steps and my Higher Power. Today is about living, *not* about using. The meetings help keep hope in my heart as I share in others' progress. For me, finding and holding onto hope has transformed life from bleak to bountiful!

~~~~~

Today, I have hope from working the Twelve Steps and from my Higher Power. I surely am blessed to know and appreciate how important hope is in my life and in my recovery. I have strength to keep hope in my heart today.

BASKING IN THE LIGHT

> . . . *we shut ourselves off from the sunlight of the Spirit.*
> Alcoholics Anonymous, *page 66*

We all have moments of clarity—those instances when our thought's light bulb ignites and we suddenly recognize some key fact from the past. For an addict like me, those moments are often related to my behavior while using.

I used to hide from the light. Not only did I hole up in my small room in the darkness, smoking crack cocaine, but I also pretended the drug *was* the light. Living in a world of shadows, I regretted the past and feared the future. With the grace of my Higher Power (the God of my understanding) and the members of our Fellowship, I began to find a way out of my solitary darkness and into the shared light of the Spirit.

Only when I started working the program found in the Steps and being of service, did I start to see more clearly. At that point, it wasn't full recovery. It was just a glimpse of the mental clarity that comes with stringing a few clean days together and being open to what might lie ahead. A taste of the true light was all I needed. I knew I'd found something better than active addiction. I am thankful for that taste and for the true light I found.

~~~~~

All living things require light to grow and flourish. My disease kept me stunted for such a very long time. May the radiance of God's spiritual light illuminate all the dark corners of my addiction.

GIVING UP THE FIGHT

Besides, we have stopped fighting anybody or anything. We have to!
Alcoholics Anonymous, *page 103*

During my active addiction, I fought everyone and everything—not always physically fighting, but emotionally, financially and spiritually-who got in the way of the next high. This included my job, family, God, and, most of all, myself. I could not stop fighting, even when other people told me I had a problem. Those people *became* the problem, and the fight would be on.

Eventually, enough trouble backed me against a wall, and I could no longer resist. To win, I had to surrender. This sounded absolutely insane to me. How do you win when you surrender? The idea opposes every human instinct, especially for a fighter like me.

However, as I worked the Steps of recovery, I learned how to "let go and let God." First, I surrendered and accepted my addiction and the fact I needed help. Then I surrendered to a Higher Power of my own understanding, asking Him daily to keep me drug-free and in the solution. Finally, I started to surrender *all* of my life to my Higher Power, not just my addiction. It was an ongoing challenge; I still sometimes find myself fighting with people or life in general. When I realize this is happening, I have to take a deep breath and surrender once again, letting God do the fighting for me.

~~~~~

I am truly grateful I lost the fight with addiction. This defeat enabled me to find a Higher Power of my own understanding so I could learn how to *surrender* to win!

SIMPLIFIED STEP TWO

> *Step Two involves open-mindedness. Having admitted we were powerless over cocaine and all other mind-altering substances, we became open-minded enough to believe that a Power greater than ourselves could remove our obsession to use and restore us to sanity. The obsession to use will be removed. This Power may be God, but does not have to be. Many of us use the Fellowship of C.A. as our Higher Power. After all, what we had failed to do alone, we are succeeding in doing together.*
>
> The First 30 Days (C.A. Pamphlet)

Step Two informed me that a "Power" greater than myself could restore me to sanity concerning drink and drugs. Having realized I have no control over any mind-altering substances and having accepted that abstinence would be a good idea, I was told that if I work the Twelve Steps, I would never again have to suffer from the terror, misery, shame and pain of addiction. The only thing necessary was for me to come to believe in a "Power greater," of which I had no understanding. Just peachy! What was I to do?

I decided I needed to counsel with my sponsor about the dilemma I was facing. I told him I was struggling with this "Power" talked about in Step Two. He asked if I believed in the Twelve Steps, C.A., meetings and the *Big Book* of Alcoholics Anonymous, to which I answered, "Yes, of course I do." Even to me, it was evident that the Twelve-Step programs had saved many people from the scrap heap. While attending meetings, I'd heard numerous stories similar to mine from people who overcame their own battle with addiction through working the Twelve Steps and attending meetings. C.A. seemed to be effectively running for many, many years now; how could I not believe?

"Exactly," my sponsor pointed out. "Is that not a Power greater than you?" Step Two states we *came to believe*. You don't have to *actually believe* at this stage; all that is needed is a *willingness to believe*. In truth, I did believe; I was complicating this simple Step. It took asking someone else for help to "Keep It Simple" that assured me a Power did exist and that anyone could access this Power as long as they were willing to believe. My only job was to remain open-minded enough to believe.

~~~~~

To those who struggle with the concept, God has sometimes been defined as "Good Orderly Direction" or "Group Of Drunks or Drug addicts." Framing the notion of Higher Power in these terms has helped many of us grab hold of a basic spiritual belief upon which to build.

AND NOW, A WORD FROM YOUR SPONSOR

Choosing strong, hard-nosed, and enthusiastic sponsorship and allowing myself to be sponsored are quite simply the most important gifts I have ever given to myself. My sponsor did not try to dictate my life, but helped me survive until I could get the hope, faith and courage to make the necessary changes.
Hope Faith & Courage Volume II, *page 36*

When I got to C.A., they told me I could only keep what I had by giving it away. So when you asked me for my phone number, I gave it to you. I asked you to call me every day, and I meant it. I didn't say "Only call me when things are fine," or "Call me when you get this thing figured out," or "Don't call me if you're afraid." I said "Call me every day," and I meant it. If you need me, there is no bad time to call. I will be available for you. Don't get me wrong. I am not your taxi service, your bank, or your marriage counselor. I am not here to fix your old life. My purpose is to offer you a new way of life, as it was shown to me. I may teach you how to make coffee and chair a meeting or instruct you on how to give out chips, but my primary job is to take you through the Twelve Steps.

Through my *actions*, I will show you how to be of service to the Fellowship. I will explain what it means to be a trusted servant, emphasizing what an honor that is. I will guide you through the Twelve Traditions. If you have questions, call anytime. I will be there for you.

I will love you, but I won't pull any punches. I will always tell you the truth. I have loads of experience to share with you, but I don't have any advice. If you can't follow suggestions, then I can't sit back and watch you die. I will not beg you to live. I won't candy-coat this thing. Some of it will hurt. When you feel scared and alone, give me a call. I will be there for you.

~~~~

You might be able to do this on your own, but I cannot. Why? Because it's a "*we*" program. Every time I reach out, someone is there for me. I have been shown the way out. For that I am forever grateful, and I must keep giving it away.

PEACE WITH MYSELF

If you have a resentment you want to be free of, if you will pray for the person or thing that you resent, you will be free. If you will ask in prayer for everything you want for yourself to be given to them, you will be free. Ask for their health, their prosperity, their happiness, and you will be free.
Alcoholics Anonymous, 4th Edition, *page 552*

Through our Twelve Steps, I was taken by the hand, guided beyond the dark world of addiction into the sunlight which is recovery. Emerging from my cocoon of isolation and pain, I now live in an atmosphere where love, forgiveness, and hope prevail. Thriving in the present, I open my wings to embrace a Power greater than myself. Then, before taking flight, I pray—trusting whatever path God has laid out before me.

In my interactions with family, co-workers, and Fellowship members, I do my best to open my heart without judgment. I need to clear resentments from my mind. When angered by another, I pray that they acquire everything in life that I would want for myself and that I be granted the patience, tolerance, and compassion I would cheerfully give a sick friend. Sounds crazy, but it works!

~~~~

Getting clean and sober is just the beginning; staying that way one day at a time is the prayer. Today, I will accept the world for what it is instead of wishing for something else.

SERVICE, THE FORGOTTEN ART

We rarely know the people our service work has touched, but somehow the anonymity of it is a blessing in humility that is required for this addict/alcoholic to stay clean and sober another day.

C.A. NewsGram, 3rd Quarter 2002

From time to time, I have forgotten the art of service. I have forgotten how service treats the spirit. I have forgotten the words of our parent Fellowship's co-founder, "For if an alcoholic failed to perfect and enlarge his spiritual life through work and self-sacrifice for others, he could not survive the certain trials and low spots ahead." (*Alcoholics Anonymous,* pages 14-15.)

Service is a full spectrum. More than making coffee, more than sponsorship, more than being a secretary, more than holding a book study, more than workshops—service is Hospitals & Institutions work; service is holding a general service commitment; service is being a responsible, productive member of the Fellowship. But most of all, service is from the heart. Page 77 in *Alcoholics Anonymous* says, "Our real purpose is to fit ourselves to be of maximum service to God and the people about us." I need to never forget this art of being of service to the C.A. Fellowship, which has given me more than I can ever give back.

C.A. has a most interesting service structure: the inverted triangle. It all starts with the groups; they are in charge. That's where I learn to be of service in C.A. When good service leaders attend the group (the grateful old-timers), an example is set with positive, meaningful, focused, spiritual-based, ready-to-participate attitudes. Newcomers are offered opportunities to engage in problem-solving, thus gaining knowledge about the specific workings of the group's activities and challenges. Quite ingeniously, service work provides the means for newcomers to develop critical thinking and spiritual enrichment.

~~~~~

Service work is the central pulse, giving life to my recovery. May I always attempt to serve willingly and from my heart, which will allow me to be of maximum service to God and my fellows in C.A.

I FOUND MY HOME IN C.A.

> *I started attending C.A. meetings, and I was willing to do anything. When I first heard* Who is a Cocaine Addict? *read, I was immediately hooked—just like the first time I tried crack. I fell in love with C.A. and felt at home immediately. I heard people share stories like mine, and since they had recovered, I got busy right away!*
>
> Hope, Faith & Courage Volume II, *page 60*

Certainly, my coming to C.A. wasn't solely to find fellowship and laughter. I suffer from the chronic, progressive and eventually fatal condition of addiction. Unless arrested in some way, that condition leads to jails, insanity and death. I came into C.A. because jails and insanity had become normal. By the grace of a Power greater than my own, I was given clarity to see the truth of my hopelessness and escape death. That same Power brought me to Cocaine Anonymous.

In recovery and in sharing my life with others, I discovered joy and joviality are commonly present. Consistent with the promise set forth in the *Big Book*, my healing began when I talked with another addict and we shared our experience, strength and hope. My first C.A. group experience took place in a car, on the way from a treatment center to a C.A. meeting. Thus began my journey to the middle of the C.A. Fellowship.

Something happens when I am centered in the program. Feelings of difference disappear, and I become joined together with others in brotherly and harmonious action. I have not had a drink or drug since my first meeting of Cocaine Anonymous. I found my home here, and I am intent on doing my part in making this home an attractive and carefree place to dwell. No doubt the most exciting and entertaining aspects of being a C.A. member are to participate in our many, varied events and to be a useful member in the groups to which I belong. I love all forms of C.A. gatherings, from pancake breakfasts, to workshops, to conventions.

~~~~

I pray I may always see clearly the nature of my disease and remember the truth about its hopelessness. I have been, and remain, exceedingly blessed to belong to a Fellowship that provides everything I need, when I need it, with love, kindness, and grace. I will continue to do my part to make our Fellowship thrive so we will all continue to have the comfort of calling C.A. our "home."

AN OVERVIEW OF THE TWELVE STEPS

> *This pamphlet is not a substitute for using the* Big Book *and a sponsor. Its purpose is to shed light on the Twelve-Step program in the* Big Book *of Alcoholics Anonymous, as it relates to our addiction.*
>
> A Guide to the 12 Steps (C.A. Pamphlet)

To help us work the Twelve Steps, Cocaine Anonymous uses a text entitled *Alcoholics Anonymous*, commonly referred to as the "*Big Book*." When studying this text, some of us find it useful to substitute the word "cocaine" for "alcohol" and the word "using" for "drinking," although, in the process, some of us discover we are alcoholics as well as addicts. Because some believe there are ways to take the Steps other than the method described in the *Big Book*, we suggest everyone seek guidance from a sponsor or an experienced C.A. member, and their Higher Power to choose a method that is right for them.

Taking the Twelve Steps prepares us to have a "spiritual awakening" or a "spiritual experience." (*Alcoholics Anonymous, 4th Edition*, page 567.) These phrases refer to the change that takes place in our thinking, attitude, and outlook after taking the Steps. This change is the catalyst that frees us from active addiction. Applying the Steps in our daily lives enables us to establish and improve our conscious contact with our Higher Power. Most in our Fellowship believe the greatest safeguard in preventing relapse lies in consistent application of the Twelve Steps.

Newcomers often ask, "When should I take the Steps?" Experience has shown delay is dangerous, and the sooner one secures the help of a sponsor in formally working the Steps, the better the likelihood of success in recovery. Of course the choice is ultimately up to the individual, and the guidance of a seasoned sponsor can best gauge the tempo at which one should proceed.

No doubt it might be possible for one to stay clean and sober strictly by attending meetings without working the Twelve Steps. However, those who choose this route are cheating themselves in understanding and adopting the full scope of recovery principles.

~~~~~

Am I missing out? Just like when my addiction was active and I didn't want to skip any parties, I want to partake in *everything* Cocaine Anonymous has to offer. God, please help me be willing to follow suggestions and work these Twelve Steps as thoroughly as I am able.

HOPE

C.A. members are people from all walks of life and from all parts of the world. The hope is that you may find recovery as we did and stay sober, one day at a time. At the spiritual center of Cocaine Anonymous is a message of hope, faith and courage.

Hope, Faith & Courage Volume II, *page v*

Since becoming a member of the C.A. Fellowship, one common principle has bound us together: hope. Hope for recovery and continued sobriety. Hope that the pain and insanity will no longer prevail. Hope for the obsession to drug and drink to be lifted. Hope for the promises to come true. Hope that the program can work for me as it has for those who came before me. Hope to begin doing the next right thing. Hope, not just for myself, but for others too.

When I started attending meetings and heard something to which I could relate, I began to identify with C.A.'s spiritual message of hope, faith, and courage. In a sense, this hope became contagious. It was transmitted to me by my prayers, by helping others, listening, practicing meditation, taking the Steps, sponsorship, and other innumerable kinds of God-centered experiences.

I experienced hope when I came in and admitted my addictions to myself in a meeting. I heard hope when members shared their experience, strength, and hope. Some of those people had experiences which were strikingly similar to my own, so that I was completely inspired. For the first time, I believed that recovery might be possible. For that brief moment during the meeting, no thoughts about the obsessive desire to use or the wreckage of my past and/or present came to me. I left the meeting feeling quite different from when I arrived—lighter and relieved. What a relief to be inspired to believe that this way of life could actually be a reality and to have a strong desire to come back and discover how other addicts have made the program work.

~~~~

May I never forget how, as a newcomer, the feeling of hope was so compelling in helping me decide to keep coming back. Please let me always be a carrier of hope—anytime I share, in my service work, and especially as I welcome newcomers into the Fellowship.

DENIAL IS THICK

He went from the brink of insanity to the leading edge of a beautiful adventure.
Hope, Faith & Courage Volume II, *page 101*

At the start of my drinking and drugging, it was fun! That's why we do it, right? In order for me to fit in with a society where drinking and drugging was socially acceptable, I *had* to do it. I was alive and finally comfortable in my own skin. I was on top of the world; what could go wrong?

As my using days continued, my so-called friends began failing in life. Lost jobs, lying, stealing, run-ins with the police, and severe illness became regular occurrences. Personally, at the time, I couldn't figure out why these people had chosen to do these things. What in the world was wrong with them? Denial is thick, and although my own addiction was progressing, I didn't correlate any of my behaviors with these people getting into trouble or getting so ill from their use.

It wasn't long before the same things that I had shunned and vowed would not happen to me began to happen. No longer could I be socially responsible or anything close to an active member of society.

Today, I am grateful for my own slow, patient downward spiral because it enabled me to hit bottom, surrender, become teachable, accept the nature of my disease and ultimately seek help. I consider myself a miracle today, and I thoroughly believe that my Higher Power has a plan for me. I discovered the solution was to join the Fellowship of C.A. and then to come back each and every day to keep what I have by giving it away.

~~~~~

Reflecting on all of the events and actions from my past certainly scares me. My sponsor tells me this is a healthy fear and an introspective process—one that will keep me from going back out. I remember that DENIAL stands for Don't Even Notice I Am Lying.

STEPS ONE & TWO UNLOCKED

> . . . *barring divine intervention, we are unable to stay away from that first hit, line, or whatever . . ., and that we will use again and again, no matter how much we want to stay sober.*
> A Guide to the 12 Steps (C.A. Pamphlet)

Step One convinced me that when it comes to cocaine and managing my life, I'm helpless on my own power. The utter desperation I felt when I got here and the unmanageability of my life were constant reminders that I need to continue on the recovery path. I was told that my First Step *must* be worked perfectly if I'm to remain clean and sober. For me, this was not difficult. My experience is that I started by grabbing another addict to share our stories about hitting bottom. No matter which drug(s) we used or what our backgrounds, Step One has proven to be the same for each of us in Cocaine Anonymous.

When it came to Step Two, I struggled with the concept of God, often loudly voicing my skepticism. My first sponsor had just relapsed, and I was flailing around, questioning everything I had learned or been told in my newly-acquired fifty days sober. A friend of mine braved my angry front to stand toe-to-toe and argue the existence of a Higher Power. "Not a human power," he yelled back at me, "a Higher Power—with a *capital* HP!" When I argued that I couldn't find written proof, even in his precious *Big Book*, my friend ripped a page from a spiral notebook and wrote "There is a God," taping it to the refrigerator. "There," he said, "written proof." That was over ten years ago, and with time, I came to believe in a Higher Power of my own understanding that continues to work for me today.

~~~~~

We tend to make this program more difficult than it has to be. Acceptance and surrender are the keys to opening the door and crossing the threshold.

THE GIFT IS MY SANITY

The minute I stopped arguing, I could begin to see and feel. Right there, Step Two gently and very gradually began to infiltrate my life.
Twelve Steps and Twelve Traditions, *page 27*

Sometimes I hear people share anger towards God. Perhaps they have lost a loved one, didn't get the job, are sick, or someone in their family is acting out. I have learned that it's okay to be angry—our feelings are our feelings!

I have been given the only thing I ever wanted from God, which was to put down the crack pipe. Believing in and applying the Power in my life has restored my sanity. I owe this to Step Two, which promises that my sanity can and will be returned. For a person who did some really crazy things for a long, long time, even the notion of sanity was elusive. I was heartened at the promise of sanity through this Step and the overall relief I feel of having another piece of my recovery puzzle put in place.

I've lost loved ones. Recovery can be trying some days. I usually turn the outcome over to God as I struggle and trudge through issues in my life. As long as I don't use any mind-altering substance, God blesses me. He blesses those I'm here to help as well.

In fact, the Power has given me more than I ever could have imagined since the first day I came to believe. The proof is in my spiritual experiences! The proof is my life today! The proof is that I don't use! The proof is that even my worst day sober is better than my best day using. The proof is that I have an understanding of a Power working on my behalf each and every moment.

The gift is my sanity.

~~~~

There's nothing wrong with getting mad at God once in a while. What's wrong is when I take back my power versus leaving it with my God. I embrace the sanity restored to me in Step Two.

MARCH

REACHING OUT

To watch people recover, to see them help others, to watch loneliness vanish, to see a fellowship grow up about you, to have a host of friends—this is an experience you must not miss.
Alcoholics Anonymous, *page 89*

"I made it into this program because someone else worked their Twelfth Step on me. Someone passed it on to me. Someone was out there after they got clean and sober, caring about others. I need to never, ever forget that. Had they simply gone on with their lives and forgotten about people like me who were still out there using and suffering, I wouldn't be here today. My gratitude begins with that fact. It is with that gratitude in mind that I reach out to others, especially the newcomers. I need to have them in my life. That is where my spirituality begins.

For me, spirituality comes from caring about others. I have found that the more I focus on improving the quality of the lives of others, the less I am into myself and my will. I feel a freedom and peace from within. The gifts I am beginning to receive in my life are greater than I could have ever imagined.

Something else I have done is that I have forgiven myself. I have forgiven myself for being an addict. I have forgiven myself for all the damage I did to my life, to my physical health, and to my career and finances. But most of all, I have forgiven myself for all the horrible, negative and unloving things I have felt about myself. It was not until I offered and accepted my own forgiveness that I was truly able to grow in my sobriety."

Reaching Out (C.A. Meeting Format reading)

~~~~

I pray that I will be able to reach out to others and pass on the experience, strength and hope that has been passed on so freely to me. I pray for continued self-forgiveness at all levels.

WHY STRUGGLE?

Lack of power, that was our dilemma. We had to find a power by which we could live, and it had to be a Power greater than ourselves. Obviously.
Alcoholics Anonymous, *page 45*

When I arrived in Cocaine Anonymous, I had no God whatsoever. I was running on self-will. My life was okay but nothing spectacular. Truthfully, I felt uneasy all the time, unsure of myself, lonely. Sure, I was working, looking after my family, going to meetings and connecting with newcomers; yet I felt an inexplicable void. Every day was a struggle, and I just didn't know why.

Then a fellow member of C.A. sat me down, and together we studied the *Big Book* chapter, *We Agnostics*. Something happened that day. My faith in God started to grow. A burden seemed to be lifted from me. I realized that without God, I would not stay clean and sober; I *could* not stay clean and sober.

Today, I am filled with God's grace. I no longer feel alone or fearful. I consult with God to help with my decision-making and to receive direction on my journey. My existence is no longer a daily struggle. I cherish the opportunities available to share with fellow members the importance of God and the amazing role He continues to play in my life.

~~~~~

The more I continue to turn my will and my life over to the care of God, the less I struggle. The less I struggle, the more peace and serenity permeate my very core.

GOD "AS I UNDERSTAND HIM"

My ideas about a Higher Power change as I grow. My
ideas aren't written in stone; they can, and will, change.
Hope Faith & Courage, *page 132*

I know everyone has their own personal conception of God/Higher Power, all with different looks and feels. Even my own understanding fluctuates with daily need and continued spiritual growth.

One of the ways I try to connect to a Higher Power is to envision a "Twelve-Step God" spinning out the principles of honesty, hope, faith, courage, integrity, willingness, humility, love, forgiveness, discipline, awareness and service.

When making life plans, I sometimes visualize my Higher Power as a large boardroom filled with six or eight members of my recovery group, a handful of prominent historical spiritual leaders (from a variety of sources), my late mom, my dad, and my spouse, all guiding me and providing input. If I had children, I imagine they would be there, too.

Always, my God is forgiving of my imperfections, allowing me to grow in the program and to thrive among the Fellowship. Through infinite love, He nurtures me into neither regretting the past nor wishing to shut the door on it.

I can always learn further about God from listening to others' experience, strength, and hope. As I mature in recovery, my God grows, too!

~~~~~

As I travel along, I pray that God (my Higher Power) continues more and more to delight and surprise me and those who share my journey.

RUNNING THE SHOW

Is he not a victim of the delusion that he can wrest satisfaction and happiness out of this world if he only manages well?
Alcoholics Anonymous, *page 61*

When I first came into these rooms, I knew that if everyone in my life could just follow my instructions. life would be fantastic. As if only I could control the *whole* performance. As if I could just manage well enough. Even with sobriety time, I often forget that I gave my life to God when I did my Third Step, so I have to do it again and again each day. I remind myself how I made a decision that God *is*. Now I need to trust that decision, get out of my own way, follow through by putting one foot in front of the other, and *do* what I believe God would want me to do. I remind myself that I am not running this show.

~~~~~

When things don't go the way I wish, I just remind myself I am not running the show. And when, I forget this fact (as we *all* do at times), my Fellowship participation soon brings me back into focus. Constantly seeking what God would want me to do is a great tool in my program.

THY WILL BE DONE, NOT MINE

> *. . . humbly saying to ourselves many times each day "Thy will be done."*
> Alcoholics Anonymous, *page 88*

Dear God, thank you for giving me this day to live clean and sober.

I humbly ask You to remove my shortcomings. Relieve me of the bondage of self that I may better do Thy will. All through the day, keep my thoughts divorced of self-pity, dishonest and self-seeking motives. Thy will be done, God, not mine.

Let me be expectant that my life will continue to get better. Let me think, act and do as if I was always in Thy presence. Let me know deeply that all is going to be well. Let me have compassion for those less fortunate. Let me see the good in all things. Let me have gratitude for what you have given me. Thy will be done, God, not mine.

Thank you God, for showing me the right path. Let me live usefully and walk humbly in your grace. Thy will be done, God, not mine.

~~~~~

I continue to pray that God's will be done, not mine. Allow me to always recognize how blessed I am to be in tune with my spirituality and with my Higher Power.

AWARENESS OF GOD

> *Let us look now upon the sea and ponder what its mystery is; and let us lift our eyes to the far horizon, beyond which we shall seek all those wonders still unseen.*
> Twelve Steps and Twelve Traditions, *page 100*

I am often asked, "Who or what is God?" The quick answer is, "I don't know." For me, like so many others, religion was a problem—but I came to understand that religion is not God. We are lucky in C.A. that we can each choose our own concept of God, one that makes sense to us!

For me, I came to believe that God is everywhere and is everything. Therefore, when I interact with the world around me, I interact with God. I can only change me and the way I am—I can't change God. Every experience can lead to spiritual growth. If I walk blindly through a beautiful place or move through the day with no care for others, then I will soon become spiritually sick. If I navigate existence with my eyes and heart open, I cannot help but grow. Before I know it, I am walking in happy unity together with others. My future is filled with endless possibilities, both inside and outside of the program.

~~~~~

I will take some time each day to see the beauty surrounding me, thinking of all the ways I can help maintain and nurture myself and this world of ours. My feet will be firmly planted on the road of happy destiny.

A MATTER OF FAITH

For we are now on a different basis; the basis of trusting and relying upon God. We trust infinite God rather than our finite selves.
Alcoholics Anonymous, *page 68*

In the darkest moments of my life, facing obstacles that I thought were insurmountable, or at times when I had to close my eyes and remind myself I was not alone, I felt a Higher Power with me. Looking back at how I came through those situations, I know for sure that I did not get through them by myself.

For me, it became simply a matter of faith. By deeply and honestly believing in something larger than myself, *it became a reality*. I can't possibly describe my feeling of relief upon realizing I was *never* alone. I feel like I am safely escorted on this path by a Higher Power who loves me. I simply need to open my eyes, my mind, and my heart to feel God's presence.

~~~~~

God, please walk with me today and keep an eye on me. Help me to be grateful for the little things. Give me the strength to do what is right and remind me that I never need to feel lonely. You have brought me here and, as always, I am in your grasp.

I AM HOME

> *I found the Fellowship of Cocaine Anonymous by accident, and I knew immediately that I had found my spiritual home—identification, laughter, and a place to belong, an instant family.*
> Hope Faith & Courage Volume II, *page 43*

When I look at the Twelve Steps in simple terms, they are a set of principles which, when lived properly, lead me to uncover major truths about myself and life. Life, for me in sobriety, means opening up to experience feelings and emotions long suppressed. It also awakens other sensations of all types. Personally, I call this the Totality of Life (you can also call it God, Creation, Universal Mind or whatever you fancy).

Sometimes I can see with clarity that *this* is it—that *right here, right now* is all we have. My spiritual practice isn't to seek gain, but *rather* to be *with* the creativity of the moment. For me, surely God is right here and right now—where else could It be? God is either everything or He is nothing. Which is it to be? What an amazing realization that God is always here, and I am not alone. I never was, and now I see that as one of the most steady and fulfilling truths in my life. I am able to experience serenity and know peace, even though I go through many changes. I am home.

~~~~~

Although thoughts, feelings and emotions come and go like clouds across the sky, something exists far beyond these changes, something I can come home to, here and now, as I breathe in and out—something some people call God.

THE SKY'S THE LIMIT

Today I believe that a Power greater than myself can, and is, restoring me to sanity in every area of my life. I have faith that this miracle will continue, as long as I keep doing the footwork.
Hope, Faith & Courage, *page 38*

Sobriety was the beginning of my new life. I learned to not just get some sober time—relief from my addiction is my only goal or purpose. I learned to use the Twelve Steps as suggested—in everyday life. If I do not start growing beyond staying sober, I will stagnate and remain that same person I was as a practicing addict. To me, becoming sober means moving forward in *all* parts of my life, not just one. Without this idea in practice, I may not use again, but my life will remain unfulfilled. I will be defeating my original purpose of recovery.

God gives me His all without hesitation. In turn, so will I. One day at a time, I will build a life with endless possibilities. Because of God's love for me, nothing is impossible, provided I'm giving my all!

~~~~~

I pray that I may heal and grow in every aspect of my being. May God show me I am not just someone who settles for a "piece of life," but that I have "*peace* in life," knowing I am doing the best I can.

RESISTING TEMPTATION

If tempted, we recoil from it as from a hot flame.
Alcoholics Anonymous, *page 84*

Addicts are not particularly skilled at resisting temptation. As a child, when my parents said not to touch the pan because it was hot, that is exactly what I felt compelled to do. In early recovery, I felt a strong desire to still use drugs. It seemed more powerful than anything else. I saw others like me give in and get high. Sometimes, it took every ounce of strength I had just to hold on and not use. I worked the Steps and went to meetings. I asked God for help, and still, nothing seemed to work to relieve those thoughts.

As time passed, I began to realize that these challenges were, in fact, opportunities for me to take responsibility for my own recovery. I made a decision to move away from destruction and towards a life of renewed hope and sanity. Cocaine and other mind-altering substances were no longer a temptation, but a repulsive thought. I felt a tremendous relief and freedom. My Higher Power had been with me the whole time. He was just waiting for me to catch on.

~~~~~

It is never too late to take responsibility for my recovery. I have choices today because I am sober. Without drugs I am free.

REWIRE MY DESIRE

> *The more we become willing to depend upon a Higher Power, the more independent we actually are. . . . Every modern house has electric wiring carrying power and light to its interior. We are delighted with this dependence; our main hope is that nothing will ever cut off the supply of current. . . . Silently and surely, electricity, that strange energy so few people understand, meets our simplest daily needs and our most desperate ones, too.*
>
> Twelve Steps and Twelve Traditions, *page 36*

Remember the power of the desire to get high? That desire would lie to me, saying, "*This time it will be different,*" totally suppressing any rational thought of just how unhealthy and toxic my behavior had become. The movement toward self-destruction from my addiction was progressive—one tiny step to the next—creeping along in such a manner that most often, I did not even notice.

My will power alone could not reverse this destructive progression. I needed to have a Power greater then myself. I had to exchange will power for willingness to accept a Higher Power. By making this decision, the process of learning dependence on God followed.

The desire to *not* desire to get high any longer was a step in the right direction for me. A desire to *retire* active addiction necessitated a *rewire* of my desire. God is one heck of an electrician. I find living in the light is much better than living in a lie.

~~~~~

Today, the current of energy I desire is available only through a spiritual connection. I pray that when I seek this connection, I will readily find it.

FAITH

Imagine life without faith! Were nothing left but pure reason, it wouldn't be life.
Alcoholics Anonymous, *page 54*

From the time I was a baby, I always had a sense of being held by a force of some kind, whether it was my mother's love and protection or a close friend's kind words. As I grew older, I started to believe that I was the one in control. My certainty in a Power greater than myself slowly diminished until, with no faith at all, I lost belief in myself and humanity. Without help I became powerless.

In recovery, God helped me shift my focus back to Him. It was only then that I could rediscover the faith of my youth, the infinite beauty of the world around me, and the vast possibilities which life has to offer.

I realize now how much God has loved me right from the start and that everything in my life is, in fact, connected to Him. Even the movement of a tree caught by the wind can speak to me and touch my soul in ways that I cannot logically explain.

~~~~~

Am I an instrument of faith? God, help me to know that with faith in You, I am not powerless. Help me to remember the loving Power that protects us all.

SHARE THE MIRACLE

I just got a great job doing what I do best, helping my
recovery by asking God to help me help someone else.
Hope, Faith & Courage, *page 148*

I was merely a "shell" before entering this program. Spiritually, emotionally and monetarily bankrupt—how true.

After embracing this new sober lifestyle and practicing C.A.'s principles, I find the things that I feared most—loneliness, abandonment, rejection and loss of control—have left my heart and mind, one day at a time. I have a place to go—meetings held in warm rooms filled with recovering people. There I can share any fears which plague me and listen to others as well. I can be myself, maybe for the first time ever. The common bond of my fellows with me allows me to share and listen. I feel secure, loved, appreciated, peaceful, safe, and even comfortable in my own skin. My Higher Power, sobriety, and the unconditional love of my new family is mine to treasure. I begin to develop the ability to accept myself just as I am and am learning to love myself. I am humble and grateful. And best of all, I can now offer these gifts to others.

~~~~

God, I know that I am loved by You and by my fellows in this program. I now even love myself! I've let go of past pain, allowing forgiveness to heal me. I try to be an example, using Your Power to recover as I share the miracle

RELAX

But just how, in these circumstances, does a fellow 'take it easy'? That's what I want to know.
Twelve Steps and Twelve Traditions, *page 26*

I had spent years and years trying to control my using and get it right, all to no avail. Eventually, I came to Cocaine Anonymous, got a sponsor, and started working the Steps.

Early on, it was revealed to me that I needed to establish contact with a Power greater than myself if I was to survive clean and free. This Power I call God. However, my desire to control was, and still sometimes is, a force with which to be reckoned!

My sponsor would say to me again and again, "Relax, God's in charge."

My impatient reply would often be, "I know, I know . . . God's in charge."

"No," he would say, "You are missing the point. *Relax!* It's no good for God to be in charge unless you are prepared to relax and let Him do His thing."

The Third-Step Prayer has become a valuable tool for me to invoke the relaxation necessary to "Let Go and Let God."

~~~~~

Can I truly *relax*, knowing God is in charge? Can I actually surrender to that notion? This is the very essence of Step Three. Control is nothing more than an illusion, so I never had it anyway!

WHO CARES?

See to it that your relationship with Him is right, and great events will come to pass for you and countless others. This is the Great Fact for us.
Alcoholics Anonymous, *page 164*

Step Three suggests we make a decision to turn our will and our lives over to the care of whatever God we can understand. Just what does that mean? Why did they use the word "care"? Care implies to me the most tender and nurturing form of love that exists, such as when I care for the sick and elderly, or when I care for my children and loved ones if they're not feeling well. As I would care for a sparrow with a hurt wing, my Higher Power cares for me.

I can quickly, easily forget my Third-Step decision and slip back into worry or remorse over the many trying situations which I face daily. My mind gets filled with financial problems, relationship worries, challenges at work, questions like "What about this?" or "Should I have done that?," to name a few. If I am still trying to control the outcome of a situation or am cleaning up the wreckage of my *future*, I have stopped believing that God has a plan. I lose sight of just how much He *cares* for me.

Today I am responsible for putting care into action. My sponsor taught me that by caring for others, I will be cared for in return. I was told that my job was to do the next right thing and that the outcome was not my business. Put my program first, and everything else will flourish.

~~~~~

Over the next twenty-four hours, I will care for others. Just as importantly, I will allow them to care for me. With Your care, dear God, may I find the balance in nurturing and being nurtured.

SHALL WE DANCE?

I enjoy real life today. I dance, I pray, I laugh, I work, I love.
Hope, Faith & Courage Volume II, *page 168*

Today, I am dancing with my Creator. I am learning to let my spirit soar up to the sky in all areas of my life. Oh yes, learning to dance without those crutches connected to my limbs was, and sometimes still is, a difficult path on my journey towards wholeness.

Breaking the crutches has led me to discover that my own personal Creator lives inside of me. I have discovered that I am a child of the Universe. I am a light, and with this light I can shine. And when I shine, my hope is to bring comfort and encouragement for others who are on their own path toward the same journey. Being able to shine allowed me to listen to my Creator when the following message was sent to my soul:

> I danced the moment I prepared you for your birth, planting a seed of love in your mother's womb for you to shine. I danced the day you were born, giving you strength for your journey. I danced through your childhood when you overcame suffering, pain, tears and phantoms running around in your mind. I danced the day you bloomed into adolescence, striving forth to show the world who you are. Oh, how I danced the day you became an adult, taking your stance upon the mountain. I danced the day you came back to Me after living in darkness, allowing My light and grace to fill you up again. I danced the day you abandoned yourself only to Me, shedding layers of fear. I will always be dancing for you, my child, watching you shine from that seed of love. Come now, dance with Me. Sway in My light. Hear the music I have planted in your heart.

~~~~~

When two people are dancing together, only one person can lead if the pair is to glide smoothly across the ballroom floor. In my dance with my Creator, may I have the faith it takes to follow so that I can feel the synchronicity of the waltz.

PART OF GOD'S FAMILY

We thought we were happiest with our cocaine, but we were not. In C.A., we learn to live a new way of life. We say that it is a spiritual, but not a religious program—our spiritual values are accessible to the atheist as well as to the devout theist.
To the Newcomer (C.A. Pamphlet)

I emerged from the dark and soulless world of addiction and loneliness where the only god that existed was the next hit of cocaine. Even if a real God did exist, I had no idea how to open a channel or cultivate any sort of personal relationship.

Inside the rooms of Cocaine Anonymous, I learned how to develop a rapport with a God of my own understanding. I now have a God I call my friend. I have come to accept the simple truth that my Higher Power loves me the same way I love my children. By reflecting upon that analogy, I better understand the depth of God's love for me. Inner peace results from my new perspective. Not a bad return.

~~~~~

I try to guide my children along the right path, shielding them from harm as best I can. God does the same for me. Today, I trust my Higher Power will love and protect me the same way I do my own children.

WILLINGNESS HAS ITS REWARDS

My willingness comes from a deep, deep sense of gratitude
that I have been helped to escape living a slow death.
Hope, Faith & Courage Volume II, *page 25*

Today I like myself deeply, from the inside out. My fear of people has been greatly reduced and continues to shrink. The areas of personal relations, daily life, and work are calm and pleasant, no longer chaotic. I enjoy the friendship of my family. It has taken several years, work, patience, hope, love, inventories, tears and honest sharing of feelings to get to this point. It would never have happened without the courage and faith I learned in the C.A. program and the guidance of the Steps in cleaning up the wreckage of my past and re-establishing relations.

Today, in my life, there is a feeling of peace and security such as I have never known. Life seems good to me today. I no longer feel self-loathing or the screaming, ragged pain in my guts, thanks to the Steps and the healing brought about by working them. I know that I am a different, much better person now than I ever was, even before I started using. All of the Promises have come true in my life. Each day sober is better than the one before, in a lot of ways.

Today, I know that I am powerless over the outcome of everything and my life is still unmanageable when left to me to run it. Today I believe that a Power greater than myself can, and is, restoring me to sanity in every area of my life. I have faith that this miracle will continue, as long as I keep doing the footwork.

~~~~~

I hope everyone can find what has been given to me. I lost nothing but my misery, which has been replaced by the most amazing gifts and insights. Help me to recognize all of life's improvements as the result of my recovery.

AN HONEST REQUEST

We feel we are on the Broad Highway, walking hand in hand with the Spirit of the Universe.
Alcoholics Anonymous, *page 75*

Open your heart and let your Higher Power in—you can feel the love instantly! Your desire for recovery strengthens, and your spirituality blossoms. You'll see things in a more positive perspective. Based on this new spirituality in your life, you will become more determined to share your experience with others. Funny how once you are on this side, you can clearly see that you have never been alone—your Higher Power has been with you all along.

Make a simple commitment to pray and meditate once a day. You will be blessed with the ability to go the distance one day at a time. With only an honest request, Higher Power is ready and willing to join you on your journey through recovery, bringing joy, peace and love to pave the way.

~~~~~

Open your heart, take that step and grasp your Higher Power by the hand. Receive the gift of spirituality. Let it grow. Make an honest request for the help you need to carry you through.

CHOOSING GOD

My friend suggested what then seemed a novel idea. He said, "Why don't you choose your own conception of God?"
Alcoholics Anonymous, *page 12*

When I was using, my life priorities did not matter to me—only my next high. As an addict, I consistently placed myself in dangerous situations that could easily have killed me. I lied, cheated, and stole to get my way, without a clue how self-destructive this behavior was or that I actually had a choice for something different. Even with near-death experiences as the result of many overdoses, nothing seemed to affect my inability to change or lessen my using patterns.

Thank goodness, a clean and sober addict took the time to show me a spiritual solution. Now, in recovery, I realize just how much my life really means, not only to me, but to my family as well. I have accepted an enormous change, and now I am ever grateful for my recovery and to be alive. Some aren't so lucky to be given that chance.

I once heard a recovering addict say, "I used to ask myself—why was *I* chosen to receive this gift of sobriety when so many others never get it?" I couldn't figure it out, and one day, I said as much to my sponsor. Immediately he had the answer, which hit me like a bomb: "You weren't chosen," he said, "*you* chose God."

~~~~

Today, may I always choose God. May I share my experience to acknowledge just how precious life is to me now in the hope that it will awaken a similar awareness in others.

83

25 YEARS CLEAN & SOBER

*I have fallen in love in this program. I have an
appreciation for my life I never had before.*
Hope, Faith & Courage, *page 184*

Something impossible has happened for me. I have not used cocaine, or any other drug, in over 25 years. I do, however, vividly remember the physical and mental obsession permeating my life before I found recovery in C.A. Using cocaine was the single most important thing in my brain. I eagerly discarded family, friends and jobs which got in the way of my using. Thank God I found my chair in the then-fledgling program of C.A., just as it was just starting to take off. We grew wings and roots simultaneously, one meeting at a time.

For the first two years of my recovery, I went to C.A. every night. I had been perpetually high, which meant life had to be relearned. Much needed to be studied and explored.

My head and my heart both began to behave differently. Although today my lessons are not the earth-shattering, brand new information that they were then, I am happy to say they still occur. I do my best to remain open and willing because spiritual principles can always be applied to my daily life. Service is ever-important to me. Bonds were formed during hours of committee work, convention planning, and tons of meetings. Monthly chips graduated into glorious annual metal coins.

I made a crucial choice to accept the gift of recovery. Even though heartache, disappointment, loss, and melancholy are sometimes inevitable, the immense joy and years of contentment far outweigh the bad. I am supremely happy with the way I have lived my life so far. Even the time prior to program is important and valuable to me. The contrast is always at hand if I need a reality check.

I have been married many years now to an addict I met my first week sober. Our lives have maneuvered all the learning curves, ups and downs inevitable with any long-term relationship. Fortunately, we've got program tools to work through the issues, giving us a distinct advantage. Thank you, C.A. for *everything*!

~~~~~

Stories of people in C.A. reaching 25 years in recovery are absolutely heartening. What a personal milestone for them and for our entire Fellowship. Who could ever imagine staying clean and sober for a quarter of a century? It is a stellar proclamation that our program works, one day at a time.

UNITED WE STAND - DIVIDED WE FALL

I have become involved in service to Cocaine Anonymous and have learned responsibility, trust, and unity. It is a privilege and an honor to be a part of C.A. and to watch this Fellowship grow and carry the message to sick and suffering addicts and alcoholics. Cocaine Anonymous opened its arms to me and gave me a safe place to be me.
Hope, Faith & Courage Volume II, *page 113*

What is unity? Ask ten people and you may get ten different opinions. Before addiction, I was raised in a large, close-knit family where we all looked out for each other. The love and unity was tangible. Somewhere along the road into young adulthood, I pulled away from my family's love and unity into addiction. As my sickness grew, I sunk deeper into myself, into isolation, loneliness, despair, self-pity, and all the other emotions we addicts experience when using.

After many emotional and spiritual bottoms, through God's grace and mercy, I found the Fellowship of Cocaine Anonymous. Skeptical at first, I kept coming back. I will admit I was somewhat amazed that this seemingly odd group of people who had found a solution would welcome me back, even after many relapses. I can't remember how or when I finally started to feel a part of, instead of apart from, the C.A. Fellowship. As I worked the Twelve Steps and got involved in service, I started to realize how sticking together was very important. Alone, I was not able to quit using. Through unity with addicts in recovery, I was shown the solution, and through working the Steps, I finally found peace with God, myself and the world.

To continue in my addiction meant a sure, slow death. Thanks to the Fellowship of C.A., I found life, hope, faith, courage and many of the Promises I had been seeking, well before I even knew they were Promises. For me, unity is best described in the old saying, "United we stand, divided we fall."

~~~~

Sticking together is *vital*, both for the Fellowship and for my personal recovery. Without a vibrant C.A. Fellowship, I can't survive, let alone recover. I pray to remain a part of the unity of C.A. so that I can continue to learn and practice the solution to my disease of addiction. Without the enthusiastic participation of its members, Cocaine Anonymous would perish.

RIGOROUS HONESTY

I have heard it well said that honesty relieves obsession. Honesty is essential if we really want to begin to recover; moreover, it remains essential to ongoing sobriety and peace of mind.

C.A. NewsGram, 2nd Quarter 2008

My path toward recovery requires honesty—honesty with myself. Can I admit defeat? Can I accept defeat? How many people have I seen admit their powerlessness, only to resume the pursuit of the tired old lie, the "insistent yearning to enjoy life as we once did and a heartbreaking obsession that some new miracle of control would enable us to do it"? (*Alcoholics Anonymous*, page 151.)

People seem to have varying ideas about honesty and, indeed, the amount of honesty needed to get by in life. For me, an addict of the hopeless variety, nothing less than *rigorous honesty* will do. Many addicts appear to get away with far less honesty than I have learned to live by. Never having been in their shoes, it would be presumptuous and arrogant to assume their lives don't have the same quality of emotional sobriety or stability that mine or anyone else who lives this program might have. Yet, it's only too clear, when speaking with those that do not practice rigorous honesty, many problems remain and very little peace of mind exists in their lives. I say this with humility rather than judgment, for I know full well I would be the same had I not surrendered completely to this program.

~~~~~

I pray for rigorous honesty in all aspects of my life, not just in my recovery. I pray for honesty in my relationships, with my sponsor, with my Fellowship friends, in service, and, most of all, with myself. I seek the ongoing serenity and peace of mind which rigorous honesty can and will provide.

RECIPE FOR SERENITY

I've learned that when I'm experiencing a lack of serenity, it's invariably because I'm not getting my way, and I need to remember to relax because God's in charge. I've learned that when I let Him, God really does do for me what I could not do for myself.
Hope, Faith & Courage Volume II, *page 99*

I was struggling, and my precious serenity was quickly becoming a memory. As always, I found the solution to my dilemma using the *Big Book*, the Steps, my sponsor, and the C.A. Fellowship. While walking a sponsee through Step Five, I was reading page 62 of the *Big Book*. Suddenly, the light came on. Maybe my resentment had more to do with me than with them! Further, on page 74, the *Big Book* suggested I go to that 'understanding person' who is not involved. "Yes!" I thought, "Surely my sponsor would sympathize and console." Our phone conversation was short and to the point. Where was I being selfish, self-centered, fearful, and inconsiderate? "Perhaps some serious and honest prayer might set your mind at ease," he suggested. "It always seemed to work for me," he said.

Finally, I took his advice and shared my on-going dilemma *du jour* at my C.A. meetings. The Fellowship provided the final course correction to move me out of my self-pity. (Imagine that?!) Somehow, every single person had the same experience, strength, and hope:

1. Make a gratitude list and reconsider my situation.
2. Recognize how my mental attitude was blocking me from the sunlight of the Spirit.
3. Pray and put the situation in God's hands, and offer my actions as an instrument.

The wise and enduring solution I needed was not what I thought I wanted. Thank you, C.A., for your united response and for helping me truly understand a clear recipe for serenity. These ingredients work for any problem impacting my recovery at any time!

~~~~

God, please help me be mindful of just how well this recipe works, time and time again, in my life and in my program.

DOUBT AS A DEFECT

It was only a matter of being willing to believe in a Power greater than myself. Nothing more was required of me to make my beginning. I saw that growth could start from that point.
Alcoholics Anonymous, page 12

The term agnostic is a combination of the Greek terminology "a" (meaning "without") and "gnosis" (meaning "knowledge"). Thus, an agnostic is one who confidently affirms, "I don't know." I have met very few real atheists in this life. Most I have met within the Fellowship seem to fall into the category of agnostic. Claiming knowledge of God is not a requirement for beginning a journey through the Steps.

Consider the quote from *Bill's Story* above. Can doubt outweigh willingness? As I look back over my life, it seems to me my *doubt* "that God could and would if He were sought" (*Alcoholics Anonymous*, page 60) kept me from being willing much more so than my lack of knowledge. Self-deprecation kept me believing that any God would surely not waste time helping a lost soul such as I, so why bother seeking Him?

The Steps are in order for a reason so we start at Step One, and move to Step Two, Step Three and so on. However, something which is described in the Fourth Step essay really helped me with my Step Three. It states that our defects are something akin to instincts that far exceed their purpose. (*Twelve Steps and Twelve Traditions*, page 42.) If I look at my *doubt* as a defect, I can plainly see where it affected me adversely by leading me into agnosticism. Realizing I had to replace doubt with willingness, I was presently able to move forward in my recovery.

~~~~~

Doubt can be a terminal anchor, holding me back from my unlimited potential in this lifetime. Today, can I be willing to believe in something yet unproven? Even myself?

THE PATH OF SERVICE

Being a product of H&I, I'm a big believer in it. I spend a lot of time going to treatment and detox centers. It puts things into perspective for me because I can relate to the guy sitting there in his foamy slippers, his eyes going different directions, shaking and sweating. And every once in a while, I meet somebody with two days, and then I'll see them years later, and they're still continuously sober, they've worked the Steps, they're a sponsor, and they have a sponsor. It's an amazing process.

Hope, Faith & Courage Volume II, page 186

The day I spoke at my first H&I panel there were 20-30 people in the room. I was so glad we had a format to follow. I closed my eyes and said to myself, "Thy will be done." I opened my eyes and looked at the patients with a smile as I introduced myself and welcomed them to Cocaine Anonymous. We opened the meeting with a moment of silence, followed by the Serenity Prayer, and before I knew it, the meeting was over.

We were received in an amazing way. The reading of *Who is a Cocaine Addict?* touched a lot of people, for they identified with it as well as our shares. When I spoke, I said something about hearing an elder statesman in our Fellowship say, "A broke brain cannot fix a broke brain; get out of the me and into the we." They loved it. Every Monday, new faces are waiting for us to bring the message of recovery via our experience, strength and hope.

I came into Cocaine Anonymous with four years sober but very little recovery. When I was introduced to this Fellowship, I felt at home. I finally found out where I belonged. People loved me until I could love myself. I got a sponsor and began to work the Steps. My sponsor asked me to become the coffee person for that meeting, which helped me get comfortable with being there. The coffee commitment started my path toward the H&I panel. For the ability to share on that first H&I panel, and all those that have followed, I remain eternally grateful.

~~~~

We never know how and when our recovery lives will connect; incidents which appear unrelated somehow intertwine, almost magically. May I be open to this as it occurs and welcome its synchronicity. In recovery, I see life as a tapestry, with all the threads of our existence woven together to create a spectacular image of depth and beauty.

WILLING TO TURN IT OVER?

How could it be that someone like me who had college degrees, money, brains, and status should be expected to stop trying to control my own life and allow someone else to do it? This was hard for me, but I was beginning to learn about willingness and God. I prayed and waited. Finally, I understood that this Step was asking me to turn my will and my life over to "the care" of God. This was something I could do.
Hope, Faith & Courage Volume II, *page 15*

Entering into recovery for the first time, I have to admit, was a little frightening! A lot of ideas were presented that didn't make sense to me; honestly, some of them flat out scared me. The idea of having a Higher Power was okay, but having to trust and pray to Him was a little too far-fetched. When my sponsor sat me down and we did my first two Steps, I had no problem admitting complete defeat and coming to believe.

However, I had a very hard time with making a decision to turn everything over to God "as I understood Him." My sponsor asked if I was willing to at least try, and I was. He proceeded to tell me, "Think of it as a God who understands *you*." This change in perspective made all the difference in the world. No doubt, back then, I didn't understand God, I just knew, as one of my truths, that many events had happened in my recovery life for which I simply had no explanation. This alone seemed to indicate a Power greater than me at work.

After I became willing to accept the ideas found in the Third Step, many other opportunities and insights revealed themselves to me. One simple way to look at it, which has helped me through a lot of trying times, is: I can't; He can; let Him. I cannot control my life. I have already tried and it doesn't work. I have come to believe that God can, so why not let Him? Once I was able to internalize this piece of the recovery puzzle, the rest of the Steps came more easily.

~~~~~

I am so grateful to have found the willingness needed for Step Three. Much of my early Step work was unlocked by this key. The means to an end doesn't really matter, only my willingness to complete this vital Step and continue working the remaining Steps.

FREEDOM FROM THE DEMONS THAT LIVE IN MY HEAD

> There is *a solution. Almost none of us liked the self-searching, the leveling of our pride, the confession of shortcomings which the process requires for its successful consummation. But we saw that it really worked in others and we had come to believe in the hopelessness and futility of life as we had been living it.*
>
> Alcoholics Anonymous, *page 25*

How long had it been since I liked myself? Believing in Something greater than me changed that. Freedom from the bondage of alcohol and drugs initiated the change.

Now that the demons in my head have quieted down, I'm finally understanding what it is to really live . . . something I haven't done for years! How did it slip away so subtly over time? Today, having surrendered to the Steps, I have found inner peace.

Trusting in my Higher Power, I've gained guidance. Letting go of my secrets freed my soul. I am amazingly aware of how the Promises are being fulfilled in my life daily. I now believe in myself, and I am learning patience. I have every faith that my path will be revealed, provided I stay honest and keep working the Steps.

~~~~~

Recipe for a good day: Be honest. Share my secret. Help a new member.

RECOVERY'S LESSONS

Many of these lessons of recovery were hard-fought. For a long time I rode a roller coaster of emotions, and yet I found that I could walk through them with a clear, uncluttered mind.
Hope, Faith & Courage Volume II, *page 106*

Life is slowly getting better, one day at a time! Recovery comes in many forms daily—a harsh reality check or a huge grin on my face for no reason whatsoever. The journey started with surrender to a real mess—drug/booze-fueled days with no happy or contented endings. Life was on hold, and good times were passing me by. Frustration and anger were constant throughout the day. When these emotions became too much to handle—more alcohol and more cocaine. I knew nothing of spiritual malady, obsession or powerlessness. I just hovered in a bad place, alone and scared.

But I didn't think I was an addict. When someone in the Fellowship took me to my first meeting, everyone welcomed me, invited me to stay a while, and told me to keep coming back. For some reason, I listened to what was said, and for the first time in many years, I finally accepted being an addict. I identified with people sharing their experiences and emotions during the meetings.

Slowly, I began to feel better. I got a day clean, then two, then a week, then a month, and here I am now, some years later, writing this small story of my journey in recovery. I strongly believe I have recovered from a hopeless state of mind and body! The program taught me to take action to combat negative feelings.

Recovery is ongoing in my life, both inside meetings as well as outside, in my work and family. Dealing with life on life's terms is hard, but in sobriety, I get results like never before. I need always remember who I was, where I came from, and the better person I am today. Without the recovery offered in C.A. meetings through the Fellowship, I wouldn't be here enjoying this freedom.

~~~~~

Recovery is possible, but I can't afford to ever do it alone. Because of this Fellowship, I am blessed with freedom from that very dark place where I dwelt before I came into the rooms of C.A.

THOUGHTS ON THE THIRD STEP

> *There is only one key, and it is called willingness.*
> Twelve Steps and Twelve Traditions, *page 34*

As stated in *Twelve Steps and Twelve Traditions,* the effectiveness of my individual program rests upon how well and earnestly I have tried to work Step Three. A lot of weight to put on a single Step! So then, what is the most effective thing I can bring to this Step to help me work it earnestly and completely? Faith? Or a leap of faith? I once heard someone say in a meeting, "I have a deep and abiding faith that comes and goes." Seriously, is faith the single best, necessary ingredient to work Step Three effectively? Apparently not.

I read in the *Twelve Steps and Twelve Traditions* (page 34) that, "Faith, to be sure, is necessary, but faith alone can avail nothing. We can have faith, yet keep God out of our lives." An interesting thought, really—and as it turns out, totally true. The program instructs me to couple faith with willingness. The willingness to relinquish self-will, one more time, in favor of God's will. My natural state is fearful running. Long-term sobriety has not changed this—for me anyway. So, the willingness to beat down self-will and turn to God's will is, most often, born from fear and desperation. You can either let go, or be dragged. Trust in God does grow over time. Yet even after all the experiences I've had, I still sometimes forget that God has my best interests at heart.

Two perspectives always facilitate my willingness to beat down self-will. The first is (as amazing as it sounds every time I think of it) that things are not necessarily going wrong because they are not going my way. Second, the Steps are not going to change *what* I go through; they will change *how* I go through it. I work Step Three most effectively when I realize what I am releasing is the results.

~~~~~

"God, I offer myself to Thee—to build with me and to do with me as Thou wilt. Relieve me of the bondage of self, that I may better do Thy will. Take away my difficulties, that victory over them may bear witness to those I would help of Thy Power, Thy Love, and Thy Way of life. May I do Thy will always." (*Alcoholics Anonymous*, page 63.)

JUST LET GO

We will suddenly realize that God is doing for us what we could not do for ourselves.
Alcoholics Anonymous, *page 84*

While playing with my two-year-old nephew, I came across one of those cars that you pull back, and then it rolls forward of its own accord. As I was showing him how it worked, he kept trying to force it to go forward, causing the wheels to spin around without the car going anywhere. I found myself repeating to him over and over, "Just let go! Pull back and just let go!"

It suddenly occurred to me—what a powerful example of the Third Step, "Made a decision to turn our will and our lives over to the care of God *as we understood Him*." Whenever I try to make things happen through my own will power, I usually find myself spinning my wheels. However, when I let my Higher Power take the reins, my life advances effortlessly and joyfully. Like the toy car, I simply need to back up and release for a smooth ride forward!

~~~~~

I will trust my Higher Power today. I will remember to let go and let God whenever I am faced with a situation, person, place, or thing that I am powerless over. I will remember that when I let go, God can do for me what I cannot do for myself.

APRIL

REWARDS OF SPONSORSHIP

*Sharing the lessons of what he or she has learned
staying sober is what a sponsor is all about.*
Choosing Your Sponsor (C.A. Pamphlet)

As a new C.A. member, I felt scared and lost. I knew nothing of the Twelve Steps or how they worked. Getting a sponsor was like engaging a guide, someone who had walked the path and could show me the way. Coming from a dark place filled with desperation, I needed someone to offer hope and steer me towards a spark of light.

Finding a good fit in a sponsor was crucial for me. Establishing a bond and developing trust in another not only took time, but also required a couple different sponsors before I found the right one. Each of my sponsors played a vital role in my recovery but after a while, it seemed I had learned all I could from them and moving on made sense. For me, finding an individual whose past held similarities with my own was important in order to maximize empathy and understanding. My current sponsor is truly a gift bestowed by my Higher Power. With this support and loving guidance, I have steadily grown—emotionally and spiritually.

Having been an active member of Cocaine Anonymous for some time now, I am blessed with the honor of working with quite a few sponsees. The knowledge and development I've gained from this type of service is incalculable.

Learning about myself through my own Step work helps me to reflect on my strengths and defects, showing me where improvement is necessary. Doing work with my sponsees gives me a different type of insight. I don't believe I have ever given a suggestion to a sponsee that I didn't need to hear myself. The lessons I receive through working with a sponsee teach me just as much as those acquired from my sponsor's ideas.

~~~~~

By sharing with another, I discover how I want to live and who I aspire to become. What greater reward could I possibly receive? I will forever be grateful to all of my sponsors and sponsees.

PERSONAL ACCEPTANCE

For the first time in my life, I was happy with myself.
Hope Faith & Courage, *page 119*

After years of self-loathing as an active addict, how do I achieve personal acceptance? It seemed the door to my innermost self was locked and someone had thrown away the key.

The Twelve Steps were the answer. Once I took that searching and fearless moral inventory, as difficult as it was, I discovered a person I never knew existed. Total honesty revealed a Higher Power within me, enabling me to be the person I truly want to be.

I am so grateful for the program because each Step has made me a better person. I can look in the mirror without shame or guilt. Don't get me wrong; I still screw things up (sometimes badly!), but as long as I continue to learn and grow from these mistakes, I can remain happy, joyous, and free.

~~~~~

By practicing the principles of the program, I can be the person I have always wanted to be. I will be honest with myself, making it easier for me to love the child of God that I am.

THE IMPORTANCE OF MEETINGS

I see a lot of people come in and out of the rooms. Today I am not willing to risk it. I know that I have to keep doing what I have been doing: meetings, the Twelve Steps, work with my sponsor, service work, all of it.
Hope, Faith & Courage Volume II, *page 175*

Even with a good bit of time in recovery, I still go to five meetings a week on a regular basis. Sometimes one of my non-addict friends will ask me why I still need meetings. This is a no-brainer! It is my *responsibility* to continue going to meetings. The fact is, if people stopped going to meetings after a few years sober, who would be there for the newcomer?

Just by being at a meeting, I can be of service to someone without even realizing it—by sharing a smile, a hug, a kind word. When I share my experience, strength, and hope with others, it shows them they aren't alone. New friends can see that someone else has felt the same way and survived. That they, too, can live a life filled with hope, faith, and courage.

Today, I *want* to go to meetings. I have gained so many true friendships in Cocaine Anonymous—I wouldn't trade those for anything! Most importantly, I am not willing to put my recovery in jeopardy. In my experience, the number one reason that people relapse is because they quit going to meetings. One day at a time, I choose to stay connected with my forever-Fellowship family.

~~~~~

When they told me to "keep comin' back," the word "until" was never mentioned. I thoroughly enjoy going to meetings even after putting some time together in the program. Meetings allow me to stay connected with my Fellowship family and keep my recovery solidified. Plus, I am there to be of service to the newcomer, which is vitally important not only to their recovery, but to mine as well.

THE REAL PROBLEM

We found ourselves scraping envelopes and baggies with razor blades, scratching the last flakes from the corners of brown bottles, snorting or smoking any white speck from the floor when we ran out.
To the Newcomer (C.A. Pamphlet)

When *Who is a Cocaine Addict?* is being read at a meeting, I feel a flood of varying emotions. At first, I am irritated by the description of drug paraphernalia. Then, I recall the desperation and hopelessness of active addiction, and I feel extreme gratitude for C.A. Also, I have to laugh when being reminded of my lofty conception of self, and how I prided myself on "my fine-tuned state of mind."

I came to the Fellowship of Cocaine Anonymous beaten and broken. Unable to carry on, I needed to find out how you all got through a day without using—how my problem with drugs could be removed.

Once I stopped using, the real problem soon presented itself. As it turns out, the problem was my disease!

In my active disease, I was useless, miserable, alone, self-centered, and dying. In sobriety, I can't say exactly when or how God snuck into my life, but I'm grateful to have received that grace. I continue to be blessed by more grace the longer I am around the Fellowship. Today, I pray that my Higher Power will "finely tune my state of mind," to help me remember that the only thing I can truly change in this life is my attitude and outlook.

~~~~~

Through the practice of C.A.'s Twelve Steps, again and again, I have been able to trace nearly all of life's problems back to their real source. I pray that I will never lose this insight.

CHOICES

I set out on what would soon prove to be the best choice of my life. I knew that night that I would never have to be alone again.
Hope Faith & Courage Volume II, *page 134*

From the moment of our birth, we are faced with choices that will determine the paths we travel upon, bringing results of joy, sorrow, ecstasy, or pain.

Life has given me many roads to explore, leading me to the present. My choices resulted in pain comparable to a sharp-edged razor cutting and tearing into my inner self, leaving a hole that I elected to fill with drugs and alcohol. They worked for a while to anesthetize the pain. The diseases of addiction and alcoholism carried me down to the depths of a bottomless pit where I felt safe in the cold darkness of my making. My disease progressed rapidly along a turbulent route of my choice. It left me feeling empty, like a seashell washed up on the shore that has been vacated by its occupant.

I had neither the tools of honesty, hope, and faith, nor the willingness to surrender and admit I was the problem. The comfort I once experienced in the darkness of that icy pit of hell was no longer available.

Just for a moment, the insanity of active addiction lifted, and a new choice became clear. Would it be life or death, darkness or light? The choice was life on life's terms. Today, with the help of Cocaine Anonymous, I have been given life and the tools needed to make healthy choices.

~~~~~

The grace which my choices have afforded me is amazing and precious from many perspectives. The ultimate choice of recovery and sobriety is a most special and enduring gift which keeps on giving as I continue to grow in my recovery. I am humbled by the opportunities I have to make choices and for the choice of life on life's terms.

LOVE IN FELLOWSHIP

After almost three decades of using, I have been
given a way of life beyond my wildest dreams.
C.A. NewsGram, 1ˢᵗ Quarter 1998

It was only a few years ago that I was practically unable to leave my house. The only time I would venture out was to score. The drugs no longer dulled the pain, but I was unable to stop. The shame I felt paralyzed me. I longed to be accepted, and loved. I was completely broken. Then God sent me a messenger. Someone I had known many years ago contacted me. He told me that he was sober, and that I no longer had to carry on killing myself daily. Help was available. I had received help in the past which include being put in a straitjacket, a padded cell, and left to withdraw in a hospital. He assured me that this would be different.

"Is there anyone new here who is clean and sober today or desires a new way of life?" they asked in a meeting. A man gave me my first chip and hugged me. I stood there and cried. What price would I have to pay for this love? Nobody gave without return in the twilight world I lived in at the time. Yet, my inner voice knew that all they wanted was to see me get well. I'd been to hell, and now I was home. It had taken so many years, but now I had found the family I had always longed to be a part of. A family who would love me for just being me, not for what I had or for what I could give them. A family who would not put expectations on me but would accept me.

What a far cry from being alone in my house. Today I am sober multiple years. I now realize that my family is worldwide. We are all so different, and yet we are all the same. I know you all without ever having met you. No matter where I go, the meetings are constant, as is the message.

~~~~~

From the depths of my disease and isolation, I can be carried to a different life of recovery which includes love, acceptance, solutions and insights beyond my wildest expectations. My vehicle for this ride is the program, which is fueled by the continuity I find in meetings everywhere I go.

THEN AND NOW

Guilt, shame, fear, disappointment, sorrow . . . we know well that we may meet again someday. But until that day we shall be walking our new path, and our companions on that journey of New Life have been promised to us; their names are Hope, Faith, and Courage. And with these new companions come . . . slowly, slowly . . . peace, true happiness, pleasure, joy, and love.
C.A. NewsGram, 1st Quarter 1999

I arrived here damaged, suffering, and in pain. My damage was different from yours, my suffering different from yours, my pain different as well. What got each of us here was different—and yet the same. Why I got here, how I got here, how long I stay here—all may be different. It doesn't matter. What matters is that I am here, others have joined with me, and I with them. We're all different, yet in many ways quite similar.

I cannot return to the past to correct anyone's mistakes. I cannot go back and right any of these wrongs. I cannot return to *then* and make right the injustices of my younger life, relationships, and experiences. What I can, and must do is to start anew—today. I go forward from *now*—free! I can start my life free from that old pain, that old suffering, that guilt and shame and damage, not by denying it, but rather by accepting and embracing it as I would a long-time acquaintance we know we may never see again.

The journey I am starting is *life*! I will walk this path with others I meet in the program because we are here and we are together in this moment *now*.

~~~~~

Listen for the similarities not the differences; remember that we all are here for a reason in this place, at this time. Even though our steps may falter, our resolve may weaken, our fears may arise . . . together we are strong. We walk together side by side, heads high, into that curious, unknown, bright future.

UNITY PROMOTES OUR PURPOSE

*When we reach our hand out to another, we may be grasping
the hand of the best of friends who only needed someone to
welcome them into our Fellowship of recovery. If we do not take
the first step toward the other, they may not receive the grace
they need and our lives and our Fellowship may be impoverished.*
C.A. NewsGram, 2nd Quarter 1998

C.A. is a Fellowship of people who, as individuals, have had their lives restored by God. Our purpose is to find ways of helping the addict who still suffers and to promote the well-being of each individual who comes through our doors. Addicts are, most often, isolated people who are looking for a Higher Power who can restore them to unity and spirituality. We now belong not only to our Higher Power, but also to a Fellowship which has welcomed us at all levels. What separated us from each other on the outside can now unite us in our rooms. Black or white, male or female, rich or poor, old or young—we all belong to the Fellowship and experience each other as brothers or sisters in recovery.

Unity is promoted by hospitality toward the newcomer. The growth of our Fellowship will depend on our loving, friendly spirit of service, which recognizes the value of each and every person. This Fellowship is for everyone who wants what our Higher Power has given to us. Let us welcome them as part of our lives and of our future service to God and humankind.

~~~~~

I always need to be mindful about reaching out to newcomers in all situations. May I always reach out to the newcomer who is different than me. May I always try to understand the outspoken old-timer or that person whose personality clashes with my own. I pray for tolerance, love, and insights in my own program and in service.

FROM THE DEPTHS OF DESPAIR TO HEAVEN ON EARTH

We came into these rooms emotionally, financially and spiritually bankrupt.
We Can Recover (C.A. Meeting Format Reading)

I have made so many mistakes along this journey called life. In my disease, I retreated from reality and never knew how to connect with my emotions. When I came to Cocaine Anonymous, many within the Fellowship not only loved me but showed me by clear example how I could love myself. Because of these lessons, I have learned to be accepting of my brokenness and to allow that acceptance to serve both as a motivating force of my continued spiritual exploration and growth. It is also an ongoing inspiration to share my lessons with others in the program so that their path might be easier than mine as a result of my newfound insights.

My troubled past using and abusing drugs and alcohol was not wasted. It was preparation for my newfound rich life of love, service, prayer, meditation, and purpose in recovery. Without all the madness and suffering, I might have missed my heaven-on-earth: the beautiful world in which I live today.

I embrace my life today. I'm getting up early and going to bed late because I don't want to miss *any* of this.

~~~~~

I'm doing the best I can, God, to use Your help to do better, to be gentler, to be humbler, to change in positive ways. May I always show patience, love, and tolerance to the newcomers I meet, as well as to my fellows both inside and outside the rooms of recovery. By fully embracing Your loving guidance, the light of hope represented by C.A. shines through my thoughts, words, prayers, and actions.

THE "WE" TEAM

We never have to be alone again. On a bad day, we find there is usually someone there who understands and who can help us get through it sober.
The Home Group (C.A. Pamphlet)

The "we" of the program is working to help me stay sober on a one-day-at-a-time basis. Of course, my morning and evening prayers to my Higher Power (whom I call God) contribute enormously to the process. God is the first member of my "we" team.

Every day, I call my sponsor plus two other recovering addicts. My job is to share how I am feeling and how my day is going. My sponsor is part of my "we" team, as are all the other Fellowship members.

In addition, I must strive to help another human being, expecting nothing in return. These combined actions keep me out of my head, which I've been told is a dangerous neighborhood, not to be visited alone.

My favorite slogan goes, "You can't *think* your way to sober living; you have to *live* your way to sober thinking."

~~~~~

Repetition is a necessary component to my program of action. All of the tools need to be used again and again for me to gain any proficiency and confidence in using them. With my "we" team's help, I can learn to become adept at practicing the principles, even when it feels totally unnatural to do so.

SERVING MY HOME GROUP

We are told that getting out of ourselves is one of the best things for us to do, and serving our home group is a wonderful way to start.
The Home Group (C.A. Pamphlet)

Recently, I was on my way to work, worrying about a certain problem and getting myself disturbed. To stop this, I turned my thoughts to my home group. The wonderful thing is I don't even have to be there to serve my home group. At the start of my recovery, my sponsor stressed upon me the important principle of "constant thoughts of others."

What can I do to make my home group the best in the world? How can I better carry the message? How do I express my experience in a way that just might make the difference to that newcomer who hasn't yet fully surrendered? How will I best set a good example to others and help maintain an atmosphere of recovery? Could I offer more support to our new secretary by sitting down on time, not sharing too long, thanking him after the meeting for a job well done, or sharing my familiarity about areas in which he might be more effective? Could I perhaps write another article for our group newsletter? If so, what topic would be most useful?

After meditating for a while on serving my home group, the problem I had been worrying about seemed to have disappeared. I had found a new perspective. On other occasions when practicing this spiritual tool, I have suddenly found solutions which previously hadn't occurred to me.

~~~~~

When disturbed, I can turn my thoughts to being of service to my home group, lifting my spirit and becoming more effective in all my affairs. I draw strength by thinking of various home group members and the experience, strength, and hope they share with me each week.

AVOID CONTROVERSY

> *"We do not wish to engage in any controversy and we neither endorse nor oppose any causes. Our primary purpose is to stay free from cocaine and all other mind-altering substances, and to help others achieve the same freedom."*
>
> (C.A. Preamble)

We all have opinions on a wide variety of matters. Sometimes, differences in opinion can be so strong, close friends or family members completely stop talking with each other.

Tradition Ten states that "Cocaine Anonymous has no opinion on outside issues; hence the C.A. name ought never be drawn into public controversy." For me, the fact that our meeting discussions don't stray into divisive issues, especially politics and religion, has always been refreshing and uplifting. I have a place where my relations with others can be focused on being useful and presenting solutions to life's challenges by the application of Twelve-Step spiritual principles. As a newcomer, I was surprised at the level of love and tolerance expressed by the people I met. Today, I know they were simply adhering to this Tradition.

~~~~~

Am I aware of how I express my opinions on controversial subjects? Do I remember to keep these topics out of discussions in C.A. meetings? Is my group committed to unity by adhering to our Traditions? Today, let me remember that controversy over outside issues destroys my usefulness to God and the people around me.

HEROES

Today I have a 13-year-old who has never seen me drunk or loaded. . . . I asked him who his hero was. Without missing a beat, he turned and looked me right in the eyes and said, "You are, Daddy."
Hope, Faith & Courage Volume II, *page 68*

After I got into recovery, I realized how unlikely it would be for me to become a famous athlete or movie star. I probably wouldn't write the great American novel either.

However, I *could* become a great father, a better brother, a caring uncle, and, above all, a loving son to the parents who had done so much for me. With a goal such as this in my life, I couldn't go wrong! My objective blossomed beautifully with my children. It went well with my sisters, brothers, nieces and nephews, too, but it was with my parents where my relationship mending brought me the most gratitude. So many times, I had taken advantage of them, filling their hearts with disappointment and sorrow. Now clean and sober, I stayed very close to my father and was able to be present for him when his health began to fail. I talked to him on the morning he died, having no regrets for anything left unsaid. I continue to stay devoted to my mother and cherish whatever time I have left with her.

Staying active in the Fellowship, I sponsor a few men, doing my best to share how the program has worked to turn my relationships and my life around. When I think about heroes, soldiers, police and firefighters who risk all to protect us come to mind. But then I realize every life sincerely lived to serve others is heroic. My duty is to help those God has placed in my path to the very best of my ability. It is the least I can do in return for His many gifts, with which I have truly been blessed.

~~~~

I've come to believe that a life lived to help others is the only life that matters. I am, through the program, able to mend relationships from my past. I believe the lessons learned and the changes I have made as a result of working on these relationships are both key to my ability to help others.

STEP FOUR GIFTS

Made a searching and fearless moral inventory of ourselves.
C.A. Step Four

Telling on myself takes down the walls that keep me from being with others—the walls of fear making me think that if people truly knew me, they would hate me. To know me was to hate me. These feelings weren't just about actions taken in the course of my life. I thought my core was rotten, that I was and had always been defective.

There can be no trust when I think I might be found out. How could others trust me? The magic of the Fourth Step is the gift of trust. I learned that I was a good person who sometimes acted badly. I learned that others sometimes acted badly but were good people. What a gift this is—the gift of being human. I learned that I and others had defects, but our defects were not who we were. I found out what it was about my actions that made me feel shame and worked to not repeat those patterns. I also discovered what makes me feel right in the world.

~~~~~

I pray that I may strive to understand the many, varied gifts of Step Four. Those gifts include trust and the affirmation that I am a good person who is human and may make mistakes from time to time. I pray that these insights may continue to be revealed to me in my recovery, and that I may work on not repeating those patterns.

CARRYING THE MESSAGE

I made it into this Program because someone else worked their Twelfth Step on me. Someone passed it on to me. Someone was out there after they got clean and sober, caring about others. I need to never, ever forget that. Had they simply gone on with their lives and forgotten about people like me who were still out there using and suffering, I wouldn't be here today. My gratitude begins with that fact. It is with that gratitude in mind that I reach out to others, especially the newcomers. I need to have them in my life. That is where my spirituality begins.

Hope, Faith and Courage, page 127
(also C.A. Meeting Format reading Reaching Out)

At my first C.A. meeting, I heard people talking openly about their secrets, which were also my secrets. It had never occurred to me that others had done those same shameful things that I was doing on a daily basis. I related to their brief shares of what it was like. I listened in amazement and horror to their laughter. They read *Who is a Cocaine Addict?* and around the banter that I couldn't follow, I heard my secrets being told: ". . . the lines got fatter; the grams went faster. . . snorting or smoking any white speck from the floor . . . Even if it made us feel miserable. . . . This time, we'd be careful. . . . We tried changing jobs, apartments, cities, lovers. . . ."

After the meeting, several women took the time to talk with me. I have no recollection of what was said, only that these women understood me without my having to explain the details. I went home that night and continued to get loaded. Weeks later, I called one of the women from that first meeting, and she took me to another C.A. meeting and then home to her own house where I began to detox. The thing I remember the most about her was that she was sober—it was such a stunning concept to me. She told me that I had what it takes to live sober too. The Twelve Steps guide us, she said.

That was the message I heard long before I got sober. It took me almost another year, which included the most violent and horrific period of using that I had ever experienced, before I was able to stand on a sobriety date. But I had heard the message, and finally, when I had been utterly defeated, it led me back to C.A.

~~~~~

I am most thankful that the message of hope and recovery somehow reached me when I needed it most. As I share the message with others, please let me remember I am planting seeds and have no control over if or when they will germinate.

CAUGHT IN A LIE

> *Those who do not recover are people who cannot or will not completely give themselves to this simple program, usually men and women who are constitutionally incapable of being honest with themselves.... They are naturally incapable of grasping and developing a manner of living which demands rigorous honesty.*
>
> Alcoholics Anonymous, *page 58*

During the early days of my recovery, I happened to watch a reality TV police program. In this particular episode, the police had handcuffed a drug user, put him in the squad car and were carting him off to jail. As they were driving away, the officer in the driver's seat was lecturing the offender about his poor judgment. He was caught in the act—buying drugs while sitting in his automobile with his children in the back seat.

Almost immediately, I took on the role of judge and convicted the man for his behavior. But then, as I sat there for another few moments, suddenly came a flood of memory, illuminating from the recesses of my mind that I'd done the very same thing, not just once, but many times! The only difference was that the offender on TV was caught by the police while I was now convicted by admitting the lie to myself.

Today, I can tell the truth. I am an addict as well as a parent, and I bought crack cocaine while my kids were sitting in the back seat of my automobile. As the result of this incident, I realized my addict behavior affected those close to me. Gradually, as I gained more sobriety, a measure of sanity crept back into my life. I began to see what I'd been missing, especially involving my parental responsibilities. Suiting up, showing up, and doing the next right thing feels far better than lying to everyone or anyone, including myself.

~~~~

Rigorous honesty is a key element in staying clean and sober one day at a time. If I frankly examine my current behavior, do I see any aspects of deceit? Can I admit to God, myself, and another human being the exact nature of my wrongs?

April 17

FROM "JUST ME" TO "PART OF"

God has touched me with many gifts: to feel loved and cared for, to feel a part of, and to feel comfortable enough in my own skin to not pick up a drink or a drug today.
Hope, Faith & Courage Volume II, *page 39*

When I came to C.A. some years back, my whole life consisted of "just me." Who did I trust? Just me. Who would I go to in time of need? Just me. Who did I want to be with and share my life with? Just me. Everything was "just me."

I had arrived in C.A. as an emotionally, spiritually, and physically bankrupt person. I went to meetings and never talked to anybody. I was mad at the world and did not trust anyone. I certainly wasn't going to share anything about myself with this bunch of junkies. It was still "just me." But then a small miracle happened. I had a roommate, and we would stay up late into the night and talk about what it was like and, more importantly, I started to tell him how I really felt. Time passed and I slowly began to believe I was not an entity unto myself. I could reach out to other human beings, and I would actually receive help!

I continued on the journey. I got a sponsor who taught me that I was a good and worthwhile person—that I was completely worthy of love and acceptance from my fellow man. Things changed. No longer was it "just me." It became "us": me, my fellows, and my God. I was now a full-fledged member of the Fellowship of Cocaine Anonymous. I had gone from being "just me" to becoming "part of." I belonged!

~~~~~

I pray that I remain mindful of the need to no longer go at life alone. The healthier, more recovered approach is to let others in and share my feelings with them. I pray for the ability to ask for help when I need it, in and out of the rooms, and to always offer help to others.

ACT NOW FOR A FREE GIFT

I was told gratitude is an action and not just a word. . . .
Hope, Faith & Courage Volume II, *page 149*

My life's goal today is one of service—to my Higher Power and to others. This is the polar opposite from the self-centered root of my disease. Here is the spiritual axiom: God reaches out to help me when I reach out to help others. It's a win-win proposition to which I am dedicated on a daily basis. To carry out my goal, I don't need money, education, people, books, diplomas, positions, power, or any resources other than my own time and willingness. My motivation stems from a deep sense of gratitude for having been helped to escape a slow death.

My bonus by-product (kind of like when you see one of those infomercials on TV, and they say, "*Act now,* and receive a free gift!") is the great joy and fulfillment I feel from helping others—always satisfying, often quite humbling. I'll continue to freely give away what was shared with me. Assisting others through the mental and spiritual process of surrender, and then showing them how to work the program is what my recovery is all about today.

~~~~~

Do I make time on a daily basis to reach out to help others? I'm not supposed to wait to be asked for my assistance. The "free gift" only comes if I *act now.*

_____

INSPIRED BY SPIRITUAL WILL

For me, this Program is about one thing—smashing my self-will and replacing it with spiritual will. I keep my faith in God and give him credit for the gifts and miracles in my life.
Hope, Faith and Courage, *page 128*

The smashing of my self-will began as I looked at the then-wreckage of my present. Humiliation, scorn, and rejection were the constant reactions from the people I regularly encountered. I felt "less than" and, at many levels, I was so.

In recovery, I soon discovered self-obsession was at my problem's root. I was the classic case of "self-will run riot," probably worse if that is possible. As I began to work the Steps, I heard about will—my will, God's will, even a spiritual will. In Step Three, the lesson was to turn my will over to the care of God. Later on, in Step Eleven, it was suggested I pray and meditate to improve my conscious contact with God, seeking the knowledge of His will for me and the power to carry that out. So the primary focus transferred completely from looking at my will to really coming to know God's will in my life.

Some have characterized this change in focus as the arch through which we pass to freedom. This is why I remain so inspired to continue doing God's will in my life. One day at a time, with practice, allowing God to be in charge becomes a natural instinct. The serenity that follows is beyond description.

~~~~~

The C.A. program of recovery—the Steps, the Fellowship, and service—has gradually transformed my self-will-driven life into one inspired by spiritual will. May I constantly be reminded that my serenity today is the direct result of grace from a loving God.

ADDICTIONS COME IN PAIRS WITH A SPARE

> *One drink is never enough, just as one hit, fix, pill or snort is never enough. We are masters at combining and substituting one drug for another to get high. Many of us never felt that alcohol was part of our problem. However, take away the drug of choice, substitute another, and eventually it becomes a problem drug.*
> Hope, Faith & Courage Volume II, *page 238*

Many of us have, as parts of our disease, addictions to more than one drug, behavior, or compulsion. When I got to the rooms, it was quite overwhelming to try and sort out my behaviors, even to know where to start. I had so many bad habits to choose from, all likely to take me to a worse place by themselves, and even lower on the downward spiral when combined with the rest.

At one of my early meetings, I shared about feeling overwhelmed. The advice I received that day was quite simple, wise and enduring: deal with the addictions in the order they would kill me. They would come as a group, and I needed to tackle them in sequence to make recovery possible. That made such sense then, and even more now.

C.A. gives me a plan to address my disease of addiction to cocaine and all other mind-altering substances, including, for me, alcohol. That is a great start and one for which I will be forever grateful. Consistently following this advice is part of my recovery. I have been able to address some of my other addictive behaviors, including nicotine addiction, challenges around working too much, eating poorly, and more. Others, too, have tackled their own mixture of alternative addictive behaviors once they were clean and sober and well into the Steps.

~~~~

Being addicted to drugs and alcohol is quite the challenge. Thank God for the C.A. program which allows me to focus on my drug and alcohol use early on, providing a solution to arrest other addictions in my life. I pray for the continued relief afforded by my C.A. recovery and the insights that working the Steps provide on how to tackle other behaviors on the periphery of my disease.

SURVIVAL OF THE FITTEST

*I am a contributing member of society, rather than a drain on its resources
. . . I see each day as an opportunity to be better than the day before.*
Hope, Faith & Courage, page 113

I love going to meetings because I am devoted to carrying the message that our C.A. program is successful. I continue to practice the Steps because they work to improve the quality of my life, my character, and my relationship with God. I persist in doing service; it's how I support the Fellowship that saved my life. I always want C.A. to be healthy and available as it was for me.

I keep studying the Traditions and Concepts to increase in wisdom about how my Group and other service bodies should work. These principles ensure the survival of our Fellowship.

I have heard my favorite wise slogans repeatedly in the rooms. These are often poignant guides for many program and Fellowship challenges, which could affect our recovery. The slogans help me keep the program simple.

I keep praying because I know I would be lost without my Higher Power. I thank God every morning and every night for any number of things, starting with my relationships with family and friends, and ending with another day clean and sober.

~~~~~

I need to be active in some part of the program (meetings, service, Step work) every day in order to receive its gifts, as well as to be able to continually give them away. It all fits together perfectly and keeps working, day after day, month after month, year after year. I need never lose sight of the perfect synchronicity.

DON'T GET DISTRACTED

A C.A. group ought never endorse, finance, or lend the C.A. name to any related facility or outside enterprise, lest problems of money, property and prestige divert us from our primary purpose.
C.A. Tradition Six

The *Big Book* of Alcoholics Anonymous states that "worldly clamors, mostly those within myself" blot out the sense of God's presence. (*Alcoholics Anonymous*, page 13.) If the solution to my problem depends on my accessing that Power which is God's presence, anything standing in the way of that contact needs to be addressed. The same principle applies to our Fellowship. Our unity depends upon striving, as a Fellowship, toward a common purpose. Our common purpose is to carry the C.A. message to the still-suffering addict. Concerns over money, property, and prestige distract groups and the Fellowship from that intent. Thus, this Tradition divides the spiritual from the material and guides our Fellowship toward a single objective.

Additionally, associations with any "outside" endeavor, no matter how well-intentioned that endeavor might be, are to be avoided. For the protection of the Fellowship, we try to avoid becoming embroiled in any disputes or controversies.

Finally, this Tradition ensures that we will always remain poor. Money is not our lifeblood; newcomers are the Fellowship's vital force.

~~~~~

Help me be aware that anything which does not fulfill our primary purpose may hurt the group. Let my thoughts be directed by God today, especially that my thinking not drift into self-pity or be driven by selfish and dishonest motives. May I have the clarity to discern the activities in life and in the Fellowship that interfere with our primary purpose, and grant me the courage to act for their removal.

SOME FOURTH~STEP THOUGHTS

When it came time to do my Fourth Step, my sponsor told me to find some place where I wouldn't be disturbed and to pray before I started writing, so that God would be in charge of what came out on the paper, not me. Writing my Fourth Step was very cathartic; it felt so good to dump what had been poisoning my spirit for so long.
Hope, Faith and Courage Volume II, page 94

I remember thinking I had to write a thorough history of every action, at least those I thought of as bad or wrong, that I had ever done in my life. I heard someone at a meeting say, "Think of it as an inventory, not a history," and, "Start in the now." What a different way of thinking that was for me. Taking stock of what was currently on the shelves was much easier to contemplate. Instead of being afraid to list a history, I began by taking inventory in the present. What's on my shelves today? What good things have I done today? What right now makes me feel less than good about myself?

I went to meetings, listened, and heard stories of things that made me think, "How awful! I never did that!" But I thought again. The person sharing was an addict just like me, courageous enough to share their experience, strength, and hope along with the good, the bad, and the ugly—not just in the Fifth Step, but in these rooms with everyone. I had to thank them for that gift of forthrightness. May their courage inspire me to be fearless and honest in my Fourth Step, so that I might enjoy the miracle of freedom and intimacy it offers, as well as the nearly instant relief it promises when completed.

~~~~~

I pray for the courage to face non-healthy actions in my past, which must be examined in order to complete my Fourth Step. During this portion of my Step work, I will go to meetings to listen to others' stories about their experiences in completing the same process. As they arise, I will share my questions and fears, working through whatever has been suggested for me to complete this process.

SPIRITUAL PRINCIPLES

As we discovered the principles by which the individual alcoholic could live, so we had to evolve principles by which the A.A. groups and A.A. as a whole could survive and function effectively.
Alcoholic Anonymous, 4th Edition, page xix

Cocaine Anonymous is a spiritual entity created for a special purpose and occupying a special place in this world. Each one of us who owes our very life to C.A. is testament to this truth. We have recovered from the seemingly hopeless state of mind and body that is addiction, in part, by the practical application of spiritual principles in all our affairs. These principles manifest in the individual through the actions of our Twelve Steps. Similarly, the structure of C.A. is organized along comparable spiritual principles, which are practiced in the Group and other service bodies through their respective adherence to the Twelve Traditions.

The Twelve Steps are principles. Consider the wording of C.A.'s Step Twelve: "Having had a spiritual awakening as the result of these Steps, we tried to carry this message to addicts, and to practice these principles in all our affairs." *Alcoholics Anonymous* (page 60) similarly states: "No one among us has been able to maintain anything like perfect adherence to these principles," and "The principles we have set down are guides to progress. We claim spiritual progress rather than spiritual perfection."

The Twelve Traditions are spiritual principles applied to the Groups and other service bodies and are key to our personal recovery. "When A.A.'s Traditions were first published, in 1946, we had become sure that an A.A. group could stand almost any amount of battering. We saw that the group, exactly like the individual, must eventually conform to whatever tested principles would guarantee survival." (*Twelve Steps and Twelve Traditions*, page 146.)

~~~~~

Many principles are referenced in the *Big Book* and throughout our C.A. program. I will seek to understand these spiritual concepts and apply them, not just in my recovery, but also in every aspect of my life. In doing so, I can claim spiritual progress on a daily basis.

SERVICE BLESSINGS

> *One of the keys to successful recovery is getting involved. Begin by taking on tasks and keeping commitments at meetings—make coffee; help clean up; put away chairs. Help yourself by helping others.*
>
> Tools of Recovery (C.A. Pamphlet)

Who is a Cocaine Addict? talks about "snorting or smoking any white speck from the floor when we ran out." For me, this was only partly true; my problem was I snorted or smoked any white speck from the floor even *before* I ran out! No matter how much dope I had left. I had become the person I used to laugh at when I saw them crawling on the floor, tweaking. I spent way too much time down there in my insanity and sickness.

Thank God I don't have to live like that anymore. It's all due to what I learned in the Fellowship of Cocaine Anonymous—attend lots of meetings, get a sponsor, work all of the Twelve Steps, find a God of my understanding, and get involved in service. A funny thing happened when I got involved in service: not only did I not crawl on the floor anymore, but the obsession to use was removed, and I had not even noticed it! It didn't take long for the service junkie in me to emerge. It started with emptying ashtrays, making coffee, sweeping floors, and helping keep our meeting hall clean. From those commitments, I had the opportunity to serve as the Group secretary, and then treasurer (I don't think they had any idea who was handling their money!), and eventually chairperson for our Group. This was repeated at the District and Area levels of service, serving on just about every committee at one time or another. Then I was elected as a World Service Conference Delegate, even though there were many others who were qualified.

What an honor to serve and to have the opportunity to give back, even in a small way, what has been so freely given to me. Service is an integral part of my program, and a very humbling exercise. For the same addict who used to crawl on the floor, to be in service to the Fellowship and others like me who have found a new way of life in Cocaine Anonymous, is indeed nothing short of a miracle.

~~~~

When I do service, I am continually blessed with a wide range of positive spiritual experiences. My obsession to use has been removed and replaced with the continued desire to be of service to our Fellowship. For that I remain ever grateful.

MY LIFE IN RECOVERY

I've learned that I'll never be done with my recovery, that it's a lifelong process, and most of all that I still have so much to learn. To be honest, I wouldn't have it any other way. I look forward to each new day of my recovery, and I am forever grateful to Cocaine Anonymous.
Hope, Faith & Courage Volume II, *page 99*

I could talk all day about the Steps and my personal adventures in life, as I never imagined it could be. I need to share how unity, service, and recovery are the means by which I've shown God my willingness. He has entered my life and heart completely, doing for me what I could never do for myself. I've had the opportunity to be of service at all the different levels, ever thanking the Fellowship for the ability to assist. I have a great relationship with the family I thought I'd lost forever. As a bonus, God sent me a wonderful spouse! Between us, we have many grandchildren, and we delight in spending time with them in our home whenever possible.

The greatest and most fabulous gift of all is that I have the honor of working with newcomers. I sit across the table from them and watch the light go on; I am able to be the guide that others were for me. Once I had no purpose or direction, and now I have found the reason God placed me on the planet. I always wished I could leave a positive mark on the world, that someone would remember me and be happy I had been here. Recovery gave me the knowledge that my experiences can benefit others. My life's objective is being fulfilled!

~~~~~

I pray that all of us who desire a solution may find our way to this path of recovery. I still can't fathom how amazing my life has become. I remain thankful for the gift of service and the opportunity to witness healing light shine in a newcomer's eyes.

SAFE AT LAST

> *No man, we saw, could believe in God and defy*
> *Him, too. Belief meant reliance, not defiance.*
> Twelve Steps and Twelve Traditions, *page 31*

Defiance is my nature. I believe I was born that way. All my life, I fought everything—every idea, every suggestion, and every bit of love, especially the limitless love of my Higher Power. Here I sit, with long-time sobriety in C.A., and I have finally given up the fight.

When I got clean and sober, I became willing—willing to work the Steps, willing to go to meetings, willing to be of service, and willing to follow suggestions, but a part of me was still continually fighting my Higher Power's grace. Why? As a child, reliance meant abuse. I learned early on to *never* rely on anyone or anything. So it has been a slow process for me to let down the guard, to quit resisting, to trust, and to finally step out of the way.

Step work, putting pen to paper, prayer, and staying close to my sponsor have all helped. So has listening to others in these rooms who share their experience, strength, and hope with me. From this solution-based process, I came to discover that *reliance* on a Higher Power is magical and is my solution! I am finally free to live a life without fear. This trustworthy Power will guide me to the sunlight of my spirit. I feel totally safe *at last!*

~~~~~

I pray to keep an open mind and to be willing, on a daily basis, to rely on my Higher Power's limitless love and guidance. May my heart continue to know that I am safe in my Higher Power's hands.

THE SCARLET "A"

Today I can love myself and look in the mirror without wanting to cry or hang my head in shame for the things I have done. Cocaine Anonymous and my Higher Power have helped me to become someone my family and friends can trust. Today I can love my family the way the program has taught me—unconditionally.

Hope, Faith & Courage Volume II, *page 31*

Toward the end of my using days, I had periods where I would feel remorse, guilt, and shame about who I had become in and around my crazy addictive behaviors. I remember, too, finally being released from treatment after I got sober, only to be inundated by an even larger dose of those feelings, particularly shame—only I no longer had any way to numb them. I despised living with the stigma of being an addict, feeling ostracized from mainstream society. I tried to be as anonymous as possible, which helped some, but a lot of my co-workers immediately noticed I quit partying, making anonymity on the job impossible.

As life settled into a routine, I started feeling some relief, but the demons and stigma still hovered close by. When I would run errands at the food market or the pharmacy, I felt everyone I encountered at those establishments saw the scarlet "A" (for addict) sewn on my shirt. Somehow they all knew my big addiction secret and that I was brand-new in recovery. I would find my only respite at C.A. meetings, where everyone had the same scarlet "A"—where it was safe, and recovery from my addiction was encouraged.

Working with a sponsor helped, as did making that initial connection with my Higher Power. Completing the resentment inventory columns in my Fourth Step also helped, as did sharing my shame and guilt in my Fifth Step. My sponsor had me begin reading the Step Nine Promises. The Promise, "We will not regret the past nor wish to shut the door on it," was instrumental in my moving past the outright shame to acceptance about my disease and addictive behaviors.

Now, with some strong clean time, the scarlet "A" is gone. Instead, I am proud to be recovering in C.A. and grateful I was lucky enough to make it into the rooms. Sharing my experience, strength, and hope gives purpose and meaning to my life, and I walk with my head held high.

~~~~~

God, I welcome my past as an integral part of who I am today. I will strive to remember and learn from the initial shame, remorse and guilt, which were so overwhelming when I got here. I am thankful for the tools within the Steps that help me to work through my feelings and keep them in proper perspective going forward.

PERSONAL CONNECTION

Each day somewhere in the world, recovery begins when one alcoholic talks with another alcoholic, sharing experience, strength, and hope.
Alcoholics Anonymous, 4th Edition, *page xxii*

During childhood and adolescence, I felt alone and cut off from the rest of the world. I began using drugs as an escape, a relief, and a way of fitting in with my peers. It was a strategy that I kept alive for many years.

As an adult, finally in recovery, going to meetings was daunting at first. I arrived just as the meeting was starting and left, seemingly unnoticed, as soon as the meeting ended. I was newly sober, scared and very lonely. The thought of meeting new people and bonding with them over my disease was a frightening proposition. I thought, "They have it all together," and "They know each other already, so they don't need me."

But then I attended my first meeting of Cocaine Anonymous, and things seemed different from the start. I was greeted warmly and I felt included right away. The people were genuine, and they were not a high school clique trying to impress each other. Those personal connections made all the difference in the world; I wasn't alone any more. We are all in this together.

~~~~~

I remember how scared I felt coming to my first C.A. meeting. Once I arrived, I felt like I belonged because of the amazing people that reached out to me. I will provide the same support to others as they attend C.A. for the first time. That is not just how the program works; that is *why* the program works.

THIRD - STEP PROMISES

> *When we sincerely took such a position, all sorts of remarkable things followed. . . . we became less and less interested in ourselves, our little plans and designs. More and more we became interested in seeing what we could contribute to life. As we felt new power flow in, as we enjoyed peace of mind, as we discovered we could face life successfully, as we became conscious of His presence, we began to lose our fear of today, tomorrow or the hereafter. We were reborn.*
>
> Alcoholics Anonymous, *page 63*

The most important choice today is whether I am going to work all Twelve Steps in my life or not.

Step Three is a decision to turn my will and my life over to the care of God as I understand Him, and it is carried out by living all Twelve Steps in my life one day at a time.

The fact that I no longer have the choice in drink or drug defines my powerlessness over cocaine and all mind-altering substances. Today my choice is to make the Third-Step decision. When I say "Yes" to this decision, I am no longer going to play God. I am going to seek the wisdom and the principles of the Twelve Steps, the counsel of my fellows, and the care of God as I understand Him. As His care unfolds and plays out in my life, I receive the gifts outlined in the Third-Step promises.

~~~~~

God, help me work the Steps in my life today. Help me turn my life and my will over to Your care. Show me how I may be useful to You and helpful to my fellows.

MAY

HONESTY

Honesty has many rewards, but the one I cherish most is the inner peace I experience as a result of being honest with myself and others.
C.A. NewsGram, 1st Quarter 1999

I happen to be my own worst critic. I try to be honest with myself regarding the actual events that occurred, without blame or justification. This softens my judgmental attitude and allows me to honor my truth and myself. Being honest with others takes courage as I learn to stand on my beliefs as shaped by my life's experience.

Sobriety has enabled me to practice honesty more than ever before in my life. Before getting sober, my drinking and using required me to entangle myself in a humiliating mass of "barbed wire lies" to cover up my self-destructive behavior. What a freedom it is to live a program of honesty as a sober member of Cocaine Anonymous.

~~~~~

Honesty has been a reward of my program, one of many. I cherish the inner peace which comes from being honest with myself and others. I get the freedom to love and live honestly as a sober member of the Fellowship.

FEAR FACTOR

Notice that the word "fear" is bracketed alongside the difficulties. . . .
This short word somehow touches about every aspect of our lives.
Alcoholics Anonymous, *page 67*

Up until it was time to take my Fifth Step, I had willingly tackled each of my sponsor's Step assignments without reservation. But on the day of my scheduled appointment to meet with my sponsor to share Step Five, my brain suddenly began inventing a multitude of excuses to put it off. Since none of these were even remotely valid, I found myself driving to my sponsor's house, gripping the steering wheel in dread with palms sweating. I knew I needed to take this vital step, but I was taken aback by the unexpected wave of terror.

My sponsor welcomed me warmly and suggested we begin with a prayer. This helped alleviate some of my trepidation, but my insides were still churning. Next, I took a deep breath . . . and started sharing what I had written. Page by page, the going got easier, and I even began to relax. My sponsor interjected some personal experiences similar to mine that helped me realize he really did understand what I was trying to convey. My fear dwindled and then vanished completely. By the time I was finished, fear had been replaced by the most amazing sense of freedom. Even now, I can't think of any words to adequately describe my emotional transformation, but I can say with utmost certainty that it was spiritual in nature.

This exercise taught me the intrinsic value in facing my fears. Knowing that I don't have to be afraid remains a key element in my program.

~~~~~

FEAR = False Evidence Appearing Real. I can walk through fear today when I remember that freedom awaits on the other side. I pray that I will always attempt to face my fears with faith in God's unfailing support and guidance.

SATURATE MY SOUL WITH SERENITY

Every day I live in the miracle.
Hope, Faith & Courage, *page 113*

As I pray to recognize God's will, I often feel a surge of overwhelming elation—a need to dance! I sense a desire welling deep inside of me, leaping and swirling to celebrate the changes I see in myself as a result of this program. No other questions I ask during the day bring me to such a perfect place of joy.

I've achieved an amazing peace and serenity from working the Twelve Steps and incorporating their principles into my daily life. I've learned to love others unconditionally, just as I believe our Creator would have us do. The walls of resistance have crumbled, melting the ice around my heart and opening my soul to solutions. Through prayer, I am finding and understanding God's grace in my life.

Each and every day, the Fellowship carries me, my sponsor guides me, and my Creator saves my life. For all of this, I am forever grateful.

~~~~~

Reflecting upon a meditation each day based on the Twelve Steps, someone's personal experience, or an inspirational quote or passage gives life to my personal spiritual journey. One day at a time, if I seek inner peace, serenity saturates my soul.

A BROAD-MINDED PERSPECTIVE

We are people who normally would not mix.
Alcoholics Anonymous, *page 17*

Accepting those around me—particularly individuals who strike me as "different"—can be a struggle some days. Old thinking can lead me to small-mindedness, which breeds a judgmental perception.

My task is much easier when I acknowledge that each of us has had our own personal journey, different paths which brought us here. Common paths keep me here, while other paths lead each of us in a unique direction toward being happy, joyous, and free.

Unity is such a beautiful gift. Our histories are diverse and unique, but we share a commonality in having found a solution that works and keeps working.

Each of us has the opportunity to make these journeys, sometimes quickly, sometimes slowly. I do not have to journey alone. "Our common welfare should come first; personal recovery depends on C.A. unity" (Tradition One). I have learned that together, we can get clean and sober, and stay that way! I have also learned that mutual respect for one another is key. Tolerance and love are the spiritual skills I need to practice in order to accept myself and others unconditionally.

~~~~~

Everyone here has earned a seat and has the right to be respected. Just because someone is fundamentally different from me doesn't mean I am better or worse. Today I will strive not to judge anyone adversely, including myself!

BUT I DON'T WANT TO

I didn't work these Steps because I cared about you; I did this stuff because my sponsor told me this was the only way out.
Hope, Faith & Courage Volume II, *page 38*

It doesn't matter why we do the Steps, so long as we do them. The Steps will work in our lives regardless of our motivation. By just doing "the next right thing," we find ourselves changing, in spite of our skepticism about how it *wasn't* going to work.

Program experience has shown me that if I take the right actions, the right thoughts will follow. Whether I set up coffee, offer a kind word to a despairing addict, overlook a co-worker's lack of consideration, help out with a program event, or drag myself into a meeting I thought I never wanted to go to, it does not matter that I was reluctant. In fact, sometimes the miracle happens exactly when I feel the least willing, yet take action anyway.

~~~~~

Today, I will move my feet so that my heart and mind will follow. My Higher Power often works though this action versus my thinking.

BE HAPPY

We are sure God wants us to be happy, joyous, and free.
Alcoholics Anonymous, *page 133*

Even when things are difficult, I can find joy.

It's easy to be happy when life is going well—when I have everything I believe I need, when everyone else is playing on the stage as I believe they should. But what about when life doesn't go my way, when the going gets tough?

The program has shown me that I can *always* find joy and happiness in something. It might be a pet's silly antic. It might be a friend's joke. It might be laughing at an old character defect that's rearing its ugly head again. It might even be laughing at myself and my behavior, perhaps for the first time. I can be happy as I recognize and honor my humanness today, rather than living without mindfulness.

~~~~~

I will consciously make a decision to be happy today, even if it's only for the fresh air I breathe. I will take a deep breath, slowly, and hold it for a moment. Then I will release it with gratitude for energizing and sustaining me. I will look for all the many reasons to be *up* instead of down. I will seek and find the gratitude and joy that this program promises me daily.

ACCOUNTABILITY

In our active addiction, we were often irresponsible and unaccountable.
We often placed blame on others and none on ourselves.

The Home Group (C.A. Pamphlet)

Today I will accept responsibility for my recovery by focusing on the issues from which I need to recover. I will pray on a daily basis for the strength and courage to face my demons of the past. I will open up that storage place in my soul where all my pain and sorrow have been hidden for so many years. I will speak about them and process my feelings with an open mind for suggestions and advice. By doing this, I can empty my storage place of angst and allow God to fill me with His love, using me to spread that goodness to all whose paths I cross.

As I begin to let go of my self-obsession, I ask God to remove the fear building up inside of me—fear of facing myself and the unknown. I redefine myself by working the Steps and using the tools I have learned to maintain forward progress in total recovery. As I begin to take responsibility and be accountable for my actions, I notice a change in the way I walk because now I am allowing God to lead my path. I notice a change in my personality and my attitude toward people, places, and things.

My ego used to control the way I thought and acted. Anger, despair, and embarrassment were among my reactions as the result. Now I understand that I have to forgive myself, allowing God to heal me as only my Creator can.

~~~~~

Accepting responsibility for my life and recovery makes me accountable for my actions. Because I am no longer under the influence of drugs and alcohol, I cannot make excuses for what I do. It feels really good to let go of blame. EGO = Edging God Out.

THE TRUTH IS WORTH THE EFFORT

Only by discussing ourselves, holding back nothing, only by being willing to take advice and accept direction could we set foot on the road to straight thinking, solid honesty, and genuine humility.
Twelve Steps and Twelve Traditions, *page 59*

I remember well the day I sat down with my sponsor to share my Step Five. Fear of what he would think of me seemed to burn through every vein, and my chest felt tight and painful. I knew I needed to take this Step because if I used again, I might not make it back. I was certain my only hope was to remain in the program of recovery I had found in Cocaine Anonymous.

Once we'd begun, the more I talked, the better I felt. As I continued to work through the fear, the less of a grip it held. Despite this new freedom, I still faltered. Thank God my sponsor could see my fear and dishonesty. He looked me in the eye and with a knowing nod said, "Come on now, the truth is worth the effort."

This early lesson has kept me in good stead for a few years now. No matter how strong the fear feels to me at the time, experience has shown me that the Power I have found in C.A. has never let me down—the truth is *always* worth the effort.

~~~~~

Until recovery, everything in my life was based on lies. No longer is that an acceptable standard. I've learned to value honesty. Just as promised, the truth has set me free!

PRECIOUS COMMODITY

I promise you will find unconditional love, happiness, and freedom when you are done.
Hope, Faith & Courage Volume II, *page 137*

When I joined the Cocaine Anonymous Fellowship, I was a young, single mother of a five-year-old who did not know his father. My life was a complete mess, and I was angry at the entire planet, blaming everyone and everything else for my situation.

Yet, right away I adhered to the program. I attended ninety meetings in ninety days, accepted a coffee commitment, found a sponsor and started working the Twelve Steps. I became teachable. Eventually, I sponsored other members and started new Groups, continuing to work the Twelve Steps in an effort to practice these principles in all my affairs. I read C.A. literature daily and got involved with service—first with the Group meetings I attended, then at the District level, and finally, at the Regional level. All of these actions molded me into a better person— stronger, wiser, and, best of all, *happier.*

Today, I am grateful and proud to be a C.A. member. When a newcomer introduces herself at a meeting, she does not leave without my telephone number. Although I am free from the shackles of active addiction, I continually remind myself that in order to be responsible for my recovery, I must give back what I received.

~~~~~

My newfound freedom is far too precious a commodity to risk by slacking off on program basics. Complacency is dangerous territory. I will persist in following the same suggestions that got me where I am today.

WEATHERING THE STORM

Let families realize, as they start their journey, that all will not be fair weather.
Alcoholics Anonymous, *page 122*

Feel the breeze as the storm clouds dissipate. A lingering shower slowly gives way to sunshine. Scars upon the landscape and scattered debris provide evidence of the tempest's fury. They remind us that another squall will inevitably come and we need to be prepared.

In the natural world, the mighty oak prepares by growing stronger roots and thicker branches; squirrels prepare by building nests within the tree's protective shelter. They both have a will to survive, yet their fate is ultimately in God's hands when the next storm hits.

As humans, we, too, prepare for such storms. We occupy sturdy homes in order to take refuge. The rains will surely come, and we must be ready. No matter how well-outfitted, we are at God's mercy.

Enduring the weather can be a great deal easier than traversing life's erratic emotional climate changes. Here, our preparation is more closely aligned with our relationship with God. Strengthening our faith through prayer, surrendering our will, being of service, and learning from others' experience assures us that we can survive whatever turmoil life may bring. Like the oak tree and the squirrel, we needn't spend our time worrying about the future. We simply do the best we can to shore up our safe haven, trusting God to handle the rest.

~~~~~

Understanding the storms of life we may encounter helps us as we prepare. Examining our scars as the reminders of past gales is part of that process and serves to heal. Feel the gentle wind sweep the clouds away. The skies clear, and God's spirit pervades as sunlight fills the day.

BIRDS OF A FEATHER

You will be bound to them with new and wonderful ties, for you will escape disaster together and you will commence shoulder to shoulder your common journey.
Alcoholics Anonymous, pages 152-153

On a crisp autumn morning as I drove my son to kindergarten, he asked, "Mom, what are all those birds doing up there on the electrical line?" Early in my sobriety, I frequently answered his questions with a "sober" reference, keeping me in the moment. "Having a meeting," I replied. "Oh, okay." He knew that I went to meetings, and that life had changed for the better ever since. He was very accepting of my answer.

To this day, whenever I see a group of birds gathered together, huddled close on an electrical line, I remember that moment in the car. It brings back fond thoughts and a warm glow. It is also a friendly reminder that I don't do this alone. And although it says we are people who wouldn't normally mix, now we do! Despite all our differences, our common bond is our recovery, as well as the feelings associated with getting and staying sober. My gratitude for the Fellowship of C.A. is overflowing. The heartfelt friendships, which provide the experience, strength, and hope I need on a daily basis, are indispensable.

~~~~~

May I remember that I can't do this by myself, and that we need one another. "We admitted we were powerless. . . ." "Our common welfare should come first. . . ." The *we* of the program gives us what we need. Being a part of this flock is God's plan for me today.

WHAT CAN I SAY?

*I go to meetings and continue to carry the message
of Cocaine Anonymous and recovery.*
Hope, Faith & Courage Volume II, *page 17*

When I go to meetings and am called upon to share, I need to keep in mind the importance of carrying the message. It is not a time for me to vent my frustrations upon those in the rooms. My sponsor or other program friends are available for that purpose.

The message is how we have worked the Twelve Steps in our lives—how life is better because of our program. I need to share as if these words may be the only message a newcomer hears, keeping them focused on my experience, strength, and hope.

~~~~~

Today I will make an effort to share what the program of C.A. has done for me as the result of my working the Twelve Steps. I will carry *this* message to the newcomer in hopes of helping them create experiences of their own to share about. It is in carrying the message that I continue to recover.

NEVER ALONE

All the same, each of us must take responsibility for our own recovery. There is no secret, no magic. We each have to quit and stay sober; but we don't have to do it alone!
To the Newcomer (C.A. Pamphlet)

I remember very clearly how frightening it felt to be a newcomer. At one of my first few meetings, someone approached me and said, "You never have to feel alone anymore." Those words resonated with me, easing my sense of isolation. That experience has always stayed with me.

As I stuck around and gained some sobriety, I heard others share about how hard it had been for them when they got to the rooms. This brought a new sense of belonging—I wasn't the only one who had felt that way!

Time went on, and I started growing spiritually. This is when I came to realize that the God of my understanding was *always* with me, no matter the circumstance. If I was feeling alone, it was my own doing because I had forgotten to pray. Telephoning a program friend was another invaluable tool for chasing away loneliness.

These days, whenever I'm in a meeting and see a newcomer standing apart, I always go talk to them, letting them know they don't have to do this recovery thing alone. We are all different types of people on the same journey—and none of us have to do it alone.

~~~~~

I welcome the feeling of relief that comes when I remember I am not alone on my recovery journey. I receive great strength from being connected to others, perhaps very different from me, who are walking the same path. I am especially grateful to have opened a spiritual connection, the ultimate bond for eliminating isolation.

SO MUCH TO LEARN

We have recovered, and have been given the power to help others.
Alcoholics Anonymous, page 132

Service to others is the highest activity to which I can aspire. Since each individual is a unique expression of God, each of our offerings to the world will look different. I may serve in ways that seem grand to the human eye, while others give their gifts in less visible ways, or vice versa. Each gift of love is God's expression in the world. I honor the person my Higher Power made me to be, a precious and irreplaceable child of God. I will strive to nurture my gifts so that I may be love's presence in the world.

Memories about my using behavior are sometimes difficult to swallow. My only thought about any given circumstance was, at the time, usually "What's in this for me?" Re-programming my thinking and related actions using spiritual tools has necessitated a lot of help from my sponsor and from God. Gradually, I also found that being of service to the Fellowship ignited a wonderful feeling of spiritual well-being. Could it be that this is what God wanted me to do? Slowly but surely, service to others took on a new perspective, becoming something I enjoyed instead of a tedious proposition.

~~~~~

Why be of service? To give back what was so freely given to us; to take on a commitment as a symbolic way of making amends; to meet other recovering addicts; to learn how to be part of a team; to learn humility by doing something selfless for someone else; to learn skills or teach others what we know; to learn responsibility (from the C.A. Pamphlet *Being of Service*).

ARE WE HAVING FUN YET?

> *But we aren't a glum lot. If newcomers could see no joy or fun in our existence, they wouldn't want it. We absolutely insist on enjoying life.*
> Alcoholics Anonymous, *page 132*

Think back to your early days of recovery. Remember wondering what on earth you would ever do to fill up the empty hours when you used to get high? We *knew* we were never going to "have fun" again! Program veterans soon discover that those empty hours quickly become filled.

Participating in life is a joyous occasion. Sports, hobbies, entertainment, education, travel, career, and family—the list goes on and on, endless choices for how to fill our days and nights. Quite frequently, our problem becomes a *lack* of time to do everything we'd like. We need to remember that sobriety must remain our number one priority. Home group meetings must always come first. Complacency is an offender for setting up a relapse. Stick with the winners—they are consistently involved with healthy, sober activities. Fun is a requirement in our Fellowship, and the laughs are guaranteed!

~~~~~

Does your home group get together for fellowship before or after the meeting? Maybe you can organize an entertaining get-together—a walk in the park, going to a museum, listening to live music, watching a movie, or even just a meal someplace fun—make it a picnic by a lake. Remember to include the newcomers. It's vitally important for newcomers to see that life after sobriety *is* enjoyable!

PRICELESS PARTNERSHIP

God doesn't want us to be miserable or sick. Trust in Him, and trust in yourself.
Hope, Faith & Courage Volume II, *page 137*

I learned in recovery that I'm supposed to live my days in partnership with God or a Higher Power. He handles ninety-nine percent, and I'm only responsible for one percent. Those percentages have given me great comfort. I thought, "I can handle one percent!" My one percent is to ask for help, go to meetings, work the Steps, pray, meditate, live in the moment, talk regularly to fellow addicts, and help others. The next day, I get up and do it all again.

No part of my one percent involves fear, worry, or obsessive thinking. These harmful behaviors never got me anywhere. God's ninety-nine percent frees me of such negative traits so I can be of maximum use to others. As I live my life this way, I find that I'm peaceful and balanced. Those two words were not in my vocabulary before recovery. What a gift.

Each day, I try to remember I'm only responsible for my one percent. If I choose to try to control and handle things which are in God's percentile, I'm taking on a world of aggravation and angst. Giving up control to an all-loving Power affords me such freedom. The only emotions that this Power wants for me are to be happy, joyous, and free. I choose every day to let go of the results, focusing and acting only on my part—my one percent. Living in the moment, while participating in and showing up for my recovery, is plenty for me to do. Why would I want to try and do more?

~~~~~

Am I willing to let go and allow God to act on my behalf? Can I focus simply on what is in front of me to do today? If I have trouble, I will ask for help, regroup, and let it go again. The more I practice these basic tools, the more I find I am at peace with myself and the world around me. A priceless gift!

MY BROKEN BRAIN

The remorse, horror and hopelessness of the next morning are unforgettable. The courage to do battle was not there. My brain raced uncontrollably and there was a terrible sense of impending calamity.
Alcoholics Anonymous, page 6

"My brain is like a bad neighborhood, I should never go there alone." This has become one of my favorite recovery slogans. It reminds me that my brain, when left alone, is likely to not think right and will surely muddle up reality to its own unique liking. This still happens from time to time, even though I have been around the program for a while.

Half the battle for me is to realize my brain remains broken, and that a level of deep rationalization, denial, general desire to stir things up or to live on the edge will always be present. I pray for a daily reprieve, and often receive one. Still without notice or warning, my brain can take me to an unsavory place that I earnestly wish to avoid.

I can rationalize, justify, assert or deny my supposed entitlement in order to make my thoughts seem right. Some people in the rooms call it "stinking thinking." My goal is to understand where it comes from, accept that it may never go away, and know I had better come up with healthy ways to respond when it happens. Likely, I will be best served by listening to others, sharing with my sponsor, praying, meditating, and seeking the experience, strength, and hope of fellow program members as they face their broken brains.

~~~~~

I pray for the ability to be aware when my broken brain takes the forefront of my thinking. May I recognize when this occurs and be able to use my program tools to counteract these thoughts.

LOVE, LIGHT AND GRATITUDE

We are all God's children, and when I am into Twelfth-Step work or being of service, I am within the will of God, and I am protected, nurtured, cherished, and loved, and I have a supreme sense of euphoric serenity.
Hope, Faith & Courage Volume II, *pages 66-67*

I can't keep it unless I give it away. I have learned so many things as a result of working the Steps, and I learn so much more by taking other people through the Steps. No words can adequately express how my life has changed for the better. Oh, sure, I could list the material things I have acquired: checking account, credit cards, car, house, etc. I do enjoy them, but, they are just things.

What has changed the most is *me*. No longer does it feel as if my gut has a huge hole in the middle. Instead, it feels as if it is filled to overflowing with love, light and gratitude. I feel a greater happiness than I ever thought possible.

The meetings expose me to such inspirational people. I have real friends, and loneliness has evaporated. With God at my side, I can cope with life's challenges as they crop up, employing wisdom heard around the tables from others who have dealt with the same or similar problems. Conversely, I'm also learning to enjoy, without hesitation, the good which consistently transpires all around. My growth process is one of constant evolution.

~~~~~

I embrace the changes in myself that spring from my Step work and in belonging to the C.A. Fellowship. If I am not growing, I soon get stagnant. God, please show me how to activate positive transformation whenever possible.

FELLOWSHIP

> *That night we gathered in the hotel's banquet hall to feast and celebrate our new Fellowship. Men and women who had only recently graced bathrooms, prisons, mental wards and treatment centers were now seated in this balloon-filled majestic room, shoulder-to-shoulder, looking and feeling alive and well.*
>
> Hope, Faith & Courage, *page xxxii*

Have you ever attended our annual CAWS Convention (or any C.A. convention for that matter)? They exemplify diversity at its finest—all ages, shapes, colors and cultures, converging on a setting so beautiful and serene, with one objective: to celebrate *life*.

We know what death is like; all of us lived in our disease as zombies. At C.A. conventions, we revel in life, greeting the day head-on, looking forward to meeting new friends from all corners of the world; listening to heartfelt stories of hope, faith and courage; laughing, crying, dancing, and sharing meals. It's an electric few days of high-voltage charging for our souls—*without* cocaine or any other mind-altering substances! We return home filled with love and wonder, somehow richer in spirit, and start saving our money for next year's event!

~~~~~

Where else but in recovery can I travel the globe and find instant friendship simply by walking into a meeting or picking up a phone to call the local hotline? Before planning my next vacation, I can check out the C.A. convention schedule on our world website (ca.org). Perhaps I'll find a destination where I can incorporate a weekend of fun and fellowship.

WE, NOT I

. . . I discovered a shared past in my similarity to other addicts and I work the same solution for recovery. Today I think myself privileged to have a changed attitude allowing me a whole host of new friends.
C.A. NewsGram, 2nd Quarter 2008

As a result of surrendering to the program of Cocaine Anonymous and allowing my sponsor to guide me into good habits, I have a new life. First, I had to get honest and admit I knew nothing about staying clean and sober. I listened and followed suggestions. I chose a sponsor who had recovered from the disease over which I had no power. I was given simple suggestions to begin immediately: pray, read the literature, contact newcomers, and keep in touch with my sponsor each day. Also, I was to cultivate gratitude for *everything*. I developed good habits and still do these things daily. Committing to a home group was compulsory—a *strong* home group. There I had to turn up early, greet people with a smile, and help with whatever service work needed doing. My home group is now one of the central principles in my recovery. It's the place where I humbly practice "we not I." It's where I learned everything I know about service, where I have practiced carrying the message, and where I continue to grow.

Under my sponsor's guidance, I have taken the Twelve Steps and now experience a freedom I never felt possible. Surrounded by a bunch of real friends in my home group, I finally know how it feels to belong. Drugs are no longer necessary because I have a spiritual center in my life. Many of my C.A. friends are people I would have shunned in my disease. I had thought I was so different, even "special." Much to my delight, I have experienced a spiritual awakening and continue to make progress. The sense of ease and comfort I looked for with drugs is mine today, sober. As long as I continue to work my program with commitment and diligence, I can stay in the "we."

~~~~~

I am an active member of Cocaine Anonymous and I am committed to continuing growth within the Fellowship. When I think less of myself and more of others, I find sufficient humility to free me from the bondage of self. It all starts with the first word of the First Step: "We."

IT IS NOT MY JOB TO "FIT IN"

Life continues to teach me what it really means to be a responsible member of society and to be of service to the suffering addict. I have finally found the strength and the faith to follow my calling regardless of where it takes me, who is with me, and who disagrees. I finally understand that it is not my job to fit in. The challenges that I face are present to teach me something that is necessary for my continued usefulness.

Hope, Faith & Courage Volume II, *page 160*

It's so easy to get caught up in trying to fit myself to the way I think others want me to be. This was especially true in early recovery. I tried, repeatedly, to mold myself into someone else's supposed expectations, possibly due to a really pesky resentment (theirs), or one of several character defects (mine). Frankly, changing myself solely to please others is a trap I cannot afford in any form whatsoever.

Even more risky to my recovery was when I tried to jump into a new lifestyle or relationship without really knowing who *I* am. This coincided with being new to the program, when my denial about my addictive behaviors was still strong. Though such actions can be recipes for disaster, they can also be recipes for growth in my life.

If I trust God, spiritual enlightenment can develop in any circumstance. I'll need to have a sponsor and other close Fellowship members with whom I can safely share my innermost thoughts and emotions. These friends can help me see that my approval-seeking nature is a subtle facet of my disease. Learning to recognize the reality of what is *really* necessary and important in my life comes with working the Twelve Steps.

~~~~

Trusting God to guide my life, actions, and decisions must take precedence over diving in to what I think I want or need. My old pattern was doing what felt good, what I thought was right, but where did it leave me? This new design for living, brought to me by the Twelve Steps, is one I can surely follow no matter what the circumstances.

RECOGNIZE YOUR TEACHERS

I thank God that I remain teachable and that my journey has
brought many wonderful people and teachers into my life.
Hope, Faith & Courage Volume II, *page 44*

I grew up wanting to be successful at life. Who doesn't? Instead, drugs and alcohol led me down a deep dark corridor, filled with nothing but rough times. I was always a follower and consistently latched onto the wrong people.

At some point, I wanted to get clean and sober, but I could never get honest enough with myself to give it a fair shake. It seemed as though all the people I met who didn't get high were too different from me. After stumbling many, many times, I finally surrendered and started attending C.A. meetings regularly. The next right move was getting a sponsor and working the Steps. This action helped me start to make good choices, like staying in school to finish my education. I am still a follower, but now I follow the winners in recovery. I have developed well-founded hope that I can accomplish many things—whatever I want to, actually!

Today I have so many teachers from all walks of life. I greet this spiritual journey each morning with anticipation, knowing that one day at a time, I can and will have the success I always wanted. I have even discovered how to be a leader sometimes, sharing my experience, strength, and hope with others who want to grow, too and who want what I have been given so freely.

~~~~~

How can we be so different on the outside but the same on the inside? Connecting with people heart-to-heart and soul-to-soul shows me how to see the good in everyone and opens my mind to learning from them. One of my greatest lessons has been to learn to recognize my teachers and their lessons in my life.

STEP FOUR INSIGHTS PART 1

Step Four was a long and painstaking process. I did what was suggested in the Big Book, and my sponsor told me to do one column at a time so I wouldn't get overwhelmed. I read everything in the book on the Step and made sure I did all the inventories. Resentments were easy; my fears and sex conduct took a bit more effort, but in the end I did a thorough job on all of them. None of it seemed scary to me. I had realized that everything was in the past, and I just had to own it, accept it, and share it.

Hope Faith & Courage Volume II, page 135

My sponsor took me out of town over a long weekend to complete my Fourth Step. I was newly sober and had previously completed the first three Steps. She told me to get my notebook and draw four columns all the way down the sheets of paper. I only did a few pages, naively thinking that I only had a "few" resentments, maybe nine or ten. I sat down to write, and I wrote a lot. I counted over a hundred names on that first list when I was done. Every horrible thing I thought anyone had ever done to me came spewing out.

The next day, my sponsor handed me some papers and told me to start writing about my fears. I wrote a lot again. I was afraid of the doctor because I hadn't been to one in six years. I was afraid of having a relationship. I was afraid of not having a relationship. I was afraid of failure, afraid of success, afraid of being too fat/thin, too smart, and too dumb. I had been living my life in fear and didn't even know it.

I then commenced to write my sexual inventory, noticing my behavior as a pattern began to emerge. Hours of writing, and so much revealed. Patterns began to materialize that I never knew existed. My defects become blazingly apparent, a revelation that inspired me to act out in anger, mad at the world and everyone in it. I heard a wise woman in this program once say, "You live in the Step you are working on." I found that to be very true for me.

When I finally sat down with my sponsor and read her my Fourth Step, I was amazed and relieved. She sat there listening, nodding and occasionally writing something. When I was finished, she handed me what she had been writing and said, "Here are your morals and values." Wow! I wasn't sure I had any, but there they were. I felt so relieved, so affirmed and, frankly, so free. I was quite motivated to continue on through the rest of my Steps.

~~~~

I remain ever so thankful for the loving guidance I received, and continue to receive, each time I complete a Fourth Step. I attribute this to the concept that I live in the Step on which I am working. This has been my experience concerning Steps Four and Five, particularly.

STEP FOUR INSIGHTS PART 2

In Step Four I began to see how nearly all my actions had placed me in positions to be harmed. I no longer had to blame the rest of the world for all my misery, and I could fix the root of my problems since they centered in me and not others. This was very freeing. I found it impossible to be a victim after doing a thorough Step Four.
Hope, Faith & Courage Volume II, *page 166*

In preparation to complete my first Fourth Step, my sponsor had me take a notebook and create nine columns in all. In addition to the traditional four columns referenced in the *Big Book*, my sponsor suggested that I include "A List of Good Things" and other columns such as "The Good I See in Others," "My Successes" and "Future Gifts from God," and yet another column entitled "Promises to God About My Program." I filled in the columns the best I could and was feeling pretty good about myself.

I completed my traditional Fourth Step that year by doing all three suggested *Big Book* inventories. The results, as for many of us, were quite profound, serving to solidify my program and desire to keep working through the Steps.

The following year, as I geared up to tackle another Fourth Step, I grabbed that same notebook and made some notes. When I compared the two years' preparatory columns, I was amazed! The first year, I had written several things in my "Future Gifts from God" column. The second year, I had placed them in "My Successes" column. I was rocketed! One year later, exact same result! Entries had moved from my "Future Gifts from God" column to "My Successes" column. I couldn't help but be ecstatic.

My sponsor assured me the reason this keeps happening is because I've kept up my "Promises to God About My Program." So when I wrote, "going to meetings, working the Steps, working with others and being of service" in that column, I could clearly see that's my part of the deal. I have been blessed with greater serenity, greater compassion and so many things I've sought, both materially and spiritually. So I keep on making a new list every year, being ever mindful of the growing gift list my program has afforded me.

~~~~~

I remain ever so grateful for my progress in this program. Working the Steps each year works quite well. I am able to measure my spiritual growth and maturity as I compare my written documentation from year to year.

YOU NEVER KNOW

Two weeks ago at my home group, a man picked up a two-year chip, came back to where I was sitting, sat down and said, "I just got out of prison this week after serving two years. Before I went down, I attended the C.A. meeting in jail that you did. I know you don't remember me, but you guys coming in every week gave me hope that I could turn my life around. I made a commitment to follow the path of recovery while I did my time and come out to find you. Thank you."
C.A. NewsGram, 1st Quarter 2009

The stories about touching another person's life by doing service are legendary throughout our Fellowship. When they occur, some of recovery's great unplanned miracles happen. We never know when or how something we say or do at a meeting, a panel, or a share may impact another, usually a newcomer, so as to inspire them to enter active recovery. Maybe it's the message of hope for freedom from the bondage of self, that they never have to pick up again, or any number of inspirational possibilities. Somehow, our words and actions give them enough strength to begin to change.

I've had people come up to me years later, asking about my daughter who did a parent-child workshop with me fifteen years ago. I know a man who saw our public information billboard, actually called our hotline number, and then got the book for being the newest newcomer at a convention. I have had sponsees, grand- and great-grand-sponsees pull out old service handouts from a workshop I conducted long ago, to which they still refer for help and guidance. The miracles are endless, and experiencing them never ceases to inspire me to do more service. The best part? As I have been giving it away, I have been blessed to keep it also.

~~~~~

I now know that when these things occur in our lives, they are not accidents. These events are validation of a Higher Power's significant participation in our recovery. For such amazing insights, I remain ever grateful.

MISTAKE NEUTRALIZER

You will make mistakes, but if you are in earnest they will not drag you down. Instead, you will capitalize them. A better way of life will emerge when they are overcome.
Alcoholics Anonymous, *page 117*

Recovery unearthed many memories riddled with a wide range of mistakes from my past. These lingering traces continued to create shame, angst, and fear, preventing me from trusting others and myself. I found myself asking whether this was the same menu of emotions that drove me to the first high. My need and desire for attention, affection, and approval brought me to my knees when I made the decision, "the mistake," to use. My disease led me to end up, like many of us, despairingly alone—a terrible place to be.

In the program, I've learned that if I reach out to others, go to meetings, am of service, ask for help, and share those memories, those mistakes, I never have to be alone again. The Fellowship loves me and has taught me to trust myself and my recovery. We all make mistakes. It is the human side of our spiritual condition. The key is learning to take these memories and use them for healing, for the spiritual lessons they provide, forgiving ourselves for our past, and then sharing our experiences in order to help newcomers come to terms with their mistakes.

~~~~~

The Steps process has a built in "mistake-neutralizer." Steps Four and Five uncover the mistakes. Steps Six and Seven help me understand why I make mistakes and how I can perhaps prevent their recurrence. Steps Eight and Nine allow me to rectify my mistakes and clear my side of the street. Step Ten keeps any future build-up of mistakes at bay. Pretty effective system, if you ask me!

HIGHER POWER

> *And the facts seem to be these: The more we became willing to*
> *depend upon a Higher Power, the more independent we actually are.*
> Twelve Steps and Twelve Traditions, *page 36*

When I came to C.A., I felt lonely, afraid, hopeless, and insane. Out of sheer desperation, I begged for help from whatever force might be meandering anywhere in our galaxy. At that time I was willing to believe in something other than me but had no idea what that could be. I reached out to people in the program and openly accepted their help. That was the beginning of inviting a Higher Power into my life.

The resources I now embrace were always available to me, but I had refused to acknowledge their significance. Now they continually provide me with guidance, strength, and love. My prayers get answered, just not necessarily according to my agenda. Sometimes when I least expect it, thoughts, ideas, and opportunities lead me in the right direction. I've discovered a powerful energy that far exceeds anything I have built alone.

~~~~~

With my addiction, I am alone. With a Higher Power, I can be the person I have always wanted to be.

GIFTS OF SPONSORSHIP

Then came my first sponsee. I got the opportunity to guide another person through the Steps. What an incredible learning experience.
Hope, Faith & Courage Volume II, *page 123*

Step 12 begins, "Having had a spiritual awakening as the result of these Steps, we tried to carry this message. . . ." One of sobriety's gifts is the precious experience of being invited into another person's heart to walk with them on their recovery path. This invitation is one of surrender, trust, and perhaps a first glimpse of humility in the new person's life.

Newly sober, I found myself in a strange new world. When I arrived in C.A. I was told that my old tools, destructive patterns of behavior, and warped thinking all stood in the way of my much-needed change. Gratefully, many have gone through this process before me and stood ready to show the way, to share their experience, strength, and hope. Because so many members of the Fellowship are willing to guide new sponsees through the Steps and the Traditions, newcomers are often quite encouraged, as I was, seeing that the program works and feeling genuine love from Fellowship members.

The sponsor can also be useful by integrating newcomers into service activities. Many show, by example, the essence of true service, giving with no expectation of reward. While service is performed selflessly, gifts of many types are received nonetheless. Service, humbly given, brings deep satisfaction—creating a sense of partnership in a noble human effort—while offering the understanding that, in God's eyes, everyone is important.

~~~~

I am grateful to be used in a way that brings myself and others freedom. Let my concerns remain centered on what I can do for the man or woman who is still suffering from the horrors of addiction. Today, I thank God for the opportunity to be of service and to share generously the lessons I learned from my sponsor.

DON'T DILUTE THE MESSAGE

> *My sponsor sold me one idea, and that was sobriety.*
> Twelve Steps and Twelve Traditions, *page 154*

I love the Fellowship of Cocaine Anonymous! If it has done for you what it has done for me and countless others, then you know what I am talking about. Because of the intense feelings I have for the program that saved my life, sometimes I get concerned for its safety.

"Each group has but one primary purpose—to carry its message to the addict who still suffers" (C.A. Tradition Five). As recovering addicts, I believe we have been given an incredible gift. It would appear those of us who've been to hell and back are the only voices others trying to escape can hear. Along with this gift comes an equally incredible responsibility.

I have to ensure the message I carry is of C.A. and not *my* message. It is important to remember as individuals and in our home groups and for the newcomer that collectively, we are Cocaine Anonymous. To our families, we are Cocaine Anonymous. As we venture out into the world outside our meetings, to those in whom we confide, we are Cocaine Anonymous.

I have a responsibility, to the newcomer, to my home group, and to the Fellowship, to pass on the message as it was given to me. Just as I didn't want you to cut my dope before I got it, I certainly don't want you to cut my message. Give it to me straight; I can take it.

~~~~

Let me always be mindful of C.A.'s true message and not dilute it with my personal message. Collectively, we are Cocaine Anonymous. May I represent our Fellowship with purity and integrity in every aspect of my program.

LOSS

As the pain subsides, a healing tranquility takes its place.
Twelve Steps and Twelve Traditions, *page 62*

Everyone experiences loss in one form or another. In sobriety, my first major loss came right away: I lost my most well-known coping mechanism and trusted friend, cocaine and all other mind-altering substances. I came into the program hurting from the disruption and destruction of this very intense and tumultuous relationship. I felt abandoned and vulnerable. My old trusted friend promised me the world, and then took it all away. It took time to develop new behaviors, to handle life, and to heal.

The Cocaine Anonymous program filled the void created by the absence of drugs. I found companionship and support both from new friends in sobriety and from my Higher Power. Moving forward, I have continued to occasionally encounter other types of loss. I grieve when someone close to me dies and when relationships end. It may be tempting to use during these emotional times, and if I do, it has the strong potential to destroy me. Or I can learn to use my new tools. I step up my meetings if possible. I reach out to people and explain honestly what I am going through and how I'm doing. I give myself permission to take special care of myself. I can go for a walk, take a hot bath, or do something else enjoyable in order to give myself some space and serenity. Healing will happen, and I will be stronger as a result.

~~~~~

May I remember that loss comes in many forms. I have a choice in how I handle grief and loss, and I don't have to go through it alone.

I AM FREE TODAY

It does work. Keep coming back. We're here and we're free.
Hope, Faith & Courage, *inside front cover*

My sobriety is all the proof I need to know Cocaine Anonymous works. I have been returning frequently since my first meeting on a Thursday night many years ago. Today, I am free from the merciless obsession and all the devastation caused by my using. I am free from the self-imposed bondage and the wreckage of my past. As a result of our program and changes I have chosen to make, that Ninth-Step Promise about knowing a new freedom and a new happiness has come true for me. I know all of the Promises will keep happening for me as long as I continue working the Steps, being of service, and relying on God's guidance.

I also am free from most of my fears and resentments, now having tools to guide me through those challenges when they arise. The *Big Book* (page 75) reminds me that my Step work is building an arch through which I shall walk a free man at last.

As an active member of our C.A. Fellowship, I'm surrounded by people joined together on a spiritual quest which includes helping still-suffering addicts find freedom too.

~~~~~

I am free to be exactly the person my Higher Power intends me to be today. I remain ever grateful for the freedoms I have found and continue to discover in C.A.

JUNE

HOW I FOUND HOPE

There truly is hope in C.A. I know that if I can stay sober you can too.
C.A. NewsGram, 2nd Quarter 1999

When I first walked into the rooms of C.A., I had no hope of ever having a life that did not include cocaine. I certainly did not believe in a Higher Power and didn't think anything could or would change my life. What I heard in that first meeting did change my life. These people had once been as hopeless as I was but said they had found a solution. As I listened to people share what had happened to them and how their lives had changed, I began to feel hope.

I actually thought that if this could work for them, and if they didn't have to get loaded in order to live and deal with life, that there certainly was hope for me. So I kept coming back to the meetings. I did what others told me to do: get a sponsor; read the *Big Book*; work the Steps of the program; and try to cultivate a belief in a Power greater than myself. I started to do these things, and soon my life began to change. I got a part-time job, my kids wanted to be around me again, and my family relationships started to heal. As time went on, I got more involved in the program, the meetings, and service work.

Carrying this same message of hope to others became an important part of my primary purpose. I have stayed sober since I walked into my first meeting nearly thirty years ago. My life has changed in so many ways. I have my family completely back, and I have a career that I love. I have friends that are always there for me no matter what, and I have relationships that are built on friendship, trust, and love. I would not have any of these things if I didn't feel the hope in that first meeting. That same sense of hope has been present in every meeting that I've attended since that first day.

~~~~~

An important part of my primary purpose is to carry the message of hope that was carried freely to me. Hope is no longer an abstract concept; it has become a reality.

CEASE FIGHTING

Giving up the struggle gradually allowed me to become as open-minded and willing as possible.
Hope, Faith & Courage Volume II, *page 92*

I gave up fighting the idea that I had any control over my drug and alcohol use years ago. For me, once I had a "First-Step experience," the understanding stuck. Nevertheless, my self-will still surfaces in the form of character defects such as judgment, the desire to be right, self-righteous indignation, and feelings of moral superiority. It is these defects which sometimes threaten to shatter my serenity and to damage important relationships.

So each day, I must return to the idea of surrender and ask myself these questions as various situations arise: "What am I fighting for? Is it worth it? What is to be gained?" This daily surrender must be accompanied by a call to my Higher Power to remove the obstacles standing in the way of my usefulness to Him and others.

~~~~~

Surrender is often still the key to my serenity. It is better to drop the sword of self-righteousness than it is to ruin even one day or destroy even one relationship. Or, as my sponsor puts it, "Would you rather be right, or would you rather be happy?"

PATIENCE IS A VIRTUE

> *We have begun to learn tolerance, patience, and*
> *good will toward all men, even our enemies. . . .*
> Alcoholics Anonymous, *page 70*

Impatience was something that followed me into recovery. I had walked through life in a very self-centered manner. My attitude was, "I want what I want, and I want it right this second!"

Learning to wait was hard. Out there, I could never wait until my next party time. I always wanted it now. My sponsor encouraged me to pray for patience. Then one day, it seemed as if everything that could go wrong, did go wrong. Family problems, car problems, and work problems—all in the same day!

That night, I went to a meeting and told everyone there about my miserable day. I wanted all my friends at the meeting to feel sorry for me. As people began to comment, each of them talked about similar bad days and how the program of Cocaine Anonymous helped them. This old timer sitting across from me said, "It sounds like God gave you many opportunities today to practice patience."

I suddenly realized it was my impatience throughout the day that had made me miserable. It was my attitude which caused the day to be so bad, not the events!

~~~~~

Awareness about how impatience impacts my serenity level is key to changing old behavior. With God's help, I can recognize the many daily opportunities for an attitude adjustment. I pray for continued patience in all situations throughout my day.

CULTIVATING LOVE AND TOLERANCE

*I learned that it's actually much easier on me when I approach
everyone and everything with an attitude of love and tolerance.*
Hope Faith & Courage Volume II, *page 95*

During my seven years in C.A., I have observed that those who follow the C.A. program with greater earnestness and zeal not only maintain sobriety, but often acquire fine characteristics and attitudes as well. One of these is tolerance, which expresses itself in a variety of ways, such as kindness and consideration toward the man or woman who is just beginning to walk a spiritual path. Another is an understanding of those who perhaps have been less fortunate in educational advantages, and empathy for those whose religious ideas may be at great variance with my own.

Without some tolerance, we could be a bit smug or superior—which, of course, is obnoxious to others. So as not to deter the advancement of another, we try to avoid a patronizing attitude.

Tolerance furnishes, as a by-product, a greater freedom from the tendency to cling to preconceived ideas and stubbornly adhered-to opinions. In other words, it often promotes an open-mindedness. This is vastly important in any line of research, scientific or spiritual.

~~~~~

Tolerance takes on many forms and can provide a vital cornerstone to my program of recovery. May I continue to strive for tolerance whenever I can and in whatever variety of situations present themselves in my daily life.

BODY, MIND AND SOUL

The mind and body are marvelous mechanisms, for mine endured this agony two more years. . . . Then came the night when the physical and mental torture was so hellish I feared I would burst through my window, sash and all.
Alcoholics Anonymous, *page 6*

For 28 years I lived life my way, getting nowhere. Many a loss was suffered at an early age within my family, out of which a pattern of abandonment grew. The desire to fit in culminated in an obsessive use of drugs and alcohol, which led to a destructive, false sense of acceptance. And so it was, until my disease firmly took hold. I can remember the exact date when delirium tremens arrived, and my prayers for all the wrong reasons began. "Why me, God? Why this? Why now? God, help!" No answer, no answer and no answer.

Thus it continued for many more years and through extensive hospital visits until, shocked back into life, I had the first awakening which the program promises. I surrendered to a program that was the only hope to counter my addiction. I found a spiritual advisor to guide me and followed simple suggestions. I began to live life day by day, and, slowly, spiritual tools and principles began to develop, ready for application. Honesty, acceptance, and willingness were the main ingredients. Then came a Higher Power who provided me with caring, understanding, patience and trust. Once I chose to believe in that Power greater than myself, promises were revealed and have continued to be revealed. Prayer and meditation keep me grounded and balanced in my spirituality. At last, I feel long-lasting true comfort within my body, mind, and soul.

~~~~~

I live a life that's simple, honest, and pure, provided by my God as I understand Him. Many have assisted me in my growth and continue to do so as I remain on my path, trudging the road of happy destiny, one day at a time. The power and sense of serenity I often experience is the direct result of doing God's work freely, simply, and without pretense so that others, too, may benefit.

DAILY REPRIEVE

What we really have is a daily reprieve contingent
on the maintenance of our spiritual condition.
Alcoholics Anonymous, *page 85*

A daily spiritual practice of consciously connecting to our Higher Power must always remain our utmost priority. Pursuit of prestige, power, and money will constantly attack and try to undermine this sacred time. This practice must be renewed, over and over again. Daily spiritual maintenance gives us a one-day-at-a-time reprieve from using. It also aids in sharpening our perception as we navigate the day, helping us to see things clearly. It helps solve many of the mysteries we face about our past, who we are and what challenges we will face in the future.

A spiritual practice does not insure that situations will always go the way we desire. We are guaranteed, however, an altered perspective and the attendant humbling lessons. Towering mountains still get in the way, but now, they appear climbable. Suffering in many forms still comes, but we are able to endure it with a peace that surpasses all understanding. Afflictive emotions arise. We rest in composure, do not engage these emotions, and they pass by. When presented with a tough decision, we quiet our mind, asking our Higher Power to inspire us with intuitive wisdom.

All these things are universally contingent upon a daily spiritual practice.

~~~~

Every morning, may I resolve to seek a conscious connection with my Higher Power through prayer and meditation. May I endeavor to reconnect throughout the day for guidance and strength. When presented with problems that overwhelm me, may I take a deep breath and ask to see things through a spiritual lens. In completing these actions, may I receive that daily reprieve which is promised to me as a vital part of my program.

_____

H.O.W.

> *The key words "entirely ready" underline the fact that*
> *we want to aim at the very best we know or can learn.*
> Twelve Steps and Twelve Traditions, *page 65*

At my first speaker meeting many years ago, a soft-spoken woman shared the acronym H.O.W.: Honesty, Open-mindedness, Willingness. That share made such a deep impact on me, and I often use H.O.W. throughout my program. For example, I consider this as I work Step Six:

Be Honest with myself, my sponsor and with the C.A. Fellowship.

Be Open to new ideas, facts or views.

Be Willing to work and step out of my comfort zone.

Another important aspect I consider related to Step Six is that we are not bad people getting good, but sick people getting well. My sponsor, a retired teacher, would say, "I know this isn't a word, but we are getting *weller*. It's an ongoing growth process."

~~~~~

I will practice H.O.W., remembering that it took me years to get sick and one day at a time to get "weller." The notion of H.O.W. can help me in many aspects of my program.

HOW DOES YOUR GARDEN GROW?

> . . . any person capable of enough willingness and honesty to try repeatedly Step Six on all his faults—without any reservations whatever—has indeed come a long way spiritually, and is therefore entitled to be called a man who is sincerely trying to grow in the image and likeness of his own Creator.
>
> Twelve Steps and Twelve Traditions, page 63

When we are born, our spirit is like a seed planted by love. Like the sun and rain, laughter and tears, this love nourishes our spiritual growth while we exist and thrive on this Earth.

Our drugging and drinking behavior touches upon all kinds of character defects, including many resentments. They multiply like weeds with deadly vines, choking the beautiful buds which should naturally develop along the plant's stem but are stifled through this abusive behavior.

By working the Steps leading up to Step Six, we are tilling the soil (admitting resentments and fears) by using honesty and open-mindedness, which are spiritual tools. Like growing perennials, we may need to perform this activity several times during our lives. It is a process wherein we can identify our resentments for the destructive weeds that they are and recognize the need to eliminate them once and for all for the sake of our spiritual health.

Once the weeds of defects are gone, our soul can flower, spreading love to the rest of the world. Others benefit from seeing radiant beauty within us. The flowers bear fruit, which provides constant nourishment to other addicts. We become, in essence, spiritual cultivators in the community garden of recovery, hope, life, and love.

~~~~~

In Step Six, "Were entirely ready to have God remove these defects of character," we prepare for our Higher Power to uproot weeds by becoming *willing*. With God as my gardener, how can I possibly go wrong?

DOESN'T MATTER WHO'S WATCHING

By working the Twelve Steps in my life, not only can I keep this gift of sobriety, but I can also strive to be the best person I can possibly be.
Hope, Faith & Courage, *page 56*

My addictive thinking and behaviors started as early as I can remember. I think I learned to lie at the same time I learned to talk. Way before I ever drank or drugged, I always had the attitude *"if no one knows and I can get away with it, then whatever it is I want to do—right or wrong—is just fine."*

One of the unexpected by-products recovery presented was my development of a conscience. The first time I ever felt it, I was taken aback and didn't really understand what was happening. Feelings, in general, were new territory and were somewhat tricky to sort out.

Through working the Steps, as my program progressed, my conscience grew. I was truly amazed to discover how wonderful it felt to do the right thing—*even when no one was watching*! Recognizing this change in my thinking was, perhaps, the first measurable indicator that a shift in my brain patterns had actually taken place.

~~~~~

My ability to do the next right thing—even if I don't *want* to do it, whether or *not* anybody is watching—is a concrete gauge of just how well I'm working my program. Today, I place a high value on honesty, especially with myself and God!

INCOMPHREHENSIBLE DEMORALIZATION

All of us felt at times that we were regaining control, but such intervals—usually brief—were inevitably followed by still less control, which led in time to pitiful and incomprehensible demoralization.
Alcoholics Anonymous, *page 30*

When I got to these rooms and started hearing this phrase used at meetings, I had no idea what it meant. My sponsor helped with this as we studied the *Big Book*. I discovered it to be a series of shameful moments which led to the horrible moral and physical sickness necessary for me to finally admit my life was completely unmanageable. In this state of utter despair, my physical allergy to drugs and alcohol had taken over. My moral compass was skewed far beyond human repair. All attempts at regaining control over my drug use and my actions led to even less control and, ultimately, incomprehensible demoralization.

This feeling, coupled with the crazy things I thought and did at that time, really defined my bottom. Everything was necessary for me to finally become teachable, to surrender, and to honestly admit my powerlessness over cocaine and all other mind-altering substances. My life was way beyond unmanageable. From there, I was able to accept that I had a serious, perhaps deadly, problem. No human solution existed, other than to embrace the C.A. program with all my heart and soul. Despite my frequent struggles against the process, ever so slowly, my feelings of pitiful and incomprehensible demoralization were replaced with hope. The many promises of true and real recovery, of which I was reminded at nearly every meeting I attended, were enough to keep me focused on going forward. One of the keys was to never forget my bottom. I haven't, and for that memory, I remain ever grateful.

~~~~~

I am thankful that I hit bottom and became teachable. I pray never to forget my moral and physical sickness from that dark time. May its memory be a poignant reminder of where my life will return if I don't stick around and continue working the program one day at a time.

H·A·L·T·S·

> *Today, when I have a problem, I don't have to run and hide in a bottle. It's all about the solution for me today, about immediately looking for that which I can change—what isn't right with me, even if it's only my acceptance of the problem.*
>
> Hope, Faith & Courage Volume II, *page 67*

One of my favorite slogans is H.A.L.T.S.: Hungry, Angry, Lonely, Tired, and Serious. When I feel any one of these feelings or emotions, I am out of sorts. When they come in multiples, I need a meeting. When more than a few rear their ugly heads (which they seem to often do as a group—imagine that), I need to be of service to get out of myself, see my sponsor, or both.

Recognizing these emotions is my key to getting past them (or at least keeping them in their proper perspective) so I don't act or say something I might later regret. Also, for most of these, when they recur, I can change my behavior to get some relief. For example: eating when I am hungry, sleeping/resting when I am tired, lightening up when I am serious, being of service or calling a friend when I am lonely. And when I am angry, I need always remember that another emotion is usually masquerading as anger, primarily fear. These seemingly simple actions will relieve my near-overwhelming angst.

I just have to keep this tool in mind when I'm feeling "off." I can quickly look for the five offenders to ascertain which one was the trigger of that particular emotional buffet. Likely others of the five will be present, although unrecognized prior to examination.

Along the way, I can pause and pray, meditate, or reach out in my private way to connect with Higher Power. On one level, I know these things and practice using these tools. Sometimes, however, the emotional rush blindsides me so suddenly that these tools are far from my first thought or resource. That's when the action(s) outlined above become crucial to my immediate serenity.

~~~~~

I pray for serenity when I feel H.A.L.T.S. I pray I can move into action to find relief from these emotions—understanding that one often triggers another and that they often appear as a group. May I ever be mindful of the tools in my kit: prayer, meditation, service work, meetings, calling my sponsor, seeking Higher Power, and, finally, remembering I am human and that it's normal to have these emotions from time to time.

UTILIZING THE "CODE"

Love and tolerance of others is our code.
Alcoholics Anonymous, *page 84*

When I was a kid, my friends and I would often invent secret codes that only we could understand. The first time I read the above quote in the *Big Book*, I remember thinking how cool it was for us as recovering people to have our own "code." And what could be a better "code" than love and tolerance?

In this program, I learned how to rid myself of resentments, *responding* to life's challenges with acceptance instead of *reacting* with negativity. In the eyes of the general public, this could certainly be construed as cryptic. "How do you do that?" I've heard non-program people ask at various times when I've employed "the code" in real-life situations that might typically elicit the opposite response. Unlike the secret codes of my childhood days, I'm always happy to share the love and tolerance philosophy of our Fellowship with anyone interested in learning a fresh perspective.

~~~~~

I can regularly be my own worst critic. May I learn to apply our code of love and tolerance not only to others in my life, but to myself as well.

_____

THE RESPONSIBILITY OF FREEDOM

> *Each group should be autonomous except in*
> *matters affecting other groups or C.A. as a whole.*
> C.A. Tradition Four

Like individuals, groups can be different. They are comprised of members with assorted backgrounds and circumstances. How a group operates is subject to God's authority expressed though the group conscience. A standardized blueprint for how a group should conduct its Twelfth-Step efforts or any other activities would be insufficient and arrogant. This Tradition frees the group to exist as it sees fit.

Autonomy and freedom bring responsibility. The group has a spiritual and practical responsibility to ensure its activities don't affect other groups or C.A. as a whole. By "affect," this Tradition really means that groups not harm other groups or the Fellowship. Engaging in some sort of group inventory process is strongly suggested to honor the spirit of Tradition Four at the group level. Regular group inventories will allow the members to be informed and to properly make decisions with respect to group affairs.

Sometimes the newcomer may think discussions about seemingly mundane issues burden the group's time and efforts, but experience has shown that consultation leads to greater understanding by the members. Greater understanding is the process which informs a group conscience, and decisions made on the basis of an informed conscience adhere to the responsibility for group actions not to affect other groups or C.A. as a whole.

~~~~~

May my thinking today include the recognition that there are many sides to every issue. Let me be a responsible member of my groups and of the Fellowship as a whole. Today, I am grateful for the principle of autonomy and recognize that this freedom brings with it serious responsibility.

GRATEFUL ADDICT =
A LIFE WORTH LIVING

I have replaced a cocaine high with a spiritual connection that comes from working the Twelve Steps and working with others. I am truly grateful to those who came before me in this Fellowship and stuck around to carry this message to me, so that I might get sober and carry it to others.

Hope, Faith & Courage Volume II, *page 84*

When I first came into the rooms of Cocaine Anonymous, I heard someone identify as a "grateful" addict/alcoholic. For the life of me, I couldn't figure out how anyone could be grateful to be an addict and an alcoholic. I thought perhaps this person was simply grateful not to be drinking and using anymore. After the meeting, I approached the grateful individual. He explained his gratitude like this, "Because if I wasn't a drug addict and an alcoholic whose life depended on working all twelve of those Steps, I never would have done it. Furthermore, by working the Twelve Steps of Cocaine Anonymous, I have not just been given *back* my life, but I've been given a life worth living."

It didn't happen overnight; I was well into my Step process before glimpsing what this outlook was all about. But because that person had expressed his gratitude so explicitly to me, I was eventually able to understand what he meant. So much in life depends on my perspective. In recovery, I know I always have a choice, and today, I choose to be a grateful recovering addict!

~~~~~

Every twist and turn on the road to recovery has been necessary for me to find my way here. If I had a chance to go back, I wouldn't change a thing. I believe I needed to hit every bump I encountered along the way to arrive at the amazing life I have today.

SERVICE THREADS GIVE LIFE TO MIRACLES

I love Step Twelve because it helps get me out of myself. I started service work at a few months sober and have been blessed to be of service at the Group, District, Area, and/or World levels ever since. As a result, I have a great respect for the Traditions and the power of the group conscience.

Hope, Faith & Courage Volume II, *page 96*

Activities within our Fellowship, seemingly unrelated to each other, are necessary to fulfill our primary purpose of carrying the message to a still-suffering addict. Home group members accept nominations and appointments to represent their Groups at District or Area meetings. Delegates are selected from Areas and represent those Areas at the C.A. World Service Conference. Trustees are elected by the Conference to stand in the shoes of the Conference throughout the year (when the Conference is not in session), and to be principal planners and administrators of overall C.A. policy and finance. Directors are selected by the Trustees to operate and administer the World Service Office and to hire and manage its employees. These and many more interactions take place within a tradition of "least possible organization."

Everywhere and every time a C.A. member gets the incredible privilege of sharing their recovery story with a new friend to our Fellowship, the sum of interactions which have taken place since C.A. was founded are present. Attending a C.A. business meeting, whether in a home group or a World Service Conference, can be challenging. Disagreements and disputes are often necessary in order to continue moving our Fellowship forward. We must painstakingly explore all methods to better serve our purpose of carrying the recovery message to the countless addicts in need of our help. Every member who contributes service *in any form* participates in the whole process. Not one service piece can be left out. In every instance, we can trust that if our motives are aligned with our primary purpose, all of our efforts will be utilized toward the Fellowship's greater good.

Therefore, don't sit in a Group business meeting and feel your opinion is unimportant. When added to the group conscience, all views are important to allow God's ultimate authority to be expressed.

~~~~~

My voice, participation and service are important to our Fellowship and my personal recovery. I now see how the many varied types of service activities are interconnected in an infinite "net of miracles" which continues to be woven, one loving action at a time.

GOD IS ALWAYS PRESENT

It has been said that in every experience is a lesson.
Hope, Faith & Courage, *page 30*

Life suits me perfectly because of the God of my understanding. This belief has helped me to stop obsessing on my past with regret, changing my perspective into a realization that God has had a hand in everything I did. I never thought I'd be one of those "grateful" recovering addicts. How could I ever be grateful for the destruction left in the wake of my disease? As I grew in my recovery, I slowly started to understand that the amazing life I have today would never have happened if I hadn't been an addict. If I hadn't hit that bottom and sought help in the rooms of C.A., I would never have discovered the peace and serenity available to me through using the Twelve Steps as a lifetime template. These days, you won't find a more grateful recovering addict than me!

God made me perfect, and all of my experiences have contributed to my character. They have made me wiser, helping to change me from someone I didn't want to be into the person I am now. *This* person can look in the mirror with acceptance, gratitude, and even courage, knowing God is always on hand to help and guide me. Certain that will never change, I look forward to the future with excitement, hope and wonder.

~~~~~

Everything that happens to me in life is either a lesson or a blessing. Usually it's both.

TODAY, I HAVE SIX MONTHS

> *Before I got here, I thought my problem was that I drank and drugged too much. What I learned was that the drugs and the booze are but symptoms of our disease. I learned that my problem is not that I drink and I drug too much, but that I'm powerless. If the problem is that I'm powerless, quite simply, the solution has got to be to find the power—to experience the spiritual awakening necessary to recover from addiction.*
>
> Hope, Faith & Courage Volume II, *page 37*

I am a grateful, recovered alcoholic/drug addict. Today is my six-month birthday. When I walked into my home group tonight, I had no solution to share. I was full of self-pity and smack in the middle of relapse mode. I am the one who means it every time someone asks me how I am, and I answer enthusiastically, "Fantastic!" The one who jumps at a chance to give out my phone number to the newcomer or share about how I've been rocketed into the fourth dimension of existence as a direct result of working these Twelve Steps. So tonight, when I was, "Just okay," or, "Not great," it was obvious to everyone something was wrong.

Looking at my program over the last few weeks, I found myself in tears several times a day, overeating, snapping at my family and friends, and not returning phone calls. I had tried to plan not just my own day, but my own life again. I had forgotten who was in charge. Slowly, I began to think I was quite capable of good ideas and didn't need spiritual guidance anymore. I wasn't putting pen to paper most nights, answering the questions on the top of page 86 of the *Big Book*. I wasn't taking someone new through the work. I wasn't repeating, "Thy will be done," over and over all day long. Not only had this backfired for me, but I was no longer useful to anyone else, in or out of these rooms!

Tonight, I was asked to read the Twelve Steps. As I read Step Three out loud, the solution hit me all over again—this thing isn't about me! It's about making the universe right and beautiful. As an addict, I don't necessarily know how that happens; but God does. This Fellowship is unapologetically about God and how we can best serve Him today. *Alcoholics Anonymous* tells us so on page 63, page 68, and countless other pages. Gratefully, I felt the fire start burning deep inside of me again.

~~~~~

When I have moments of complacency in my recovery, I need to return to the basics—either move on with my Step work or, if it has been a while, start on my next go-round through the Steps. I have to keep doing the work again and again to stay enthused. In order to feel "rocketed," I need to live the program daily. I have to work closely with my sponsees so I can tell them what *I* need to hear. Asking God to relieve me of the bondage of self that I may better do His will, I can live this miraculous program for the rest of my life.

WATCHING LONELINESS VANISH

I can't say enough about what the C.A. Fellowship has done for me. I finally feel "a part of" instead of "apart from." The first C.A. meeting I went to has been my home group ever since. I've made better friends in C.A. than I ever thought I'd have—or deserved. They have loved and supported me through the few really bad times I've had in sobriety and have been there for the many, many good times.

Hope, Faith & Courage Volume II, *page 98*

I was early in sobriety when I first heard the term "tortured loneliness," immediately connecting with the speaker and the feeling. This term described my primary condition for as long as I could remember. Throughout the many years of active addiction, drugs and alcohol seemed to "cure" this condition. I was part of life, and I had a reliable friend. Being loaded gave me the impression I could tap into the creative and imaginative part of myself that I didn't believe I could access on my own. When confronted with problems, the pipe appeared to help me regain my fierce determination to win, if only to do what was necessary to get more. Always, whether alone or in a crowd, the feeling of loneliness would overwhelm me. I was experiencing life as if I were on the outside, an observer rather than a real participant.

Over time, I've discovered this is a common feeling frequently shared by addicts. One hears it from almost every single person who tells their story. When I heard it for the first time at a C.A. meeting, I knew right there and then I was no longer alone. Recovery has since produced a host of friends from all walks of life. I am wealthy beyond measure in this commodity—the polar opposite from whence I came.

Our annual C.A. World Service Convention illustrates the epitome of countless wonderful relationships for me. It happens in the spring, and as the earth renews itself (as it does every year), I renew myself. I look forward to reconnecting with old friends and get excited to meet new ones. On the evening of the final banquet, the attendant member with the longest length of sobriety will stand with someone who has the shortest clean time, perhaps a courageous newcomer with only 24 hours. Together, they will represent all of recovery through unity and service, the miracle which takes place in our Fellowship each and every day. As for me, I am moved just knowing that I'm right where I'm supposed to be, connected with the most amazing group of people—my Cocaine Anonymous family!

~~~~

The Fellowship I now crave has become an incomparable replacement for my old den of loneliness. Life has taken on new meaning. It just keeps getting better! It is so exciting to know the most satisfactory years of my existence lie ahead.

SEARCHING AND FEARLESS INVENTORY

> . . . it could have little permanent effect unless at once
> followed by a strenuous effort to face, and to be rid of
> the things in ourselves which had been blocking us.
>
> Alcoholics Anonymous, page 64

Inventory is stage one in the "strenuous effort" referred to in the *Big Book*. A thorough inventory process enabled me to identify and take action toward removing obstructions keeping me from God. As difficult as the exercise appeared, especially when I was in the middle of it, once on the other side, enormous relief ensued. I gained valuable insight about my character and more about the nature of my disease.

Three different manifestations of self are addressed in this suggested inventory process—resentment, fear, and shame. In my case, I needed to complete not one but three separate inventories, the groundwork of each having been carefully laid out in these pages. Working with my sponsor through this process, I was diligent about being as thorough as possible in anticipation of the relief promised to me when I was finished.

I learned much about my addiction and its attendant behaviors. Being in resentment blocks me from God because when resentful, I take on God's role. Being in fear blocks me from God because in fear, I am relying on self rather than God, and any faith I might be trying to hold onto is hugely diminished. Being in shame blocks me from God because in shame, I have unconsciously decided I am not worthy of God. None of these patterns make any sense. I also completed a sex inventory according to the *Big Book* instruction. This helped me to get clear on the appropriateness of my behaviors and the ideals I choose to seek around sex.

Courage and my sponsor's guidance were essential ingredients for me to complete a searching and fearless moral inventory. The end result made every ounce of strenuous effort worthwhile.

~~~~~

Inventory opens a clear channel for me to cultivate conscious contact with my Higher Power. God, help me vigorously exert the energy required to do a thorough job.

FULL CIRCLE

> *I developed a passion for carrying the message via Hospitals & Institutions and Public Information (H&I and PI) because I know there are many others like me who are worried and have no clue C.A. is here. Being involved in service and working the Steps . . . is absolutely vital to my recovery.*
>
> Hope, Faith & Courage Volume II, *page 26*

At around eight or nine months clean, I started speaking on Hospitals & Institutions Committee panels. Initially, I was terrified of speaking in front of a group, but when I was finished, some of the clients came and thanked me! They even said parts of my story had inspired them. To think that something from my experience could actually help another suffering addict on his or her path— perhaps lessen their pain and give them strength to continue onward—was a wonderful feeling! For the very first time, I was able to understand the Promise, "No matter how far down the scale we have gone, we will see how our experience can benefit others." (*Alcoholics Anonymous,* page 84.) When I left the facility that night, I felt amazing—extremely happy and elevated. It was a natural "high." I now know this comes regularly from giving back. Fortunately, this kind of high doesn't affect our sobriety date! Addict that I am, I obviously loved this feeling and wanted *more!* Grateful for my recovery life, I'm blessed by the ability to share my hope with others who need to hear the message, just as I had when I came to C.A.

Like many addicts, when I look at my using past with its variety of attendant horrors at so many levels, it seems to be a miracle that I survived. I used to wonder why I was so lucky to have escaped death and the grips of active addiction. I now believe it was necessary for me to survive the lowest depths of my disease to properly and effectively reach others by sharing my experience, strength, and hope. By giving back what others so generously gave, my life is filled with purpose.

Particularly fulfilling is returning to my roots by speaking on a C.A. panel at the facility where I started my journey. This is the place where I discovered C.A. when panel members came and shared their experience, strength, and hope with me.

~~~~~

An incredible spiritual reward is to know something I have done has touched the life of another. I've had the enormous good fortune to occasionally run into people who have heard me share through H&I. Humbled by hearing them describe the positive impact one of my talks had on their lives, I gratefully thank God again and again and again.

_____

LOVE

You will learn the full meaning of "Love thy neighbor as thyself."
Alcoholics Anonymous, _page 153_

When we got here, few of us knew much, or even thought a lot, about love. Many amongst us did not come from households where healthy love was encouraged, explored, or even existed. It took time, for some longer than others, to begin to grasp the notion of love in recovery. I frequently remarked that I would not know what "love" was if it landed on the seat next to me. But today, I have learned that love is an important part of my program and our Fellowship on so many levels.

Tradition Two references a "loving" God as He may express himself in our group conscience. What does it mean to be "loving" of ourselves, of our God, and our fellows? How can we stay on our own respective spiritual paths while being of service in a loving way, while taking care of ourselves, and still giving away what we have found in order that we might be able to keep it?

From the rooms, I have come to use two definitions for "love" that guide me to understand the concept of love and of a loving God. First, a loving condition exists when the care and concern I have for you equals or approximates the care and concern I have for myself. Secondly, love is doing something for another human being so that they might become the finest person that their Higher Power intended.

Early on my sponsor and I often joked that I had no working definition of love—no idea what it was or how it applied in my life, in my Steps and beyond. So we looked for some definitions and came up with one more idea: love is a deep, tender, special feeling of affection and solicitude toward a person, the program, God or the Fellowship. It arises from recognition of attractive qualities, kinship, or perhaps a sense of underlying oneness/unity. I think I can understand that one perfectly!

~~~~~

At some point in working the program, there is a clear milestone when we really start to _feel_ God's love. I remain ever thankful for the ongoing lessons about love taught by the program and our Fellowship.

PREACHING OLD-TIMER –
OR MISUNDERSTOOD?

Don't start out as an evangelist or reformer.
Alcoholics Anonymous, *page 89*

Being an old-timer with many years of recovery, I tend to forget how hard it was to get sober. I don't ever think about drinking or using—the obsession has been relieved, and my job is simply to pass it on. It's a rough feeling to know some are going to get it and some aren't, and I have to offer my resources where I can do the most good.

We all want so badly for the newcomer to succeed. Over the years, I've watched so many people come in and out, sometimes it feels to me like we are failing.

I remember sharing in a meeting that I was 0 for 12 sponsoring people—apparently nobody wanted what I had! Afterwards, my sponsor pointed out, "No, you are 12 and 0 because you never drank over any of them!" I didn't understand what he meant for a long time, until one day, I sponsored someone and did everything I could to get him sober. From helping him work the Steps, to finding him jobs, giving him rides places, and interfacing with his family to help them understand our disease. I tried it all, but he never got sober. I guess our claim to fame is that we just don't ever give up hope on the newcomer. Through this particular sponsee, however, I came to understand that I can't engineer anyone's sobriety. Whether they drink or stay sober is not my doing; that's between them and God.

So if it seems like those of us with some time under our belts tend to preach sometimes, please understand it's only because we want the newcomer to stick around and find out what we have discovered. Recovery *is* possible, and, happily, we never toss anyone aside

~~~~

God, let my words to the newcomer always be encouraging. May I show them by my actions and example what it means to be a sober member of our Fellowship. Help me to recognize when I cross the line from offering suggestions to preaching.

SILENCE IS GOLDEN

So we clean house with the family, asking each morning in meditation that our Creator show us the way of patience, tolerance, kindliness and love.
Alcoholics Anonymous, *page 83*

I was dying when I came to C.A.—broken down, not a clue how to live life, stealing from my family and my infant son. I knew I was failing as a father and couldn't imagine how much worse it might get if I continued on the same path.

Cocaine Anonymous and the God of my understanding have gradually taught me I don't have to live that way anymore. I make it to meetings, work Steps, sponsor others, and, most incredibly, pray first thing every morning. I need God in my head before I start my day. I read a morning meditation book. The further I progress in my recovery, the more I see a need to quiet my mind and search inside my heart. This period of silent reflection produces a peace so deep inside me, it is impossible to describe. Next I pray—for my son, his mom and lots of other people. I say the Third-Step Prayer and the Seventh-Step Prayer, asking for God's help throughout the day. I make my bed, stretch, and am ready to deal with whatever life throws at me in the next 24 hours.

This practice is not always easy, but placing God squarely in my head as soon as I wake up has become a way of life. I know with certainty it's what I must do to stay rooted in the solution. Thank you, Higher Power and C.A., for showing me the intrinsic value in greeting each day with a quiet mind.

~~~~~

Silence is golden. God's presence is a present. All I need do is to open my heart and receive the gifts of peace and love.

SERVICE SYNCHRONICITY

> *My sponsor then led me into being of service. It started with getting to meetings early and helping set up, then staying late and cleaning up before going to coffee. In the beginning, I didn't understand the need for this. As time went on, I came to realize that it is these types of actions that rebuild my self-esteem.*
>
> Hope, Faith & Courage Volume II, *page 123*

Service provides me with a way to think of others. From my second meeting, I was encouraged to stand out on the doorstep, ready to welcome the newcomer. My sponsor suggested I arrive early to help set up the chairs and stay behind to clean up ashtrays after the meeting had finished. Under the guidance of my sponsor, I worked my way through the C.A. service structure, starting at Group level, and now I'm a trusted servant of the Area. During the entire process, I have been guided by the literature and have followed the experience of those in our Fellowship who have gone before me. Had I been given just any old job to do, perhaps without the required sobriety time or experience, it could have been harmful to Cocaine Anonymous and, frankly, to me as well.

The long form of Tradition One states, in part, that C.A. ". . . must continue to live or most of us will surely die. Hence our common welfare comes first. But individual welfare follows close afterward." (*Twelve Steps and Twelve Traditions*, page 189.)

~~~~~

I truly appreciate the continued loving guidance of my sponsor in so many parts of my program. The wisdom imparted as experience, strength, and hope shared in relation to doing service work, both in my early recovery and yet today, has been remarkably spot-on. At any particular time, I seem to be presented with the exact lessons I need to learn.

NO PAST REGRETS

Very deep, sometimes quite forgotten, damaging emotional conflicts persist below the level of consciousness. At the time of these occurrences, they may actually have given our emotions violent twists which have since discolored our personalities and altered our lives for the worse.
Twelve Steps and Twelve Traditions, *pages 79-80*

I have heard many stories about C.A. members' active addiction, and I have to honestly say that my using past isn't as horrific as most stories I hear. I was only 19 when I got sober, but my past is mine, and it got me to the program. Remembering what it was like is money in my recovery bank. After working Steps Four and Five with my first sponsor, I no longer feared the episodes of my using past. Because I got sober at such a young age, I believe I have a unique ability to talk to the young people showing up at our doorsteps today, letting them know it's possible to get and stay clean as a teenager.

Just because I'm sober many years now, however, doesn't mean I don't still fall prey to damaging *emotional* conflicts. Sometimes these lie dormant for a long time before bubbling to the surface. When they finally erupt, I have recovery tools to work through the pain. Growth is always involved. I'm grateful to recognize these experiences for what they are: another opportunity to share life's lessons learned with fellow program members and to grow in my relationship with my Higher Power.

When I hear someone sharing at a meeting, I listen. Sometimes I hear emotions, obsessions, and abnormal thinking with which I can relate. Other times I'm given a chance to see how someone tackles and overcomes a life issue using the Twelve-Step process. I file this experience away in case I ever run into the same thing someday either in myself or with a sponsee. This is how I work my program. The more I see myself in others, the more I learn about myself. The more I share about myself with others, the more I can offer to help them. It is a *we* program, and I never have to be alone—yet another deposit in my bank of recovery!

~~~~~

Everything that happens to me, good and bad, is an opportunity to share experience, strength, and hope. Today, I am able to laugh at most things from my past, a sure sign of acceptance. This joy is further proof to another suffering addict that life gets better!

MY SEVENTH TRADITION EXPERIENCE

. . . it was high time we now—sober—paid our own way.
Twelve Steps and Twelve Traditions, *page 160*

As a newcomer in C.A., I kept hearing the Twelve Traditions read at most meetings I attended. I found myself curious about all of the Traditions and was particularly confused by the Seventh Tradition including the practice of passing the basket, the idea that a group had to be self-supporting, not accepting outside contributions.

I asked my sponsor for guidance, and he explained that the Seventh Tradition was, in fact, quite spiritual and meant much more than just putting some money in the basket at each meeting. He shared his experience that the Seventh Tradition included members contributing their time and talents to support the group. Also, members contribute by attending meetings and when appropriate, sharing experience, strength, and hope.

I learned that this Tradition was created to ensure the group would not receive funds from people, businesses, and institutions outside of C.A. He had me reference the *Twelve Steps and Twelve Traditions* writings on Tradition Seven (pages 160-165) where I learned that declining outside contributions insured the group's independence, and how it was wise always for the group to remain with little funds, sending excess funds to appropriate service bodies to support Fellowship-wide unity.

In studying the Seventh Tradition, I see how the notion of being self-supporting is vital to this equation. It allows the groups to flourish and to support other service bodies, including the World Service Office, which discharges program services to ensure that the primary purpose of carrying the C.A. message to the still-suffering addict is supported.

I also meditate often about what else can I do to carry the message and to make sure that the groups are supported by my efforts and contributions. I also meditate about what I can do to honor the second part of Tradition Seven which references declining outside contributions. The longer I am around C.A.'s rooms, the more this Tradition seems to overlap many key personal recovery and service-based principles and practices.

~~~~~

Am I doing all I can to support the key parts of Tradition Seven? Am I contributing my time and appropriate resources to help my group stay strong and to decline outside contributions? Can I begin to see how this Tradition ties together with other Traditions and my own recovery program?

SPIRITUAL EXPERIENCE

> *With few exceptions our members find that they have tapped an unsuspected inner resource which they presently identify with their own conception of a Power greater than themselves.*
> Alcoholic Anonymous, 4th Edition, *pages 567-568*

In my opinion, Appendix II is one of the most influential *Big Book* segments. By carefully studying this scant page and a half, I have truly come to understand the profound changes spirituality generates. *Alcoholics Anonymous, 4th Edition*, page 568 states, "Most of us think this awareness of a Power greater than ourselves is the essence of spiritual experience. Our more religious members call it 'God-consciousness.' . . . We find that no one need have difficulty with the spirituality of the program. *Willingness, honesty and open mindedness are the essentials of recovery. But these are indispensable.*"

Many tools are available for cultivating my spirituality. Some are outlined in Alcoholics Anonymous, not just in Appendix II—Chapters 4 through 6 include many of them. Other means are self-developed through personal prayer and meditation. For me, yet another avenue for honing my spirituality is practicing my faith.

Faith is a glorious gift, an ever-growing, privileged connection with the God of my understanding. Spirituality emerges in many forms. For some, it can be as simple as the lighting of a candle. Music does the trick for others. Whatever the ritual, I must remember that its practice is personally unique to each of us. Our Fellowship encourages respect and sensitivity toward everyone's diverse beliefs.

~~~~~

When I go to a meeting, I want to hear how the God of your understanding has worked in your life today. I want to know what spiritual tools you have used to grow towards living a more serene existence. These lessons and insights provide the fuel for my own spiritual development.

ENTIRELY READY?

> *We shall need to raise our eyes toward perfection, and be willing to walk in that direction. It will seldom matter how haltingly we walk. The only question will be "Are we ready?"*
> Twelve Steps and Twelve Traditions, *page 68*

I did not realize the magnitude of my character defects until I did a Fourth and Fifth Step. Having identified them and acknowledged their existence in my life, I became willing to do something about them by asking my Higher Power to remove them all. Willingness is the foundation of Step Six. If I wanted to bask in the sunlight of the Spirit, I had to remove all the blockades. I had to examine what had been written and revealed in Steps Four and Five, and what I then found as I looked closely at my defects in Step Six.

I could not shy away from reality. In fact, I had to use it as an instrument of freedom. By doing a daily inventory, more has been revealed to me. I've learned that character is built and shortcomings removed through patience, self-esteem and humility.

~~~~~

Dear God, I am ready for your help in removing my defects of character which are obstacles to my recovery. Please, help me to continue being honest with myself while you guide me toward further spiritual growth.

I FOUND A NEW MANAGER

There was nothing left for me in my life. Cocaine was my master.
Hope, Faith & Courage Volume II, *page 75*

For me, admitting I was powerless was a simple thing to do. I could easily recognize my inability to handle cocaine. Once I started to use it, I could not stop.

On the other hand, realizing my life was unmanageable was not so effortless. I didn't understand my being uneducated and jobless was unmanageable. I was going nowhere fast. I couldn't even see that stealing from stores to support my habit was unmanageable because I never got arrested. This fact contributed to my delusion of being above the law, only fostering my unmanageability blind spot. My "normal" lifestyle went like this: come to, steal for money, buy drugs, pass out, and start again. Very manageable, or so it seemed to me.

When I finally got into the rooms of Cocaine Anonymous, I found out my life truly was unmanageable, and if I wanted to stop living that way, I was going to have to get a new Manager. I wasn't sure what this meant, but my sponsor explained it to me. It meant I was going to have to find a Power greater than myself to manage my life in all areas at all times.

I was told if I could find this new Manager, I would be restored to sanity. Wow! What a promise! I began to practice Step One in my daily life, and as I progressed through the Steps, I did find that new Manager. Not only did that Power restore me to sanity, It gave me the life I had always dreamed of having.

~~~~

I pray I never forget not only the powerlessness of my disease, but just how unmanageable my life became as a result. I need to always remember those confusing times and how important they were in igniting my ability to surrender. Allowing my Higher Power to become my Manager was the best move I could possibly make.

DECISION

> *I realized that I really was powerless; that whether I was*
> *to live or die was not within my control. At that moment, I*
> *wanted to live more than I ever had in my whole life.*
> Hope, Faith & Courage, page 171

After years of painful struggle with relapse, I was left with nothing except my sickened soul. I had reached a turning point with one decision to make and two options: Either jump off the ledge of life or jump into the arms of recovery. Somewhere deep down I wanted to live. I surrendered, admitting complete defeat. I was finally willing to do anything to stay sober. It was as if a large weight had been lifted.

My decision to be sober was a beginning, but of course it didn't stop there. I had to take direction from my sponsor. I had to show up at meetings even when I was tired or didn't feel like going. I had to be brutally honest as I worked the Steps, which was difficult considering I spent years perfecting dishonesty and denial. Like the refresh button on my computer, I have needed to remind myself of my decision to choose life and to work for it on a daily basis.

~~~~~

My instinct is to run from the truth and painful emotion, but my Higher Power gives me the strength to stay put and face it all.

JULY

HUMILITY AND GRATITUDE:
KEYS TO LONG-LASTING SOBRIETY

As the pain subsides, a healing tranquility takes its place. And when humility and serenity are so combined, something else of great moment is apt to occur.
Twelve Steps and Twelve Traditions, *page 62*

Ancient spiritual wisdom offers: "all is vanity." In other words, "Who do I think I am?" In still other words, "Don't sweat the small stuff . . . and it's all small stuff."

I often wonder what secret ingredients allow some to maintain quality sobriety and grow in recovery while others never "get it" and continue to suffer from the disease of addiction. I believe that humility and gratitude may be those secret ingredients. My definition of humility is the ability to remain down-to-earth and to fully embrace the process and the principles of recovery, relying on a Higher Power as opposed to self-will. Few, if any I've seen, fail to recover who have remained humble about the power of their disease and the futility of their own self-will.

Continued gratitude, even on bad days, is another key ingredient to long-term sobriety. I occasionally suffer from perspective loss and fall into the victim ("poor me") syndrome. Self-importance, pride and ego sometimes cloud my thinking and block me from seeing clearly why I should be grateful. In truth, I am simply an addict who could be dead, or at least alone and miserable, if not for the gift of sobriety afforded by my Higher Power, the Twelve Steps, and the Fellowship of C.A. All is else is vanity.

~~~~~

Tomorrow, I may forget this lesson—but, for today, let me remain humble and grateful for another day alive, clean, and sober.

SELF~DISCOVERY

We ask Him to remove our fear and direct our attention to what He would have us be. At once, we commence to outgrow fear.
Alcoholics Anonymous, *page 68*

In the past, all through my clueless childhood and especially in those dark days of addiction, I never had the self-esteem to show the real me. Instead, the world dealt with my facade. I never seemed to have the chance to try the authentic me out in the world. How do I occupy space without the confines of fear? This is something I'm learning more each and every day from my recovery.

In the past, I lived in a fantasy world, a ghost life devoid of originality and perhaps without the nature of texture and flesh. Today, I live within the spontaneity of others, in and around C.A. and society as a whole, sharing what it is to be alive. Apart from witnessing and feeling all that is human, good and bad, my fellows are my teachers, shining a light on what it is to be me, and exposing darkened corners of my psyche, real or imagined. Without other Fellowship members in my life, I am ignorant of who I am and who I am not—of what needs to be overcome in order to maintain my recovery. This knowledge of self is critical if I'm to grow, keep spiritually fit, and to be of maximum service to God and to my fellows. This self-discovery is necessary in order that I may hold up the mirror for others needing the same insights.

~~~~~

I pray to continue nurturing and maintaining the self-understanding I have come to experience from my recovery. May I keep evolving spiritually as the result of this new awareness.

BEEN THERE, DONE THAT

I still have fear, but it doesn't run my life anymore. By facing fears, they have less and less power over me.
Hope Faith & Courage, *page 180*

It's been a bad day. But I have been here before. Pre-recovery, I lived perpetually in this frame of mind: denial; always focusing on someone else's business so I wouldn't have to deal with my own; chronically caretaking to the point of self-neglect; blaming others (certainly none of this is *my* fault); full of fear!

What's different today is that I've done Steps Six and Seven, which enable me to see my character defects relatively clearly. I desire to change, and I am a willing participant seeking transformation, praying for direction and the power to carry it out.

Even though I have been here before, today is the only day that counts. Today I understand that just because *I'm* changing doesn't mean others around me will. Letting go of some of my character defects is terrifying. When I admit that, the acknowledgement diminishes my fear. I have been dependent and co-dependent my whole life, mentally isolating from everyone and everything (because *you* don't understand—*I'm different!*). Thank God and Cocaine Anonymous that I no longer have to do this alone.

~~~~~

Having learned how to take responsibility for myself and my character defects, I must quit giving in to them by staying in today and realizing that I am not alone in this effort. Both God and C.A. are with me.

GOD IS IN CHARGE

If we ask, God will certainly forgive our derelictions.
But in no case does He render us white as snow. . . .
Twelve Steps and Twelve Traditions, *page 65*

After years in the rooms of C.A., I've come to realize there are no doctors here, only patients. Granted, some of us are in intensive care while others are laughing it up in the lobby, but in recovery, no one is in charge except God.

Knowing we are all addicts, I try to always remember not to put my sponsor on a pedestal. He is another addict, just like me, only with more experience. I also realize that founders of our Fellowship are not gods, just drunks/addicts who recovered from a seemingly hopeless state of mind and body and then shared their experience with others. I also try to remind my sponsees not to place me on a pedestal because if they do, I will surely disappoint them.

I'm a recovered addict but a flawed human being and so is my sponsor—thank God! It is this collective admission of imperfection that first attracted me to the program of C.A. and has given me a realistic expectation for growth.

~~~~~

I pray to remain mindful that God is in charge. I need to remember that my sponsor, my sponsees, and I are all flawed humans seeking spiritual experiences, and that no one, in or out of recovery, should be placed on a pedestal.

HOW FAR WILL I GO?

> *If you have decided you want what we have and are willing to go to any length to get it—then you are ready to take certain steps.*
> Alcoholics Anonymous, *page 58*

The first time I sat down with my sponsor to look at the Twelve Steps of Cocaine Anonymous, he asked me, "Are you prepared to go to any lengths?" At the time, I didn't have a clue what "any lengths" meant. All I knew was I could no longer continue my disease's destructive path. We began working the Steps together. Since then, my life keeps changing, day after day.

I have to be willing to have all my character defects removed, not hanging on to any of them. The longer I cling to these behaviors, the worse they become. My Higher Power wants me to have an abundant life, unencumbered by this type of negative energy. I need to make the decision daily to turn these behaviors over to Him.

I used to be troubled, hating my life and everything about myself. Not only was I void of self-love and self-respect, I had none for anyone else either. Alcohol and drugs blinded me; but today, through the grace of God and the C.A. program, I'm starting to understand the truth that I am lovable, worthy of recovery and God's grace.

I am learning to accept God's will. As I come to know and love myself, I am also coming to know a loving God. As I pray for willingness to let go of the old me, my open-minded attitude broadens and strengthens my spiritual connection and further enhances my recovery.

~~~~~

I believe that, for me, "any lengths" is simply the best I can honestly do at any given point. What lengths will I go to today to stay sober, to be of service, and further deepen my understanding of my disease?

PROGRESS, NOT PERFECTION

Selfishness—self-centeredness! That, we think, is the root of our troubles.
Alcoholics Anonymous, page 62

In our active addiction, it was no surprise how many of us were selfish. We did not want to share our drugs (unless we wanted something in return!). Everyone else we knew operated in the same manner. Why be friendly to others unless they could help us get drugs, offer us money or shelter, or save us from the loneliness that was killing us inside?

Once we were free from mind-altering substances, we thought we would be fine. Much to our surprise, however, we discovered our powerlessness over the "hundred forms of fear, self-delusion, self-seeking, and self-pity" (*Alcoholics Anonymous*, page 62) that overran our no-longer-altered minds. We felt resentful of those who were more successful than us. We judged our friends in the meeting. We pitied ourselves when our relationships dissolved or simply didn't exist in the first place. We stirred things up unnecessarily. Worse yet, we dreaded the boredom and lack of edge and excitement that threatened to fill our days. We began to realize that we were not simply powerless over substances, but over our many defects of character as well. Envy, sloth, pride, fear, and resentment all took turns on center stage of our lives. By working the Steps and by coming back continually, we learned how to turn these hindrances around. Awareness is more than half the solution.

~~~~~

May I accept my defects of character and realize that I am not, nor will I ever be perfect. May I always be mindful that I have a Higher Power and a recovery program to help me let go of these shortcomings, growing towards a new way of life, one day at a time.

CHAOS
(OR MAMA SAID THERE'D BE DAYS LIKE THIS!)

My life got to be about as unmanageable as possible. . . .
Hope, Faith & Courage, *page 39*

I've been taught in the rooms that serenity is not the absence of calamity, but rather the ability to remain calm and connected on the days and moments that test my composure. It is during these chaotic, frustrating, and seemingly unbearable times that I must pause and remember—life sometimes *does* give me more than I can handle *on my own*. After all, I am often powerless to control other people, situations, and life events. Experience shows me that my self-will and self-sufficiency proved inadequate long ago. Now, in addition to a set of spiritual tools to help me navigate the storm, I also have a Higher Power to call upon when life comes raining down on my shoulders and the weight seems too much to bear. Today I have faith that the principles I've learned through the process of the Twelve Steps can guide me through any situation, no matter how trying.

~~~~~

Serenity is not floating on a pink cloud of happiness. Rather, serenity is sailing through life's inevitable storms knowing that if I trust my Higher Power and remain calm, I will eventually reach the safety of the shore.

HUMILITY

> *To get completely away from our aversion to the idea of being humble, to gain a vision of humility as the avenue to the true freedom of the human spirit, to be willing to work for humility as something to be desired for itself, takes most of us a long, long time. A whole lifetime geared to self-centeredness cannot be set in reverse all at once.*
> Twelve Steps and Twelve Traditions, *page 73*

When I was using, I had no humility. I thought it was a weakness. I was who I was, and I knew best. My way was the right way. Everyone else should defer to *me*— after all, I was doing just fine in my drug addiction, with a lack of respect for most things and with no sense of direction or belonging. More accurately, I simply did not have a clue as to the meaning of the word humility, nor how it could affect my actions. Frankly, I didn't care.

People I met in recovery were different. For starters, they were calm and focused, greeting me with a smile and a welcoming handshake. They showed interest in my story and listened to my problems. They treated each other and (even more surprisingly) *me* with dignity and honor. They showed respect for the meetings, for each other and for the Fellowship itself. Most amazingly, they were staying clean and sober. I began to realize this respect was a by-product of humility.

Today, I do my utmost to remember who I am and what I am doing in every situation. It begins with being honest with my sponsor. I've learned to listen, doing the best I can to follow suggestions. I give the group and its trusted servants my respect because all are important teachers in my quest to understand and adopt an attitude of humility.

~~~~~

What I reap is what I sow, and as I give, so I receive. I am in a better place today as a result of a new attitude of humility, something much simpler than my head used to lead me to believe.

FINDING GOD

> *No one comes into Cocaine Anonymous to find God. We come to these rooms to get rid of a terrifying drug habit.*
> A Higher Power (C.A. Pamphlet)

When I first got to Cocaine Anonymous, I did not believe there was a God, and I certainly didn't want any help in changing myself. What I did want was to be clean and sober, so I did what everybody said I needed to do—I got a sponsor. After allowing him to guide me through the Steps and then spending some time practicing the principles, I found I no longer wanted to use (the good news!). Unfortunately, I still felt unable to handle my shortcomings (bummer).

One day, while suffering from an ongoing problem with which I had been struggling, I got down on my knees in desperation to pray for some relief. I knew not what I was praying to, nor did I believe anything was really there. I said, "When are you going to help me with these defects?" Right then, I felt something say, "*I am.*" This experience was my first real conscious contact with a God of my own understanding. Suddenly, I had the conviction that God would do for me what I could not do for myself. Inner peace immediately flowed into my being.

~~~~~

Through taking the actions described in the Steps and suggested by my sponsor, I have gone from being a person who never wanted or believed in a Higher Power to living in a God-centered world. This transformation is available for all who are willing to try.

BLAME BE GONE

Our liquor was but a symptom. So we had to get down to causes and conditions.
Alcoholics Anonymous, *page 64*

It was a revelation—a spiritual experience—to discover through the *Big Book* that alcohol and drugs were not the root cause of my problem. I could no longer deny that I had allowed my stinking thinking to lead to many unacceptable behaviors over a long period of time. I began to understand that I couldn't blame anyone or anything, especially drugs and alcohol, for any of my problems—past or present.

Much work would be required to get down to causes and conditions: working the Twelve Steps; working with my sponsor; seeking outside help (where necessary); dropping the resentments that I still carried. I also needed to address my many character defects to decrease their number and intensity.

Only when I empty out the toxic negativity and clear away the wreckage of my past, *and* only when I am willing to do the work, can I fill back up with the positive energy offered by the program.

~~~~~

God, please direct my thoughts and actions to reflect the Step work I have done to finally get down to causes and conditions. Help me please to stop blaming chemicals and liquor for my problems. I want the gifts and promises of the program and the freedom they bring.

TRAGEDY TRANSFORMED

We missed the reality and the beauty of the forest because
we were diverted by the ugliness of some of its trees.
Alcoholics Anonymous, *page 50*

When I was using, my life was defined by sometimes daily tragedies. Even if circumstances occasionally seemed to get better, they inevitably returned to the worst. I tried to forget the nightmare of these terrifying experiences, but I lived in fear of the next calamity, which I was certain was just around the corner.

Upon entering recovery, I often remained a victim of this ceaseless obsession—unable to shake the idea that sooner or later, the other shoe would drop.

By focusing my energy on the fears of tomorrow, I continued to rob myself of the current day's true beauty. Because the incessant dread that "it will ultimately fall apart" was all I'd ever known, I failed to see many of the countless gifts which my Higher Power had granted me through the grace and gift of sobriety.

Fortunately, Steps Four through Seven enabled me to recognize the counterproductive nature of these fears. With God's help, I began believing the future holds bright opportunity and promise. I was released from the fear-based beliefs, which kept me stagnant.

~~~~~

I will not allow trepidation about tomorrow to divert me from life's magnificence today. As a symbol of my gratitude, I will call or contact those people who have helped me find recovery and thank them for being a part of my life. By putting gratitude into action, I not only pay tribute to my sobriety and those who went before me, but I am reminded to stay firmly rooted in the reality of the present moment.

H & I HIGH

I realized that if I show up to be of service to someone, even though I'm there to help another addict out of his or her pain, I get an opportunity to learn and heal. Those things are what have created a spiritual change in who I am.
Hope, Faith & Courage Volume II, page 129

Being a product of Hospitals & Institutions (H&I), I deeply wish to thank any member of C.A. who has ever done any H&I service work. H&I meetings brought into my treatment center planted a seed of hope, causing me to seek out the rooms of recovery. Having recovered from a seemingly hopeless state of mind and body thanks to the Twelve Steps, I can now say that seed of hope which H&I planted has taken root, grown, and flourished in my life.

Because of my gratitude to H&I, carrying the message into treatment centers is one of the biggest joys in my life and perhaps the greatest gift I've received through being of service to C.A. My goal is to keep growing in effectiveness and understanding, to keep learning from others with more experience, and to continue reaching out the hand of C.A. to the still-suffering addict.

I have had the extreme joy of meeting addicts in detox units and, upon their release, watching them join this Fellowship, get C.A. sponsors, work all Twelve Steps and become sponsors themselves. This is the progression of passing it on. At a recent C.A. World Service Convention, through my own tears of gratitude, I watched rehab patients brought in by H&I weep with joy. I was, again, indescribably moved by what I call my H&I high. My gratitude for the ability to serve in this capacity is immense.

~~~~

Service is a key component of my recovery. I am blessed to experience the true joy when newcomers I meet latch onto the program and stick around. Perhaps I may even have said or done something that played a part in their awakening. Being able to relay our spiritual message in this way is absolutely priceless.

_____

FAITH WITHOUT WORKS IS DEAD

Faith without works was dead, he said. And how appallingly true for the alcoholic! For if an alcoholic failed to perfect and enlarge his spiritual life through work and self-sacrifice for others, he could not survive the certain trials and low spots ahead. If he did not work, he would surely drink again, and if he drank, he would surely die. Then faith would be dead indeed. With us it is just like that.
Alcoholics Anonymous, *pages 14-15*

Even if I believe that my Higher Power can do for me what I can't do for myself, I need to keep trudging forward in my program and in my recovery. I just can't sit idly by and wait for my life to improve and for the answers to my confusion to come to me. I must take action, no matter how difficult that may be. I have to participate in my recovery rather than wait for it to happen.

As I complete Step Seven, *Alcoholics Anonymous,* page 76 reminds me that I need more action, without which, I believe that faith without works is dead. This requires me to promptly work Steps Eight and Nine to the best of my ability, after which I can then receive the Ninth-Step Promises.

Even more action is suggested as I start working Step Ten and incorporate daily prayer and meditative process into my life. *Alcoholics Anonymous* warns me here not to let up on my actions (page 85) or rest on my laurels. It urges me to go further, and that means yet more action—working Step Eleven on a daily basis. Even then, I am reminded again that there is action and more action needed (page 88). Step Twelve and the *Alcoholics Anonymous* chapter *Working With Others* are all about further action. Here, all the promises of the program, including the "spiritual awakening," will come to me, *if* I remain in action.

~~~~~

I pray for the faith to guide me in my program that I may remain diligent in working the Steps. I must remain in "action" throughout the last key Steps for ultimate relief and awareness and for the promises to come true in my life.

MEASURING UP

> We had lacked the perspective to see that character-building and spiritual values had to come first, and that material satisfactions were not the purpose of living.
> Twelve Steps and Twelve Traditions, page 71

My entire life, I compared myself to others and what they had. I began using cocaine as a means of measuring up, but in the long run, my use and abuse stole any chance of that ever happening. At the time, I had no way of knowing I was comparing my insides to everyone else's outsides.

Working the program, especially Steps Six and Seven, has led me to realize self-worth is built upon the development of my spirituality. As I cultivate my relationship with the God of my understanding, my character becomes stronger; I become more confident and truly at peace with myself. The more I can build my character, the better I can serve my Higher Power, my fellows in Cocaine Anonymous, and the addict who still suffers. This also allows me to forgive myself and move forward in my recovery.

~~~~~

I pray that I may step out of my own way so I can continue to gain spiritual guidance. This is the best means by which to develop my character and to be able to serve others.

EMBRACING REALITY

A.A. led me from this fantasizing to embrace reality with open arms. And I found it beautiful! For, at last, I was at peace with myself. And with others. And with God.
Alcoholics Anonymous, 4th Edition, *page 559*

Pain, angst, horror, and loss comprised my basic reality before I found C.A. and recovery. In trying to escape this quagmire by using and drinking, I invariably found that it only compounded my problems. The ensuing nightmares integrated themselves into my altered frame of reference.

After I found the rooms and started working the Steps, my reality shifted to something more authentic. Life got hard for a while, leaving me with confusion and fear—not only about where I *had* been, but the direction I might be headed if I didn't work through these challenges. My sponsor helped with some clarity and grounding, as did others in our Fellowship whom I met doing service work. I began to grow and change in a positive way, with no ulterior motive except to learn to do the next right thing. I was helped to understand what it means to "not regret the past nor wish to shut the door on it." (*Alcoholics Anonymous*, page 83.) Accepting the truth, without magnifying, rationalizing or denying the full scope of my actions, was totally new behavior for me. I began to embrace life on life's terms in a responsible manner without any drama.

After a time in sobriety, I acknowledge that none of us are immune from life's sometimes harsh realities. Even while I know God does not give us more than we can handle, sometimes what we do get can be particularly daunting. Realities such as loss of family or friends, challenges at work, health issues, and financial insecurity have all graced my plate recently. When these circumstances arise, the same tools necessarily come out—namely, go to meetings, pray, and seek guidance from others who have made it through a similar challenge. The big difference is that I don't use over these matters. Rather, I face them, one day at a time, empowered by a partnership with God and the wisdom of those in our rooms who share their strength, hope, and particularly their *experience* with me.

Today, recovery insights and promises come true throughout my journey and provide a strong foundation for me to perceive life's realities just as they are.

~~~~

I am truly humbled and thankful for having grasped a reality which is grounded in truth, faith, doing the next right thing, and a conscious contact with the God of my understanding. I never dreamed just how wonderful a gift this would be in the overall scope of my recovery.

SHOW ME THE MONEY

Every C.A. group ought to be fully self-supporting, declining outside contributions.
C.A. Tradition Seven

In being responsible for every aspect of our group's activities, including making sure that its bills are paid, we discover an inner resource. I realize that in many areas of my life, I have depended on the actions of others to bring me happiness. Often, I found myself frustrated at the inability of those around me to act according to my internal wishes. By participating in the group principle of self-support, I found that the true source of happiness is to live usefully and humbly. Every time I contribute when the group passes the basket, I can know, at my deepest level, that I am participating in a unifying principle.

Tradition Seven may also be applied to personal lives. Recovery enables responsible, gainful employment. In turn, the ability to provide for oneself is possible, perhaps for the first time ever. The resulting by-products of a deeper sense of security and well-being add yet another positive element to my new, drug-free world.

~~~~~

Today, let me participate in life by doing the things necessary to support my group, including making contributions so that it can meet its financial responsibilities. Help me to remember how much I used to spend on my drugs that I may give with gratitude for all I've received in recovery.

_____

BUILDING SELF-WORTH THROUGH SERVICE

> *Cocaine Anonymous is a Fellowship of men and women who share their experience, strength, and hope with each other that they may solve their common problem and help others recover from their addiction.*
>
> Hope, Faith & Courage Volume II, *page 227*
> *(taken from C.A. Preamble)*

I walked in the doors of C.A. broken and shattered. I felt no worth as a human being and didn't believe I could ever be saved from myself. Very quickly, the miracles started. I learned there was hope, even for me. As I attended meetings, I was amazed to see many laughing, happy people. At first, I thought it had to be a big scam and that soon enough, everyone would try to get over on me somehow. I decided to stick around long enough to figure out the catch.

But the miracles kept on coming. Even though my self-esteem was in the bucket, they kept assigning me service positions. I still felt unworthy but began to be humbled by the fact that these people trusted me to show up and do what I was supposed to do. The "catch" I was looking for never appeared. Instead, I quickly got drawn into the Fellowship structure—meeting lots of new friends and discovering that no matter how horrible you feel about yourself, the people in C.A. will accept you and love you unconditionally. They'll stick with you, no matter what your problems and situations may be. They will show you how to be a loving, kind, considerate, and caring human being even if you didn't believe that was possible. The miracles can happen for anyone who is willing to give it a chance and get involved.

~~~~

Very few of us have any self-respect when we arrive at the doors of C.A. Earning the trust of our fellows by being responsible to a service commitment lays the foundation upon which a positive sense of worth can begin to grow.

THE POWER OF MY AMENDS

It is the beginning of the end of isolation from our fellows and from God.
Twelve Steps and Twelve Traditions, *page 82*

Almost all addicts suffer from the harm caused by our behaviors in our active addictions, causing hurt in the lives of the people we love and care about the most. We are extremely remorseful and often quite fearful about having to face many of these people and accept responsibility for our actions. In fact, the very thought of facing them has caused some of us to either stall out in our programs or worse, to relapse.

In tackling our amends, many of us learn that shame had been our constant companion, along with guilt and remorse. Many of these amends are born of our resentment and fear in some combination with our more perilous character defects. Recovery in C.A. gives us the opportunity to repair these broken relations and to clear our side of the street. We can approach the people we have harmed with confidence, knowing that our Higher Power is right there with us.

Addressing these challenging amends is quite empowering. In fact, many program gifts and insights are received in addition to the Step Nine Promises we hear about most often in meetings. Many of us experience equally powerful promises. We learn how to forgive ourselves and learn from our mistakes. We are gifted with the chance to make living, ongoing amends for the years of abuse to our bodies and spirits. We will find within ourselves, perhaps for the first time ever, a peace and serenity to sustain us through all emergencies and trying times which will follow throughout our recoveries. Self-obsession will be removed, and we will genuinely know how to be of altruistic service to others. We will place our transgressions in a healthy perspective and move past their paralyzing effects. We will confirm the fact that our Higher Powers are managing our lives far better than we ever could ourselves.

In facing these amends, we remember that we are not after an apology; rather, we are seeking the cleansing, the lessons, and the spiritual experience.

~~~~

Have I made all my Step Nine amends? Am I now willing to approach somebody I have harmed whom I did not want to face? God, please give me the strength to repair my broken relationships to enter into a new life of freedom and usefulness.

MOVING DOWN THE SERVICE LADDER

Adopt the attitude of service without reward.
Being of Service (C.A. Pamphlet)

Learning about service work at levels outside your home group is an educational experience. However, local District or Area positions often go unfilled for lack of warm willing bodies. Why is that?

The biggest excuse usually heard generally has to do with being "too busy." But how much time and energy did we spend getting high? How much time and energy did others who were clean and sober in the program before us contribute to make sure *we* had a place to go and that the Fellowship would keep on growing?

Don't ever assume "someone else will do it." The future of C.A. rests in the hands of its members. If you are feeling a pang of guilt right now because you are not doing anything to help, find out who to call. If you are saying to yourself, "Gosh, I ought to be more pro-active in the C.A. service structure," don't just say it—*do it!* It's an opportunity you can't afford to miss.

~~~~~

Let me spend some time today considering the type of service work for which I'd be best suited. I will talk to my sponsor about his/her experience with service and ask for suggestions. God, please help me not to make excuses.

AS DEADLY AS THEY COME

Perhaps we saw a cocaine friend die of respiratory arrest, and still *we went on using!*
To the Newcomer (C.A. Pamphlet)

My sister, a nurse, repeatedly tried to save me from myself. She would search the cesspools where I hung out, dragging me home whenever she could. She never gave up on me, and eventually I found recovery.

When I was five years clean and sober, my sister got cancer. It was a tough battle during which twice she lost all vital signs and had to be resuscitated. Following these experiences, she told me it felt as if she were on a giant cloud. She heard a voice she believes was God saying everything would be okay. She said she thought of me and wished they had a Twelve-Step program that could put her cancer in remission like C.A. did for my disease.

I started to think about that and imagine how people with cancer and other serious life-threatening diseases would approach the Twelve Steps if working them would arrest their disease. I'll bet very few, if any, would ever leave the program or fail to apply the Steps! They would be too grateful to be free from their symptoms. It made me realize how flippantly I had treated the gift of sobriety!

My sister asked me to promise her I would never quit going to Twelve-Step meetings, because they gave me back to her. I made that promise, and one day at a time, I plan to keep it.

~~~~~

Addiction is incurable, but unlike many deadly diseases, we have a treatment that works (the Steps). My gratitude for this fact must never diminish.

FUELING OUR BODIES

Some of us hit a physical bottom.
To the Newcomer (C.A. Pamphlet)

Our bodies house our souls and mind. They are the vehicles in which we travel through our lives. Like a well-maintained automobile, if we pay attention to how we take care of them, the better they will take us through our life's journey, and the more energetic we will be. We will have more mental clarity if we aren't distracted by unnecessary aches and pains because we haven't had enough water today or because we've eaten something that doesn't agree with us.

When we get a new car, there's a manual that comes with it to tell us how to care for every part of our new vehicle. It tells us what kind of fuel to use and what types of oils and other fluids to keep at specified levels. It warns against dropping below a certain level of air pressure in the tires. It even instructs us on what cleaning solutions to use on the surface of the car, inside and out. There's also a detailed maintenance schedule that when followed, increases the life and value of the automobile over the years. How we treat and maintain our car determines how long it will serve us and how well.

Our body can serve us best if we respect and honor how we maintain it. Our "body vehicle" needs the right fuel and care if we want it to "run well." We don't have the advantage of being born with our own unique how-to manual, but we can learn what works and what doesn't work by educating ourselves, asking others, being awake to how we feel, and by making adjustments when we need to.

~~~~~

As I move through this day, let me be open to how my body is feeling and how my actions impact it. Let me listen to my body's messages and be as thoughtful about fueling and caring for it as I am about my car. Let me have respect for my body and physical health today.

GRATITUDE/RELIEF

I always thought I had a pretty good life. Now I know there is more to it than the selfish, materialistic point of view I used to hold. Because of this Program, I have been blessed with an "attitude of gratitude."
Hope, Faith & Courage, *page 56*

Gratitude and relief are both valid words which I can use to describe my sobriety. I have not always been clear which description applied.

Gratitude is a virtue, with elements of unselfishness, and is often connected to an outpouring of grace. Gratitude directs my attention away from me and my needy, demanding side, and allows me to nurture a different aspect of myself that had long been dormant until I stumbled onto this path of recovery.

In the beginning, I could not truly experience or express gratitude, but I did experience relief as the physical, emotional, and spiritual pains were lifted and I began to re-awaken. Relief is not a bad thing; I needed to experience some pleasures of sobriety for myself before I could be of any real service. But in my view, relief always ends with *me* and, therefore, is not gratitude.

Gratitude lists can be good tools, provided I expound on my thoughts to delve into the real essence of what makes me grateful. For example: "I am grateful that I am employed." By itself, this is not true gratitude. However, "I am grateful I am employed because I can put gas in my car and offer a ride to the meeting to that newcomer who lost his license and lives outside of town, which is too far for most people to travel," or "I am grateful I am employed because I was able to take my fellow home group member whose car is unreliable up to the state prison to visit his son who is doing eight to ten years." Now, *that* is understanding the true spirit of gratitude.

~~~~~

Like everything else, the tools are only as good as I allow them to be. I often take my employment for granted, but when I shine the right light on it, I can grow in gratitude. Gratitude *always* gets me out of myself and into a mindset of helping others.

NOW HEAR THIS

We are often surprised how the right answers come. . . .
Alcoholics Anonymous, *page 86*

One of my favorite prayers is short and to the point: "Okay, God, what am I supposed to learn from *this?*"

Typically, I use it most often when things aren't going my way, when some unexpected obstacle has planted itself right in my path, or when I am faced with a dilemma. If I say it sincerely, with my heart open, I'll frequently get an immediate answer—often one that surprises me and makes me laugh. Usually simple and straightforward, words that are not my own pop right into my head. For example:

"You just never know what's going to happen next," or "Be grateful! Things can always be worse!"

These are just two replies I've received over the years. Each pearl of wisdom has been profoundly embedded in my soul. I've also been able to pass them along to family, friends, co-workers, sponsees and other members of the Fellowship when *they* have lost perspective. Everybody benefits!

~~~~~

When I stay in the *now*, asking to *hear* God's input, this simple re-centering of myself generally puts things in a different light. Whatever it is I'm supposed to learn becomes clear.

REPAYING THE DEBT

I have been handed this great gift from God and the Fellowship, an exciting new life full of unlimited adventure and discovery. That's a debt that no matter how hard I try, I will never have the ability to repay.
Hope, Faith & Courage Volume II, *page 107*

When I finally got to the rooms of C.A., I was greeted by Fellowship members who asked only that I stick around and receive the gifts which had been freely given to them. Frankly, it was like they were giving me something I could never hope to repay by virtue of their support, kindness and non-judgmental love. For the longest time, I did not fully understand their motivation for being so earnest in their desire to see me make it.

The longer I stuck around, the clearer all this became. It was about me and paying it forward, but it was also about their paying a debt to C.A. for getting their lives back with new clarity. I now understand that they wanted to see me find myself in sobriety, get answers to the unanswered questions in my life, and find some inner peace and serenity. They did this by inviting me to work the Steps, be of service and, ultimately, to join forces with them in our recoveries. They showed me how to walk the path toward a happy, joyous and free life, collectively trudging the road of happy destiny.

When I give back through service, my rewards are immeasurable. How can I repay consistent peace of mind? How can I account for the promises coming to me, continually? Is there a price I can put on restoration of the many important relations in my life? How do I value a deep sense of purpose and freedom? How do I ever thank the Fellowship for the relative ease and comfort I now have living in my own skin? With sanity restored as a direct result of the Steps, I am able to recognize that true freedom comes from giving. The C.A. Fellowship is a perfect and necessary place for me to give back all that I can.

~~~~~

Today, I will focus on how I can carry the C.A. message of recovery and freedom. I will strive to repay the debt as others before me have done with hope, gratitude, and humility.

AMENDS ~ THE FINE PRINT

> *There are still some people that I have to make amends to, and as long as I continue to have the willingness, God often puts them in my path. I've had old friends or girlfriends find my name in the phone book and just call me up. My experience is that my amends never work out the way I think they will; I talk, and then they talk, and then we have healing around a new relationship. I'm really grateful for that.*
>
> Hope, Faith & Courage Volume II, *page 185*

If I pass up an opportunity to make an amends, a long time might pass before I get another chance to see that person. In fact, I might *never* get another opportunity. Thus, it is best to make my amends as soon as I possibly can. Often times, my Higher Power will bring me into contact with those I need to see, and it's important to seize the moment.

Shortly after starting Step Nine, I was sitting in one of my regular meetings. A few minutes before the meeting ended, a man walked in and took a seat in the back of the room. I turned to see who it was and, to my utter amazement, recognized my first sponsor, to whom I owed an amends.

As soon as the meeting ended, I approached my former sponsor and made my amends. I had never seen him there before, and have not seen him anywhere else since. I am convinced God brought him into my life that day to give me the opportunity to make things right. I am very grateful I didn't hesitate, and the incident still stands out as one of my first truly spiritual experiences.

The Ninth Step offers a door through which we may pass to greater freedom. We must remember as we approach this door our agreement at the outset of sobriety that we were willing to go to any lengths, keeping also in mind, "If we are painstaking about this phase of our development, we will be amazed before we are halfway through." (*Alcoholics Anonymous*, page 83.)

~~~~~

It's not by chance that the Promises are listed with the Ninth Step in *Alcoholics Anonymous*. At this point in our recovery, they start to come true. Shortly after starting to work this Step, we begin to realize that God truly is doing for us what we could never do for ourselves. I pray for the willingness to make amends when the opportunity presents itself. I know it is no accident when someone to whom I owe amends appears unexpectedly.

COOPERATION THROUGH PARTICIPATION

The final responsibility and the ultimate authority for C.A. World Services should always reside in the collective conscience of our whole fellowship.
C.A. Concept One

The foundation of this Concept is rooted in that part of Tradition Two which provides: "For our group purpose there is but one ultimate authority—a loving God as He may express Himself in our group conscience."

The heart of this Concept lies in the Fellowship of Cocaine Anonymous. It's found in the members who search out C.A. on a daily basis. It's rooted in those who have a willingness to attend meetings. It's seen in those who share their experience with the Twelve Steps and Twelve Traditions, and in those who desire to explore change and progress through participation.

At the various service levels of our C.A. Fellowship, this Concept is always present. It reveals itself through the group inventory, being always mindful of the manner in which group conscience is implemented and how C.A. as a whole may be affected. It holds true in our Groups' participation by their Group Service Representatives, and by other trusted servants at larger Area, Regional and World levels.

These trusted servants remain responsible, respectable, and reliable when serving the Fellowship of C.A. Their position in the "upside-down pyramid" of service reflects the collective conscience of C.A. Groups. The actions taken at the World Service Conference each year indicate decisions on matters which, at times, the Fellowship and/or Groups cannot readily accomplish for themselves.

~~~~~

Concept One, the "collective conscience," has been characterized as one of enough enlightenment, enough responsibility, and enough love of man and God to insure that our democracy of World Service will work. I will make time in my program to learn about the Concepts in order to become an informed and responsible Fellowship member.

LET THE LIGHT SHINE AND THE MUSIC RING

So cooperate; never criticize. To be helpful is our only aim.
Alcoholics Anonymous, *page 89*

The darkness of alcoholism and drug addiction continues to ravage the lives of addicts, their families and, in truth, all those with whom it comes in contact. One addict at a time, the darkness is lifted when C.A.'s music is sung and heard. C.A.'s symphony is played in the key of "service." Service, in its purest form, is the activity in which a spirit awakened through recovery meets others in fellowship.

When a candle is lit in a darkened room, the darkness disappears. In 1934, a candle was lit in the dark room that was alcoholism and drug addiction. In 1935, Bill W. shared his light with Dr. Bob, and the glow strengthened. That light continued to be shared, alcoholic to alcoholic, until Cocaine Anonymous was born in 1982. Struggling to honor the A.A. singleness of purpose tradition, the new Fellowship recognized that freedom from cocaine and all other mind-altering substances was its unifying element. What Cocaine Anonymous is today has simply resulted from a long line of service.

Service requires addicts to sacrifice in the interest of others. Without the destruction of ego through recovery, sacrifice in the interest of others can be challenging. The straightforward quote from the *Big Book* above is a guiding principle to service. It is a useful instruction for all levels of service—from guiding a sponsee through the Steps, to home group members discussing changes to their meeting format, to Group Service Representatives exchanging ideas at an Area meeting, to Delegates debating a motion on the floor at the C.A. World Service Conference.

I can never *force* an outcome in any of these service settings. Instead, I find myself open to the resolution God intends through the informed group conscience. Inevitably, love and tolerance prevail.

~~~~

Is C.A.'s melody always near to me? I hope its service refrain plays on in my heart and soul forever and that the light from my recovery candle is never extinguished.

CARING AND FRIENDLY

Most of us feel we need look no further for Utopia. We have it with us right here and now. Each day my friend's simple talk in our kitchen multiplies itself in a widening circle of peace on earth and good will to men.
Alcoholics Anonymous, *page 16*

I came to Cocaine Anonymous with many decades in another Twelve-Step program already under my belt. At my first C.A. meeting, my sponsor was speaking. Before the meeting started, a man came in looking for a different Twelve-Step meeting. The C.A. members invited him to stay. He accepted the invitation and even shared during the meeting. I was shocked by their invitation to this individual who didn't even have an apparent addiction issue.

Months earlier, I had lost my mother-in-law, with whom I had been extremely close. Still very raw emotionally, I remember thinking, "I don't want to share because I will lose it." Of course my sponsor's talk was helpful that night, but I was still hurting. Then I got "the look," and with a nod of my sponsor's head, I knew I had to share. As soon as I opened up, tears started flowing. The C.A. members were so caring and friendly, extending many comforting condolences—they really made me feel better! They didn't ask who, what, or where anybody came from. There was no judgment, just pure love to me and to the others in the room, including the guest from another Twelve-Step program. Our C.A. Fellowship is so open to helping addicts as well as their friends and family. The warmth I feel towards C.A. has never faded. Now I attend many C.A. meetings, and I find the same kindness and compassion at each one.

~~~~~

I've learned I never stop growing and that my recovery can always get better, no matter how long I stay clean and sober. My C.A. exposure helped me to become more caring and friendly, not just at meetings, but in my everyday life as well.

COMMITTEES WORKING OVERTIME

To be able to think that clearly and precisely, to have only one thought rather than a hundred raging voices, is one of the greatest gifts recovery handed me.
Hope, Faith & Courage Volume II, *page 106*

Why is it so difficult to live in the moment? Committees in my brain love to work overtime, that's why! The "Shoulda Done It" commission reviews every word I say and all of my actions, replaying the scenarios of my life over and over again, submitting endless proposals on how things could or should have gone differently. Then, of course, the "What's Gonna Happen?" executive board convenes, primarily in charge of charting my future. All types of worst-case scenarios must be carefully plotted and rehearsed in my head's virtual conference room. Unfortunately, the poor "Let's Enjoy Right Now" group can't ever seem to get any meeting space time. The schedule is perpetually booked up by the other two entities.

Whatever I may have done yesterday or plan to do tomorrow will never be as important as what I do today. If I strive to do what God has intended for me today, then when today becomes yesterday, I will have done God's will. Tomorrow, I simply do the same! Each day, if I utilize what is freely given, I will be blessed with an appreciation for the most precious gift that is today.

~~~~

I pray to always remember where I have been and to honor tomorrow, but to dwell in today. Yesterday is history. Tomorrow's a mystery. Today is a gift—that's why it's called the *present*!

BOUNDARIES

I can take responsibility for my life and make choices. I learned to stand up for my boundaries.
Hope, Faith & Courage Volume II, *page 24*

Before I got into recovery, there were no such things as boundaries and nothing I would not attempt. The extreme was common; I was *too* everything. I hurt too much. I sought too much. I was too angry, too sad, too scared, too courageous. I was also much, much too judgmental and many times I remember being too right. Those were the times I wound up in jail, hurt, or losing someone and/or something I loved *too* much. In a nutshell, I was too self-serving!

My recovery has been about seeking to find and set healthy boundaries because past experience has taught me that to not have them is foolhardy, dangerous, and completely self-destructive. In the process of this change, I'm learning that these limitations are what help create a balance in life.

As I seek through prayer and meditation to improve my conscious contact with God, knowledge of His will for me illuminates right choices about the boundaries available to me in my new life. I know today that as I set wise boundaries, my serenity will remain steady or improve as a direct result.

~~~~~

I pray that through self-forgetting, I may find that self which God would have me be. May I see clearly the boundaries which must be crafted and then honored.

FORGIVENESS

It was not until I offered and accepted my own forgiveness, that I was truly able to grow in my sobriety.
Hope, Faith & Courage, *pages 127-128*
(also C.A. Meeting Format reading Reaching Out*)*

When I first got into recovery, I felt consumed by guilt and shame over all the horrible things I had done while I was using. I wanted others to forgive me so badly that I became a doormat. I never said "no," and I did not have any boundaries. I got hurt often as a result, and I felt even worse about myself and my relationships. Even though I was sober and working the Steps, my insides were in a continued state of turmoil.

In recovery, I learned that I had never forgiven myself, both for my actions before I got sober, as well as my lack of boundaries after I made it into the rooms. I saw myself so lowly as to not even be worth my seat at the tables, and, frankly, I treated myself that way. I eventually hit a different kind of bottom.

Today, I know that I am worthy of sobriety and healthy relationships. It is important to be kind and loving towards myself. I can be more accepting of all my parts—the ones needing some work and the ones that shine brightly. I know I've made huge mistakes in my life and hurt people I love, but if I can't forgive myself then no one else will either.

~~~~~

Today, I will remember that we are all worthy of love and acceptance.

AUGUST

August I

JUST PRAY ANYWAY

You start with belief, your experience will come.
A Higher Power (C.A. Pamphlet)

I was new in the program and was told that I needed a sponsor. Although I was looking, I couldn't seem to find anyone who seemed right for the job. One of my counselors suggested I just pray about it. I had been resistant about the spiritual part of the program, and I shared that with my counselor. "Just pray anyway," he responded.

So that's what I did. What the heck—it couldn't hurt to try even the simplest of prayers.

A few hours later, a man I'd never seen before came into our meeting. Turns out he was the speaker, and as he told his story, he might as well have been telling mine. Right then and there, I understood I had a Higher Power looking out for me.

This man became my sponsor, and we immediately began working the Steps. The first thing I noticed was that a lot of my burden and stress went away almost immediately. I found it easier to do everyday things, including fall asleep, or even face the day each morning. I soon learned that by talking about my problems, whether it was with another person in the Fellowship, my sponsor, or my Higher Power, my life became and has remained much more manageable.

~~~~~

If I hadn't been willing to try praying in spite of my misgivings, I might still be drifting aimlessly, and I'm relatively certain that I would not be in recovery today. I have come to believe my Higher Power is always with me. It's comforting to know I am never alone. It is also comforting to know that I might be just a prayer away from the solution(s) to whatever my needs or problems are at any given moment.

LIGHTEN UP

Rule #62. . . . "Don't take yourself too damn seriously."
Twelve Steps and Twelve Traditions, *page 149*

When I expect too much of myself, I am usually disappointed.

How many times have I begun a new project or venture, or taken a class to enrich my life, only to beat myself down when I don't perfect it within the first five minutes? All of my experiences, both positive and negative, are part of my journey.

I've learned it's okay that I dropped a stitch when crocheting a blanket for a loved one. It's okay that I sometimes missed the target in karate. It's okay when I forget to mail the birthday card and it arrives late. It's okay that I do not have all the answers to my problems today—or even any of them. God is okay with these things; I just need to be okay with them as well.

I am able to learn, to love, and to laugh at myself, whether I make mistakes or not. I've learned not take life and my recovery journey too seriously.

~~~~~

Life is a journey to be experienced, not perfected. I can never perform everything I do perfectly. I can only keep trudging as I go—enjoying each and every step, lesson, and moment to the fullest.

_____

RELAX AND TAKE IT EASY

> . . . we ask God for inspiration, an intuitive thought or a
> decision. We relax and take it easy. We don't struggle.
> Alcoholics Anonymous, page 86

Always fascinated with the idea of spiritual bliss and peace of mind, I learned to concentrate on my third eye (the spot between my eyebrows) at an early age, visualizing beautiful waterfalls, flowers and rainbows. Later on, I realized I was using my imagination to avoid feelings of sadness, remorse, and not ever being "good enough." After my introduction to drugs, escape was faster, and I felt temporarily on top of the world. I could continually find a good excuse to be loaded and escape reality. I didn't have a clue I would almost lose my life through the insanity of my alcohol and cocaine use. My hopes and dreams slipped rapidly through my grasp, and I was living strictly to get high.

When I found the rooms of Cocaine Anonymous, I internalized the meaning of surrender and real peace of mind. I re-learned how to meditate and stop fighting the world—breathing slowly, with a smile on my face, regardless of my circumstances and fears. I surrendered often, at many levels. I enlisted each moment to communicate with my Higher Power, and put my life in His hands on a daily basis. I found a more enduring form of spiritual bliss and peace of mind, which has served as my program's foundation.

~~~~~

I will find time today to slow down and take deep breaths, rejecting any thought of worry or anxiety, with the complete certainty that my God will handle *all* of my problems. I will find a peaceful place, meditate or use other recovery tools to quiet the clamor in my head. I will diligently practice Steps Three and Eleven, trusting that my life is getting better in sobriety, even if I don't always see it.

THE LESSON OF A HUG

I started to find some answers from the very first hug at the door of that very first meeting. . . .
Hope, Faith & Courage Volume II, *page 104*

A hug. Some of us don't put a lot of thought into it. For many of us, it's almost an unconscious act. It's just a hug.

It's been said that each human being needs to receive at least three or four hugs every day. Positive physical contact with another person is vital to our overall mental and spiritual well-being. Mentally, hugs help draw us out of ourselves, even if only for a few seconds. Spiritually, hugs can be an expression of the sort of unconditional and non-judgmental love that we need to give and get in order to recover.

Hugs received at meetings help newcomers learn they are neither untouchable nor unlovable. Many of us arrive at the doors of Cocaine Anonymous with a feeling of self-loathing. We find it hard to imagine anyone would want us around, let alone want to hug us. Even if we don't believe the words, "I love you," and, "Keep coming back," the implication of love and caring from a hug will be impressed upon our subconscious. Giving and receiving hugs can also teach us that it is possible to have caring, physical contact without any sexual or violent overtones. Quite a few of us have been abused physically, sexually, or emotionally, so this concept may be completely foreign.

It's just a hug—a simple, little thing, really—and yet it can teach us all so very much.

~~~~~

I welcome hugs in my program, both as the recipient from members of the Fellowship and as the person seeking to share that expression of kindness and reaching out. Hugs have taught me a lot about my program and about myself. H.U.G. = Healing Unconditional Goodwill.

OPEN PUZZLE

. . . it's the way I feel inside that's the real miracle.
Hope, Faith & Courage Volume II, *page 98*

My relationship with my son is fundamental to my sobriety. Of course, he's not a sponsor—I have one of those, and it's the work I do with my sponsor that keeps me centered in the principles. What I get from my son is different. He inspires me to grow, helps me to understand, and evokes the experience of selfless love.

We often talk about the Serenity Prayer, what it means, and how it relates to particular moments in our lives. He's only eight, so I have to keep it simple (not so much for him as for me!). He can recite the prayer, and his understanding seems to increase as he sees me practicing it in my life. Likewise, I believe the more he is able to put these principles into his life from such an early age, the more likely he will be to develop serenity and spiritual fulfillment.

Recently, we were talking about some problematic situation. We discussed the incident in terms of what we could do about it, what we couldn't do, and what we needed to leave up to God. During our discussion, my son suggested perhaps we should look at this "puzzle" as something to be solved from the inside out! In that moment, a light bulb came on, and I realized this was more than just a way to solve the immediate problem. My entire life in sobriety could be related to his perspective.

When I entered the program, I read the *Big Book* and quickly assumed I could put a frame around the puzzle of addiction and recovery. I was wrong. Now I see that sobriety, like an open puzzle, is an ongoing process of spiritual development—from the inside out!

~~~~~

Let me approach my sobriety as an open puzzle that I begin from the inside, working outward. If I presume to know the puzzle's boundaries before I begin, am I not "boxing" myself into expectations for the future? The more I practice the principles, the more the pieces fall into place, and the more I see there is to work on.

NO GREATER GIFT

> *After you are around the program for a few weeks and months,*
> *you will begin to see changes in your thinking. You will begin to*
> *feel better. You will see changes in the other newcomers that*
> *come in with you. We call those changes miracles.*
>
> A Higher Power (C.A. Pamphlet)

On this great journey of recovery, I have been given countless gifts. One of my favorites is that I have "recovered from a seemingly hopeless state of mind and body." (*Alcoholics Anonymous*, 4th Edition, page xiii.) No longer do I travel that vicious circle of insanity produced from drinking and using. While once my time was totally consumed with thoughts of getting my next high, now my thinking is occupied by real-life material—often spiritually inspired.

Related to this same gift is a bonus prize. How precious it is to watch the transformation of other members who come into the rooms with the same empty look I once wore. I call them dead eyes—empty sockets with no spark for living anymore. When I look deeply into those dead eyes, I can see fear of the unknown. It's a terrifying proposition to walk this new course without drugs or alcohol— what will happen now? Then, if they stick around and follow a few simple suggestions, those once-dead eyes soften, unveiling a person who has discovered a passion for living. What joy comes from watching the spirit come alive in those eyes, ignited by their own Higher Power. One can't purchase such a gift.

~~~~~

Today, I will remain conscious of all God has given and will continue to give me. The gifts are infinite, provided I keep following the simple suggestions so generously offered. I will not hoard my gifts but will share them with all who desire release from that "hopeless state."

SPARK OF HOPE

> . . . *once having formed the habit and found they cannot break it, once having lost their self-confidence, their reliance upon things human, their problems pile up on them and become astonishingly difficult to solve.*
> Alcoholics Anonymous, 4th Edition, *page xxviii*

Like most addicts, I had many problems when I got to C.A. I despaired over how to attack solving all or even one of them. I couldn't even figure out how to get started. Whenever I thought about the real troubles facing me, I would double over in pain, wanting only to get loaded and not have to feel any of it. But then I saw and heard others who had similarly despaired—others who were now clean and sober and whose lives had become manageable once again. I could not deny it; a spark of hope was lit.

Although it has taken over seven years, I have been able to solve most of the challenges I had when I got here. My job now is to share that message with others in order to give *them* hope—hope that they, too, can recover and solve *their* problems and the wreckage of their pasts, whatever they might be—no matter how confused or despondent they feel at the present time.

~~~~~

When I was a child, my father would sometimes buy "sparklers" in the summertime. I remember how as soon as he'd light one, dazzling bright embers would cascade from the end of the wire in a brilliant burst of colored light. I pray that my example in recovery ignites similar sparks of hope for every newcomer. I pray, too, that I always remember when the initial spark of hope was lit in my own life.

A~OKAY

Where before I walked around with a constant feeling that something terrible was about to happen, today I walk around with a constant feeling that everything is going to be OK.
C.A. NewsGram, 2nd Quarter 2001

In recovery, I am a friend to many. I've often been told that God has given me a gift. It is a gift I continue to try and give away. I may not be a saint, but I am a grateful, active member of Cocaine Anonymous. Thanks to all of the old-timers who did their share to make sure these doors were open for me when I got here.

Having a sponsor, growing through the Twelve Steps, building a relationship with a Higher Power, going to meetings, keeping commitments, working with others, and daily prayer are a few of the essentials that keep me separated from cocaine, alcohol and other drugs. If you are new, or a member who is going through a rough spot, don't miss the opportunity to make it to the other side. Don't lose the chance to see someone come in after you and watch what a Higher Power does in that person's recovery. Thanks to Cocaine Anonymous, I now have a satisfying life far better than anything I could have dreamed up for myself.

~~~~~

God, thank you for the continued gift of this program, and for allowing me to be of service to You and to our Fellowship. Thanks, too, for the opportunity to see a new member join us, and for the ability to recognize what you do for that person's recovery.

NO SPOKESPERSON REQUIRED

Our public relations policy is based on attraction rather than promotion; we need always maintain personal anonymity at the level of press, radio, television and films.
C.A. Tradition Eleven

Personal anonymity is stressed as vital to creating and maintaining unity. Unity is the goal of the Traditions and each Tradition is a principle which allows deeper surrender by the individual member. By maintaining my own anonymity at the public level, I avoid the temptation to become a spokesperson for our Fellowship, and I continue the surrender of my ego. At a deeper level, I remain aware of the truth that my sobriety and joy in living today are not the result of my direct efforts. I am sober by grace.

This Tradition does not intend for me to keep silent about my life having been radically transformed by C.A., its program, the Fellowship and the opportunity to be of service. Many of us have chosen to inform our friends, neighbors, co-workers, and relevant people with whom we come in contact that we are members of C.A. With my ideals grounded in a Power greater than myself, my life has been re-created, and this is an attraction to others who may still be suffering the ravages of addiction. "Attraction rather than promotion" *is* the basis of this Tradition.

~~~~~

Let my life be an attraction. May victory over my difficulties bear witness to God's power, love and grace. I am grateful for the quality of living I have today, and I know that when my life continues to be re-created, it becomes one of re-creation.

EYES THAT LOVE

I got to build my own sobriety by working with people whose sobriety I liked, whose happiness rang through in their voices and shone in their eyes.
Hope, Faith & Courage Volume II, *page 66*

While I was using, someone told me that my eyes were lifeless—totally dead. No surprise, really. My eyes simply reflected my physical and spiritual condition at the time.

Now that I'm clean and sober, sometimes I look into another's eyes and feel confused and often sad as I sense anger, fear, loss, or uncertainty. When this happens, I take my sponsor's suggestion by praying for that person. Whether or not the look in their eyes changes, I always feel a lessening of the unsettling emotion in me as I pray. Better yet, I often experience a sense of compassion that, wonder of wonders, feels a lot like love.

As a sober parent, I was looking into the eyes of my child one day, overwhelmingly grateful for recovery and a family bond which was previously non-existent. Continuing to gaze into those eyes, I suddenly connected my enormous love for my child with the long-gone parents who loved me very much in the same capacity. Marvelously, the eyes that bestow love are also eyes that gather love. In that precious moment, I acquired something I pray I can hold onto for a lifetime— one day at a time.

~~~~~

One Eleventh-Step Prayer suggests that it is better to comfort than to be comforted; to understand than to be understood; to love than to be loved. Simply stated—in giving, we receive; in receiving, we are blessed.

THE FREEDOM OF FORGIVENESS

. . . make me a channel of thy peace—that where there is hatred, I may bring love—that where there is wrong, I might bring the spirit of forgiveness.
Twelve Steps and Twelve Traditions, page 99

In recovery, I discovered that being addicted to drugs—especially cocaine—was only part of the problem. After two years of sobriety, I still wasn't happy! I had worked the Twelve Steps (or so I thought). I was going to meetings, and I was active in the Fellowship through service commitments. What could possibly be the problem now? It wasn't supposed to be like this!

I asked an old-timer, "Is that all there is to sobriety?" He said "This is all there is—if this is all *you* are willing to do." A novel answer that I didn't understand, but it had an immediate impact on me. I became willing to go to the next level of recovery. I became as willing as I was when I first came to Cocaine Anonymous. The hunger returned once again!

I ventured to re-work the Steps I thought I had already taken and found it was totally different! When I reached Step Eight, I discovered that not only had I been selfish, inconsiderate, and basically intolerant in *all* my relations with others, but I didn't even understand true forgiveness! Step Eight gave me an opportunity to fully absolve others *and* myself. I become ready to correct my wrongs and thus be free from the baggage I had been carrying with me in sobriety. Step Eight has proven to be the beginning of a newfound freedom in every single one of my relationships.

~~~~~

Thankfully, Step Eight exists to provide relief in my program—to allow me to get past many of the issues with which I had been struggling even after I got sober. If I become willing to go to the next level of recovery and rework the Steps, I gain further insights into my side of the street and where I was wrong. More importantly, I comprehend the necessary action in each instance to make things right. Learning about true forgiveness has afforded a newfound freedom.

LEAP OF FAITH

. . . A.A.'s tread innumerable paths in their quest for faith. If you don't care for the one I've suggested, you'll be sure to discover one that suits if only you look and listen.
Twelve Steps and Twelve Traditions, *page 27*

What does faith mean to you? If many different people were asked, you might well receive just as many variations in their answers. I have heard faith defined as "confidence or trust in a person or thing." Personally, I view faith as my *willingness* to believe in my Higher Power's ability to affect the outcome, or at the very least, my perception of the outcome.

In other words, something happens in my life. If it's a good thing, acceptance and gratitude come easily. If it's something unpleasant, faith gives me the option to look for a positive result in spite of a negative impression. Have you ever heard of someone taking a "leap of faith"? This means trusting in your Higher Power and taking that step (which seems so impossible) by leaping into His arms. Hand Him the reins and be amazed at the guidance and love you will surely receive.

~~~~~

Are there circumstances happening in my life today that require a leap of faith? Can I ask God for help in altering my perception to notice a benefit rather than a detriment?

CLASHING COLORS

> *All members of the family should meet upon the*
> *common ground of tolerance, understanding and love.*
> Alcoholics Anonymous, *page 122*

I'm many years clean and sober in C.A. I have my very own spiritual tool kit and use those tools quite proficiently in most all of my affairs. The thing that puzzles me, however, is why it is most difficult to practice these principles with my spouse. We both came into recovery at about the same time and, miraculously, the marriage survived. We're best friends, yet no one else knows and pushes my buttons so well!

It's not just me. I've observed over the years how easily many people lose patience and serenity when it comes to immediate family issues. Why is that? Perhaps it's because we feel comfortable letting our true colors show. If my colors clash, maybe I need to change my outfit!

A wise program member I know says we need to show the same amount of courtesy, kindness, and respect to our families at home as we do to the grocery store checkout person. This sounds perfectly logical, but I have to work extra hard, being particularly mindful, to pull this off. The result is well worth the extra effort—but I also have to remember, progress not perfection.

~~~~~

My immediate family, especially the members I live with, are the most important people in the world to me. God, help me to communicate patience, love and understanding to them as the rule rather than the exception.

ON THE ROAD AGAIN

Those of us who travel drop in as often as we can.
Alcoholics Anonymous, *page 162*

Now that we're no longer spending all our money on drugs and alcohol, it's amazing how we can afford to do other things like travel! Ever since early recovery, I've made it a point to attend meetings when I am on the road. I'll never forget my very first out-of-town meeting. I walked in and there was one guy with a huge 50-cup coffeepot. He was so happy to see me! Three more people wandered in and we started chatting. We soon discovered that none of us had even a year of sobriety yet. If I remember correctly, I was the "old-timer" of the crew at about seven or eight months.

The meeting began and the topic evolved as relapse because apparently it was one thing we all had in common. By the time everyone got done sharing, the last girl to speak said, "Boy, this has been a powerful meeting. I feel this is what it must have been like back when Bill and Bob were just getting started, and it was simply the blind leading the blind!" Another guy (who had been sent by the court system) said, "I've been going to these meetings a few times now and I always see people nodding when someone is talking. I scornfully labeled them 'swivel heads' because they reminded me of those funny dogs with bobbing heads that you see in some people's rear car window. Now here I am, and during this meeting, damned if I didn't find myself nodding my head!" We all left that day full of hope and gratitude, and I'll never forget what a special bond we shared for that one hour.

Since that time, I've had the opportunity to attend meetings in at least twenty different states and on two other continents. With internet capabilities these days, finding a meeting out of town or abroad gets easier and easier. My trip highlights always include making new friends around the tables.

~~~~~

Wherever I travel, I seek out meetings. I love to interact with new faces and experience interesting meeting format variations. No matter how far away I am from where I live, I'm always at home in a Twelve-Step meeting.

SELF-WILL RUN RIOT

. . . the alcoholic is an extreme example of self-will run riot, though he usually doesn't think so. Above everything, we alcoholics must be rid of this selfishness. We must, or it kills us! God makes that possible.
Alcoholics Anonymous, *page 62*

In the rooms, we talk a lot about our will, God's will, and self-will. At various stages through the Steps, our focus on each of these becomes paramount. In Step Three, we talk about turning "our will" over to the care of God. In Step Eleven, we reference praying only for the knowledge of "God's will" for us and the power to carry that out. We also explore the notion of "self-will" gone bad, as it connotes our will being used inappropriately to the point where it's descriptively characterized as "self-will run riot."

I remember the first time I heard that phrase. I saw it written on the lecture room white board in the treatment center where I was a patient. I didn't know then where the phrase came from. All I knew was it described, almost too perfectly, the state of my behaviors when my recovery began.

As I started working the Steps and found myself at Step Three, my sponsor had me thoroughly examine my self-will. *Alcoholics Anonymous*, page 61, states, "The first requirement is that we be convinced that any life run on self-will can hardly be a success." How had I been the actor? How had that worked out for me? What could I learn? What could I change? This exercise was a study all about me! Once I was convinced that my life run on self-will would never be a success, the selfishness had to go. It would kill me if I didn't get rid of it.

Next, it was explained to me nothing that I could do by myself would reduce this self-centeredness—I had to find God's help. I had to quit playing God, and let the God of my understanding have that role once and for all. I had to be, as the *Big Book* suggests, "reborn."

~~~~~

I pray that I can, and will, shift from "self-will run riot" to a healthy reliance on my Higher Power. I pray to lose, once and for all, my fear of today, tomorrow, or the hereafter. I pray to be relieved of the bondage of self, that I may better do my God's will.

MORE ABOUT HONESTY

The fact remained that our lives had become unmanageable. Not until we got honest with ourselves and surrendered, did we begin to know peace.
Hope, Faith & Courage Volume II, *page 204*

When I found C.A., I started going to meetings and working the Steps. It seemed all of those early meetings, the Steps and readings in the *Big Book* centered on honesty in one form or another. I have struggled with honesty pretty much my whole life and well into my recovery. I often would lie when it was just as easy to tell the truth. Therefore, I spent much-needed time trying to place my arms around honesty and how it applies in my program, both in the rooms of C.A. and all the other parts of my life—job, relationships, etc. The *Big Book* and sharing from Fellowship members have provided some impeccable gems.

Honesty dispels the resurging ego, which is constantly fighting against my initial surrender. The investment in honesty can be likened to my commitment to daily surrender.

Further, when I begin to practice honesty, it may often seem alien, and I rapidly fall short on the notion of "absolute honesty." When this happens, I know not to be discouraged, but to remain mindful of the *Big Book* wisdom: "No one among us has been able to maintain anything like perfect adherence to these principles. We are not saints. The point is, that we are willing to grow along spiritual lines. The principles we have set down are guides to progress. We claim spiritual progress, rather than spiritual perfection." (*Alcoholics Anonymous,* page 60).

I have learned to simply try as best I can, diligently staying aware not to rest on my laurels or allow myself to justify and rationalize conduct I know to be wrong.

~~~~~

When we practice honesty, we begin to look the world in the eye and rest in good conscience. Once we have sincerely understood and taken Step One, open-mindedness follows. "Faced with alcoholic destruction, we soon became as open-minded on spiritual matters as we had tried to be on other questions." (*Alcoholics Anonymous,* page 48).

TO THINE OWN SELF BE TRUE

I also try to remember that I'm not doing anyone any good by keeping my problems to myself because I somehow feel my length of sobriety means I have to look and sound a certain way. The truth is, life still happens, and sometimes am a bit of a mess—and sharing that I'm working through it sober is actually the best way to carry the message that the program does work.

Hope, Faith & Courage Volume II, *page 97*

"To thine own self be true" is a slogan I have heard around the tables. I've struggled mightily over the years to grasp its meaning. What I have discovered finally makes sense to me and in my program: if I am not true to myself—if I do not take care of my needs—then I will be of no service to myself, God, my family, or my Fellowship. I have to start with me when I seek to be truthful, spiritual, recovering, responsible and, especially, respectful.

Today, I am not afraid of who I have been or how I show up for life. I no longer live a life of fear about my past, my character defects, my still unmade amends, or even the ongoing amends to myself. I embrace who I am and stand proud on my path in recovery. I don't regret my past—its pain or its lessons. I can make decisions for myself, but at the same time, I am cognizant of when I need to ask for help. I can take suggestions from others now in ways I couldn't even imagine previously.

I know I must take care of myself. I must make sure that I eat properly; take care of my body, mind and spirit; and strive for true happiness. I must continue to give away what I have found and what has been gifted to me in our rooms, and I must also continue to work the Steps, go to meetings and be of service. I need to always remember the link between my understanding of God and how I had that moment of clarity, surrendering to the program, my powerlessness, and the unmanageability of my disease.

~~~~~

My life is amazing today. I still have a long way to go, and I am by no means perfect, but I am true to myself. Since I thought I would live my entire life in shame, dread and fear, this is nothing short of a miracle.

EMBRACING CONNECTION

We admitted our lack of power and accepted that we could not recover alone.
Unity (C.A. Pamphlet)

All my life, I tried to go it alone, refusing to ask for help. Weaklings asked for help, and I took vast pride in being totally self-sufficient. As my addiction progressed, keeping a handle on everything became increasingly problematic. Finally (thank God!) unmanageability prevailed, and I admitted defeat—seeking relief from the lunacy through C.A. Twelve-Step recovery.

Today, I stand convinced that I can no longer be a solitary creature. I *must* have a network of clean and sober friends, a program family, especially when I am feeling particularly weak and alone. This is not to say that I don't need to love and take care of myself. A healthy attitude of self-respect and independence generates an overall feeling of well-being. I completely understand the importance of including Higher Power in the equation, consistently asking for help and guidance in knowing the difference between my will and God's.

I've heard that there is no such thing as a self-made man. We are each a highly unique composite, influenced by thousands of others whose lives we've encountered. Everyone who has ever done a kind deed or spoken one word of encouragement has entered into the positive make-up of my character, and I strive to return the favor for those with whom I share the journey.

~~~~~

God, may I embrace my connection with You and other people. I will not allow fear to drive me back into a self-imposed prison of isolation. I recognize my ability to ask for help as positive growth in my recovery.

August 19

HEARING THE MESSAGE

So I'm here with my sponsees and other enthusiastic sober folks, continuing to take the actions, work with others, and carry the message of hope, faith, and courage.
Hope, Faith & Courage Volume II, *page 39*

When I hit bottom, I had nothing but a life full of mess. I knew that I needed help, I even knew where to find help, but the fear of actually reaching out paralyzed me. After a several-day bender, I just knew I could not live this way any longer. I got online and searched for Cocaine Anonymous. I found an online meeting and quickly signed up, asking someone to send me some C.A. literature. At that point in time, I fully intended to work this program by myself. Someone in the group agreed to send me the literature I requested, which was the beginning of my hearing the message. This person was definitely carrying out our Fellowship's primary purpose.

Staying connected with this online meeting, I slowly began to understand what the Twelve Steps and the program of Cocaine Anonymous were all about. As I shared what was going on in my world, others shared their experience, strength and hope with me in return. I began to learn about the Steps, what they meant and how they had worked in many people's lives. I became encouraged as to how the Steps could work in my life. No one forced me to stay, no one tried to convince me to practice a certain religion, no one talked of anything besides how they got through the very same life stuff I was facing by using the Twelve Steps. Because of their sharing of the message, I started relating to these people, and I began to do the things I heard they were doing. By working the Steps in earnest, I have come to understand how important it is that a clear message of Cocaine Anonymous be carried to the addicts who still suffer. Thus, in turn, a newcomer can relate and no longer feel alone, can gain hope that there is a solution, can hear and understand, maybe for the first time, that recovery is a *fact*, possible through the Steps. We learn to live a different way, far deeper and more satisfying than anything we could have ever imagined while still practicing our addiction.

~~~~~

C.A. Tradition Five plays a big part in my recovery: "Each group has but one primary purpose—to carry its message to the addict who still suffers." I pray that I will always do my best to carry the message of recovery to the still-suffering addict. May my message remain pure in C.A. principles to keep our Fellowship strong and healthy.

242

LOOKING AT MY RECOVERY

In Cocaine Anonymous, I see God's work all around. We are men and women who, prior to Twelve-Step recovery, had been hopeless, often homeless or institutionalized. We were dying. Now we in recovery are men and women righting the wrongs of our past; regaining the respect of friends, peers, and colleagues; thinking about the welfare of others; paying our bills; and acting as good parents, spouses, and responsible members of our communities.

Hope, Faith & Courage Volume II, *page 84*

I looked up the word "recovery," and the definitions I liked the best were a gradual healing after sickness or injury, the act of regaining or saving something lost, or restoration to a former or better condition. All of those accurately describe phases of my life as a sober member of Cocaine Anonymous.

Drugs and alcohol brought me to my knees. Most of my teenage years and all of my pre-program adult life revolved around getting and staying loaded, medicated from my feelings. What started out as fun, rebellion, and what I thought was independence turned into a seemingly inescapable prison of my own making. Life was unbearable, and I didn't know how to change it. The "sickness or injury" in the first definition fit me perfectly, and I needed healing desperately.

Enter the treatment facility that led me to the rooms of recovery and a seat in C.A. I thank God for both. Treatment wasn't recovery, but it was a place to rest, to gradually let my body and spirit heal from all the abuse I had inflicted upon it, and to be exposed to people who could guide me to a solution. These individuals would come in on H&I panels, with service commitments at the open meetings, as speakers, or as former patients who wanted to share that what they found could work for us. These saving souls were indispensable for me! I never knew anyone had thought or felt like me, yet here they were—the truth resonating in their whole demeanor—a bright and undeniable light in the dark! I found a sponsor, and my journey began.

Just being sober was a beginning, but I quickly ascertained that "simply sober" would never be enough. So much had been lost—my dignity, my dreams, my self-respect, my relationships with family—that regaining any of it seemed impossible. Slowly, sometimes painfully, through working the Twelve Steps and seeking a relationship with a Power greater than myself, restoration of the authentic me began to take place—not to my former condition, but to a better one.

~~~~~

My recovery has been nothing short of miraculous. I vividly remember where I came from and have not lost sight of that former self. I humbly honor my position in life today and the recovered person I have become.

243

HARD CHOICES

My challenges help me become a more compassionate person and to be of greater service. I've learned to keep my eye on God's plan, not mine, that my choices and behaviors need to reflect my priorities and values, and that out of everything I perceive to be negative, something incredible emerges.
Hope, Faith & Courage Volume II, *page 160*

When I become willing and ready to make the hard choices in favor of healthy self-love and guidance from my Higher Power, the resulting freedom and joy are priceless. Sometimes I may be stuck in a situation (job, relationship, service position, etc.) which I convince myself is acceptable; but in time, I realize that remaining any longer will be really harmful, not only to my spirit, but to my overall recovery. God will reveal the truth to me countless times, yet so often, I do not want to see that which may be obvious to others.

Alternatively, I may not want to risk being alone or face a particular truth about myself. Trusting God to take care of me in these situations smooths the course, eases the path toward understanding and enfolds me in a safety net of love, converting any pain into an opportunity for growth and spiritual lessons. With God, I am never alone, there are no accidents, and things happen for a reason. Once I become willing to go to any lengths to improve my relationship with my Higher Power and myself, I am given the courage I need to move forward. The sunlight of the Spirit never shines so bright as when I trust God and let go. The outcome really doesn't matter, as long as I believe.

~~~~~

I will commit myself to God's will today, trusting Him to teach me and paying close attention to my lessons. Even though I may face hard decisions, His loving help and sage guidance will carry me through.

ONE SUGGESTED READING PLAN

I was introduced to Cocaine Anonymous through an H&I panel. Two guys came into the detox on a Saturday afternoon. They handed me pamphlets about finding A Higher Power, The First 30 Days, and one for newcomers. They shared what working the program in their lives had done for them and told us they got support from the Fellowship.

Hope, Faith & Courage Volume II, *page 134*

There are a variety of ways to work the Steps and to be of service in our Fellowship. Different sponsors introduce a comprehensive bibliography of program readings at assorted times along our respective recovery journeys. My first sponsor kept my reading program quite simple, sticking to the *Big Book* and *Twelve Steps and Twelve Traditions*. That sponsor moved away, and I had to seek a second one. The person I connected with next had an entirely different perspective on the readings, Step work, and even service. Imagine my surprise (and relief) when I realized that they both could be correct. My new sponsor had me read some other materials to supplement our ongoing *Big Book* and Twelve-Step study. These were a perfect enhancement for me as I continued to grow through working the Steps.

The following is the reading plan suggested by my second sponsor, which I found particularly helpful:

1. A.A.'s *Twelve Steps and Twelve Traditions*;
2. C.A.'s pamphlets *The Home Group* and *Being of Service* (before becoming Group secretary);
3. The *C.A. World Service Manual* (once I became Group secretary); and
4. The *A.A. World Service Manual Combined With 12 Concepts for World Service* (before doing service at District or Area levels).

By sticking to a structured means of introducing people into service, we are caring for the welfare of the individual. Positions at the District and Area levels involve a huge amount of responsibility. It seems unfair to place inexperienced people under that much pressure.

~~~~~

It is nice to be aware of the many materials available for my further C.A. recovery study. I have truly been blessed with insightful sponsors who cared enough to require that I do my "service homework" as part of my ongoing program.

August 23

TOOLS TO THE RESCUE

In the C.A. fellowship, you are among recovering cocaine abusers who are living without drugs. Make use of us!
To the Newcomer (C.A. Pamphlet)

While in my addiction, I experienced rare moments when "rush hour" paused for me. During these respites, a simple thought would enter my mind, a voice not my own, assuring me of a solution to return my life to normality. Today, I know it was God whispering in my ear, nudging me, ever so gently—even if it was to just have my spirit opened to the suggestion that recovery could or would work for me.

Eventually, someone (one of God's angels!) introduced me to Cocaine Anonymous. I began attending meetings regularly. I had been given my first tool in recovery. As I observed members making coffee, chairing, exchanging phone numbers, telling their stories without a trace of remorse, I felt the strong sense of wanting what they had. They talked the talk of recovery, but even more importantly, they walked the walk. They were all trudging on their respective paths of happy destiny. The Twelve Steps and Twelve Traditions; the suggestions; the loving, tolerant environment; God's omnipresence, even the group conscience, all produced such a desire within me.

I stuck around. Days clean and sober have turned into years. I am accountable today and understand the importance of moral values, enabling me to wisely practice the principles of recovery in all my affairs. As promised, God has returned my life to normal.

~~~~

Tried and proven by countless addicts, our invaluable program tools led me to what I call "the beginning of an end." Daily use and practice has produced new habits allowing the promises of the program to come true throughout my life.

LOGICAL REASONING

If crack cocaine made us feel miserable, why did so many of us continue to use? Ask a hundred cocaine addicts that same question and you will probably get a hundred different answers. . . .
Crack (C.A. Pamphlet)

Cocaine impaired my ability to reason logically. The excuses I gave to justify my addiction were often circular. When thinking in these circles, the possibility of escape from my habit seemed impossible. With all of the thousands of reasons I had for perpetuating my miseries, I nonetheless found they shared a common solution! The moment I elected to make an appeal to a Higher Power, the downward spiral was snapped. It made no difference whatsoever that I didn't understand and wasn't yet sure I believed in this Higher Power; my sanity had begun to be restored.

We rely on our good reasoning to navigate daily living, but we mustn't forget to recognize that its power is limited. There is One who has all Power, and I'm eternally grateful to turn my will and my life over on a daily basis to the Higher Power of my understanding. This finally makes sense to me.

In spite of my logic, in spite of my reasoning that this can't or won't work, that I am not worthy of it working, or that I did so many things which were wrong and horrible that I am prevented from getting this, I trudge on. No more excuses or rationalizations; instead, these have been replaced by God's grace and the reality that if I do these simple things, and whatever else is suggested to me along my recovery path, the compulsion to use will leave and be replaced by a true desire to do God's will in my life every day.

~~~~~

When is a reason not a reason? When it's an excuse! For God, all things are possible. Trusting God, I can question the logic of my reasoning but still surrender to His will for me.

August 25

TWELVE TRADITIONS – A VITAL LINK IN MY PROGRAM

> . . . *trusting and relying upon Him through prayer and meditation allows for the conscious awareness of the Principles associated with the Traditions and their presence in my life.*
> C.A. NewsGram, 4th Quarter 2004

Quite often, my program links directly to any one or several of C.A.'s Twelve Traditions. As I study and pray about the lessons and insights behind the Traditions, I often see a direct relationship between my thoughts and actions around what a specific Tradition suggests. This observation is helpful when my character defects start cropping up—my ability to rationalize, over-think, or fail to consider all the options in any given circumstance.

When I'm concentrating on money or other material goods, or when I'm busy "resting on my laurels," then I'm not seeking to enlarge my spiritual status. Many an opportunity to participate in our primary purpose is overlooked while I'm operating in this mode.

As a humble servant, respecting the Twelve Traditions is as important to me as living the Twelve Steps. The Traditions are in place to establish boundaries, preventing me from thinking I know what's best, or not, for C.A. as a whole. I use the Traditions as a checkpoint—an opportunity to act with humility, and to be able to admit that not all of my ideas are the greatest.

A good question which I've incorporated into my daily prayer and meditation is, "What Tradition am I living today?"

~~~~~

The Twelve Traditions ensure our common welfare, and as such, are a key component to my personal program. I've learned to recognize which Tradition I am "living." May I remain mindful of the connection between the Traditions, Steps, and my sobriety.

THE ANSWER TO ALL MY PROBLEMS

Acceptance is the key to my relationship with God today. I never just sit and do nothing while waiting for him to tell me what to do. Rather, I do whatever is in front of me to be done, and I leave the results up to Him; however it turns out, that's God's will for me.
Alcoholics Anonymous, 4th Edition, *page 420*

One of the early concepts introduced when I made it to C.A. was acceptance being the answer to all my problems, no matter their origin. My sponsor guided me to the *Big Book* story written by a doctor who was an alcoholic and an addict where the well-known "acceptance" passage originates. It turns out this individual had, in fact, spoken at many C.A. conventions and workshops. In my early Step work, I found it helpful to study these passages, learning to incorporate the acceptance principle into my recovery.

From this work, I discovered much about myself. Some basic points made sense right away—specifically, until I could accept my addiction, I could not stay clean and sober. Furthermore, I must accept the precept that nothing in God's world happens by mistake, that it is all linked together in the big picture. If I want to be happy, I must completely accept life on life's terms—simple enough.

The harder parts were much more confusing at the outset. For example: ". . . perhaps the best thing of all for me to remember is that my serenity is inversely proportional to my expectations." (*Alcoholics Anonymous,* 4th Edition, page 420.) Additionally, I am guided to concentrate on what needs to be changed in myself and my attitudes versus what the world should do differently. Then came the proposal about "a bit of good in the worst of us and a bit of bad in the best of us; that we are all children of God and each have a right to be here." (*Alcoholics Anonymous,* 4th Edition, page 417.) This puzzled me for a longer time.

As I began to personally experience the wisdom of acceptance, other parts of the equation made sense and ultimately enhanced my recovery. Today I understand that acceptance is a journey and an ongoing process. Acceptance has to be applied over and over again to each new challenge and condition in every part of my life. In recovery, if practiced well, acceptance becomes an instinctive response.

~~~~~

I first accepted that I could live an honest, vibrant, spiritual life in recovery without ever using drugs or alcohol again. That initial acceptance guided me to a wonderful path where I was ready to receive whatever the Universe placed in front of me.

FOLLOW THROUGH

> *I truly love Cocaine Anonymous. . . . I now understand the concept of "the greater good" as reflected in Tradition One: "Our common welfare should come first; personal recovery depends upon C.A. unity." So how do I hold that unity? How do I make sure a meeting exists? How do I make sure that people consider the Traditions? How do I ensure that C.A. is going to be here for the newcomer? It's my responsibility, and for that I will show up.*
>
> Hope, Faith & Courage Volume II, *page 130*

My first elected service commitment was Group secretary. Since the meeting was small, it seemed very important to me to be there every week. At the time when I became secretary, the group seemed to be struggling with unity. I felt it was my responsibility to change that.

I made sure the coffee was always ready, chips stocked in the box, books and literature available for newcomers, and regular members took turns sharing. The meeting began to grow. By holding regular group consciences, our service positions were all filled. When I rotated out as secretary, the meeting felt unified to me and was well-attended. Unity works.

Over the years that followed, I have held numerous service positions. I have to be consistent in my approach to these various commitments, both in my behavior and in adhering to our applicable service manuals.

Following through on every service obligation has been essential to my recovery—being reliable and finishing what I start. Doing so not only serves to reprogram my formerly irresponsible behavior, but it sets a good example for those next in line who will fill the various service positions.

~~~~~

I am grateful for the service opportunities provided by the Fellowship. I am honored whenever my service increases unity within our Fellowship. I am humbled by appreciation for the change in my perspective which this service work has given me.

MAKING AMENDS TO LIGHTEN THE BURDEN

Making amends has allowed me to hold my head high and look people in the eye. When I find myself balking at the Steps, especially the Ninth Step, I am reminded of my sponsor's words, "How free do you want to be?"
Hope, Faith & Courage Volume II, *page 167*

I had caused harm to a teacher when I was still in primary school. I had embarrassed the teacher horribly and never made it right. Carrying guilt with me for many years, the burden got even worse when, a few years later, I happened to run into him and did nothing to make things right.

Some time afterward while dining out, I again saw the teacher. By this time, I was in recovery and working Steps. I immediately knew what to do. Asking the teacher for a minute of his time, I reminded him I had been in his class when in my early teens. I shared my Twelve-Step program involvement and explained that part of my recovery included making amends to those I had harmed along the way. I touched on the incident and expressed my regret in causing him pain or embarrassment. When I finished, he smiled at me and said, "It's okay, you were just being a teenager."

I thanked him and we parted. Suddenly, I realized the huge weight I had been carrying around for those many years was gone entirely. It had been replaced with a memory and a lesson. I felt lighter and so very relieved. The truth was, while it felt good for him to say what he did to me, his forgiveness mattered less than my finally dropping the heavy load on my shoulders.

~~~~~

Sometimes making a difficult amend is quite empowering. When completed, no matter how long ago the wrong was committed, a sense of perspective about the harm is achieved. Heart-felt relief replaces guilt and shame, and I take with me a valuable lesson learned. I can draw from this lesson for future amends.

ANOTHER CHANCE AT LIFE

We cannot be helpful to all people, but at least God will show us how to take a kindly and tolerant view of each and every one.
Alcoholics Anonymous, *page 67*

It is one thing being kind to loved ones close to us. It is quite another to be kind to the person ahead of us in traffic who sits through a green light! With road rage being a character defect of mine, this example came easily. But what about co-workers, friends, police officers, the tax collector, etc.? What about the newcomer who I think is not serious enough? Judging others is also a defect. There is a fine line between constructive criticism and judgment.

I look back at my using career and it proves that my judgment leaves much to be desired. I would like to believe that in recovery, my intuition is based more in reality. My Higher Power has shown me the true meaning of unconditional love. When I have one finger pointing at you, three are pointing back at me. Forgiving myself and others is possible because I know the God of my understanding is not judging me. Who are we not to forgive ourselves?

It is by God's grace and Cocaine Anonymous that I have been given another chance at life. Today, I have a chance to live, not just exist, and to help others in their recovery.

~~~~

Help me to recognize quickly those behaviors in me that are my will and not God's. I will pray consistently to make whatever personal changes are necessary to keep this gift of sobriety.

A DUAL~HEADED MONSTER

There have been numerous times when I have thought about taking a drink. Such thinking usually began with thoughts of the pleasant drinking of my youth. I learned early in my A.A. life that I could not afford to fondle such thoughts, as you might fondle a pet, because this particular pet could grow into a monster.
Alcoholics Anonymous, 4th Edition, pages 256-257

The Twelve Steps embody the practical program of action intended and crafted to free us from self-centered obsession and bring us into contact with a Power greater than ourselves. Step One simply describes the dual-headed monster with which I am dealing: an abnormal physical reaction, coupled with the lack of a mental defense against picking up. The conclusion I draw about my addiction is that both heads alternately snarl, bare their teeth, and threaten to kill me. Step Two is the enlightenment I receive to shield me from the beast. In Step Three I make a decision to ask for help in protecting myself, based on the precepts I've learned in the first two Steps.

Steps Four through Eleven put my Third-Step decision into action. The result is a personality change sufficient to overcome my fiendish addiction. Having taken the first eleven Steps, I am now at Step Twelve and am ready to carry the message to other still-suffering addicts. The monster will always be lurking, never running out of unsuspecting victims who'll need help.

In addition to carrying the message to other addicts, Step Twelve involves practicing these principles in all areas of my life. If addicts who relapse are fortunate enough to return to the program and analyze what happened, they invariably find they had stopped practicing these principles in all their affairs. They admit having ceased examining their motives, reviewing their days, praying, or carrying the message. The result? They weaken and fall prey to the monster once again. Sadly, some succumb, unable to break free from its deadly grasp.

~~~~~

The program has instilled in me a healthy fear of the monstrous beast I knew as addiction. Let me practice these principles in all my affairs to keep it at bay. Help me remember my spiritual awakening can always go deeper. The broader my conscious contact with my Higher Power, the greater my protection.

NO TEST REQUIRED

> . . . perhaps you chose to avoid a Higher Power
> because you were taught about a punishing God.
> A Higher Power (C.A. Pamphlet)

When I was new, I always shared how I truly believed God had been punishing me most of my life. Even after I'd stuck around for a while and begun to change my thinking, I still talked about how I thought perhaps God was testing me when I was going through a particularly frightening medical crisis.

Someone kindly disclosed their own personal experience in discovering the God of their understanding does *for* them, rather than *to* them.

This seemingly simply statement had a profound impact on me. It not only opened my mind, but it brought me to a place of great comfort and peace. The more I contemplated the idea of a loving God, the more it made perfect sense! Surely the God who was helping me to stay sober would not chastise or test me.

From then on, whenever I am going through difficult or disturbing times, I remember what I learned that day, calmly reassured in knowing that I am in good hands—God's hands!

~~~~~

I trust that God is doing *for* me, not *to* me.

SEPTEMBER

THE PROMISES

The Promises have come true for me, and I have faith that they will come true for you. Give yourself a chance. Do the Steps, and find out how wonderful life can be. . . .
Hope, Faith & Courage Volume II, *pages 136-137*

If we are painstaking about this phase of our development, we will be amazed before we are half way through. We are going to know a new freedom and a new happiness. We will not regret the past nor wish to shut the door on it. We will comprehend the word serenity and we will know peace. No matter how far down the scale we have gone, we will see how our experience can benefit others. That feeling of uselessness and self-pity will disappear. We will lose interest in selfish things and gain interest in our fellows. Self-seeking will slip away. Our whole attitude and outlook upon life will change. Fear of people and of economic insecurity will leave us. We will intuitively know how to handle situations which used to baffle us. We will suddenly realize that God is doing for us what we could not do for ourselves.

Are these extravagant promises? We think not. They are being fulfilled among us—sometimes quickly, sometimes slowly. They will always materialize if we work for them. (*Alcoholics Anonymous*, pages 83-84.)

~~~~~

I pray that I may be open to receive and understand the Promises as they are revealed to me in my program. I know they will materialize in that perfect manner and time as God plans. Where do I already see the Promises coming true in my life?

THOUGHTS ON HUMILITY

Now I have experienced love—unconditional love.
Hope, Faith & Courage Volume II, *page 24*

True humility is a product of love. Consequences do not make me humble. Being rejected, jailed, or fired does not make me humble. I don't become humble by being humiliated. I may be shamed into avoiding the behavior that merited the consequence—but that's not humility, it's fear. If humiliation made me humble, then jails would turn out nothing but winners.

Only love humbles. When I arrived hopeless and helpless and was met with love and respect, I was lifted beyond my failings, beyond my addictions. I became able to change, to recover. If I am guilty, it's hard to look into the eyes of a person who scorns; but when my eyes are met by a clear, peaceful gaze, one that does not judge, then my spirit is filled with hope. I can no longer wallow in shame and self-pity. In the eyes of the Fellowship, I see the person I truly am reflected. I know that it's right to let that person shine.

~~~~~

I pray that God will give me eyes of compassion for the people who show up in the rooms of Cocaine Anonymous. I pray that I may see myself and others through His eyes of unconditional love.

LIGHT AND LOVE

> *Today, in my life, there is a feeling of peace and security*
> *such as I have never known. Life seems good to me today.*
> *I haven't felt the self-loathing or the screaming, ragged*
> *pain in my guts at all for a couple of years now, thanks to*
> *the Steps and the healing brought about by working them.*
>
> Hope, Faith & Courage, *page 37*

I have learned so many things as a result of working the Steps, far too many to mention. Many who stick around have heard it shared that, "If when I got here I had made a list of what I expected to get from the program, I would have severely short-changed myself." It just keeps getting better the longer I am in the program.

I have seen the Fellowship change and grow for the good and I believe that I too have changed in a variety of positive ways. I no longer feel like there is a huge hole in my gut that I've felt has been there my whole life. I have some answers and occasionally might even know the right question with the wisdom that only comes from sticking around the program for a while. I am graced with God's light and God's love daily. The promises really do come true, all of them, and more is revealed to me on a continual basis. I realize and then affirm that God is doing for me what I could not do for myself. As a result, I know a greater happiness than I ever thought possible.

~~~~~

I pray that I am able to *live* the program every day of my recovery. May I always remain aware of the many gifts and insights that the Steps have produced and continue to manifest in all aspects of my life.

MONEY CAN'T BUY HAPPINESS

Fear of people and of economic insecurity will leave us.
Alcoholics Anonymous, *page 84*

When I got into recovery, I heard the Promises read at every meeting. I was quite excited at the prospect of some of those coming true in my life.

At two years sober, I attended a convention workshop on the Promises. By the end of the workshop, I had only one question to ask the presenter—when was I going to be free of economic insecurity? I mean, *really* . . . I was two years clean and sober, and some of the Promises had already started coming true. I felt good and believed I was in a place where I was ready for the dough to start rolling in. I was employed and had begun clearing up past wreckage. Quite frankly, I wanted to be certain I could live more prosperously than my current economic status. The presenter took me aside, instructing me to take a deep breath and hear something important. What was pointed out was that if I truly turned my life over to my Higher Power on a daily basis, the *fear* of economic insecurity would leave me. I could become comfortable in the knowing that even though I might not have everything I thought I wanted, I would certainly have everything I needed. I would feel peace in knowing my Higher Power was caring for my well-being: emotionally, mentally, and spiritually. I would be happy, joyous and free.

What a concept! I had been so focused on the idea of buying everything I wanted, I forgot to remember what I had heard ever since I was a child: that money can't buy happiness. Nor can it buy recovery.

~~~~

May I always trust in my Higher Power to provide everything I need to stay clean and sober and to enjoy a life of freedom, a life even better than I could have ever imagined. May I come to learn that peace, serenity, and acceptance are always my most valuable assets.

BEING PRESENT IN MY SOBRIETY

I live life as it happens in the present, not yesterday or tomorrow, but fully in the moment.
Hope, Faith & Courage Volume II, *page 168*

When I came through the doors, I was too unfocused to see much of anything, much less "be in the moment," as the saying goes. If anything, doing drugs is about *evading* the moment. For me, my use was an escape from the recollection of yesterday and a flight from the responsibility of tomorrow. My insanity was thinking that the crack-induced nuclear explosion inside my head each time I hit the pipe was all that I needed to know about the present.

After being clean for a while, I began to wake up, like some Rip Van Winkle who'd been sleeping his life away. I started to see, experience, and hear things I'd been missing. Without the seductive urge for cocaine, I was able to just sit still in the present. Willingness, honesty, and openness began to expand the boundaries of the moment I had been avoiding. As a result, I've been able to look at my past with more acceptance and less shame, and toward my future goals with hope.

~~~~

Being present in my sobriety is about experiencing the reality of my life without the need for any mind-altering substance. It's not about what I've done or what I hope to do, though both can offer perspective to guide my actions. It's about staying aware of exactly what is happening—at the moment it happens—and accepting it just as it is.

NEVER GIVING UP

> *Steps Eight and Nine are concerned with personal relations. . . . we consider how, with our newfound knowledge of ourselves, we may develop the best possible relations with every human being we know.*
> Twelve Steps and Twelve Traditions, page 77

Today, I no longer take, take, take from my relationships. Rather, I look to see where I can provide anything to improve relations. I try not to be concerned about what the other person is doing, except when my personal boundaries are crossed. Through working Step Eight, I have found what it means to truly forgive, to be humble, non-judgmental, and remain in harmonious brotherly love with most of my fellow men and women.

With these Step Eight revelations, I have been able to acquire and maintain a happy marriage. It's not one hundred percent perfect (nothing ever is!), but we really try to bring our best to each other.

I've learned to give freely of myself without expecting anything in return. If something comes back, then I see it as an unexpected gift. No longer am I critical and judgmental of everyone, including myself. Only through the strength given to me by my God, the Twelve Steps, and the Fellowship of Cocaine Anonymous could I have found this freedom. Liberty to be the person I really want to be—my Higher Power's messenger, charged to share my hope, faith and courage with those just like me. Thank God for the Fellowship not giving up on me, and for me not giving up on the power of the Fellowship!

~~~~~

Am I continually aware of the ongoing revelations brought about by working each of the Steps again and again? What does my message of hope, faith, and courage sound like? Has my desire to be a better person translated into unselfish actions? I seek continued forgiveness and to remain in harmonious brotherly love with those sharing my recovery path.

BELONGING

I identified with the feelings and the stories of the people at the C.A. meetings I started to attend. I found comfort there and finally felt at ease and at home.
Hope Faith & Courage, *page 141*

I was forced to attend a Cocaine Anonymous meeting while in rehab. Narrow-mindedly, I squirmed in my seat thinking, "I am *not* a cocaine addict." However, once I heard the phrase, "Nothing mattered more to us than the straw, the pipe, the needle" from the reading *Who is a Cocaine Addict?*, I suddenly knew a calmness that only coming home brings.

It's true that one can miss our intended C.A. message if we are distracted by the messenger. It is suggested to listen for your message, and I found mine when the word "pipe" was read. I have learned regardless of how I used, or what I used, as long as I have a desire to stay free from cocaine and all other mind-altering substances, I belong in the C.A. Fellowship. To me, this is a wonderful freedom.

~~~~~

I pray that the broad message of recovery presented in C.A. may reach everyone having the desire to stay free from cocaine and all other mind-altering substances so that they may join in and share the countless gifts offered by our program and our Fellowship. May I be a shining example in order to attract others to the home where they belong.

STEP UP TO THE PLATE

Self-supporting alcoholics? Who ever heard of such a thing? Yet we find that's what we have to be. This principle is telling evidence of the profound change that A.A. has wrought in all of us.
Twelve Steps and Twelve Traditions, *page 160*

Our Seventh Tradition states, "Every C.A. group ought to be fully self-supporting, declining outside contributions." Sounds like I've got to stop depending on mama and daddy to take care of me, huh? Quite a chunk of humility is required to put my hand back in my pocket and keep it there instead of holding it out, expecting you or anybody else to pay my way. Life requires so much, so it obviously owes me something back, right? I can lie and cheat my way through the system because the things I need shouldn't cost so much anyway, right? *Wrong!* It is time to grow up and take responsibility.

This same principle applies with our Groups. When we decide to have fundraisers, we need to have realistic expectations about who should participate—not the people on the job, our neighbors, or family members. That we are "fully self-supporting through our own contributions" means I need to get my home group members to buy a few raffle tickets, go to the barbeque, and participate at the District and Area levels. We must carry our Fellowship and not expect outside affiliations to get us through. It's time to step up to the plate and be counted—and not just in dollars. Time, too, is so utterly important to keep the Fellowship strong. Give some back. *Please.*

~~~~~

When I think about how much C.A. has given to me, how can I not want to give something back? When the basket is being passed at my home group, a line in our format reads, "Give as generously as you are able—remember how much we used to spend on our drugs." The group responds as one voice, in a loud chorus, "*All of it!*" Everyone laughs, and lots of people dig a little deeper in their wallets.

STEP NINE

> *. . . we tell him that we will never get over our drinking
> until we have done our utmost to straighten out the past.*
> Alcoholics Anonymous, *page 77*

It was time for me to make amends with my ex-mother-in-law. My sponsor told me to listen for the Eighth-Step sound. If I didn't hear it, I needed to hightail it out of there because I wasn't willing! When I asked what the Eighth-Step sound was, he knocked on his desk and said, "It's you knocking on her door with the money in your hand."

With cash in hand, I knocked on her door. When she answered, I handed her the money and said, "I am an alcoholic and addict staying sober today on a spiritual basis. I can never get over drinking and using until I have done my utmost to right the wrongs I have caused people. I believe I have harmed you by hurting your son and never paying you the money for the car you helped me with. I believe I owe you a lot of money. It's all there."

At this point, she started crying and had to leave the room. When she returned, I was sure she was going to try to get more money out of me or something. To my surprise, she never mentioned the money. Instead, she said, "My family is all that I have. When you hurt them, you hurt me." But it wasn't her voice I heard. It was my own mother's voice. Mom had said the exact same thing just a week or two before about someone hurting *me*. Suddenly, it dawned on me—this woman isn't a witch, she is just somebody's mom!

I left there feeling greater freedom than I had in my entire life. And true to what it says in the *Big Book*, that is when I first noticed the Ninth-Step Promises materializing for me. Thank goodness I was willing to follow my sponsor's direction in order to experience this unexpected wonderful revelation. I'd never have guessed what amazing benefits cleaning up my side of the street could bring.

~~~~~

I hope to build stronger recovery through my own personal experiences in the amends process. As I keep clearing up the wreckage of my past, more and more Promises keep coming true.

HOPES AND DREAMS

Make your recovery your number one priority. All your hopes and plans, even your very survival, depend on a drug-free you. Staying away from cocaine and all other mind-altering substances may be the greatest challenge you will ever face.
Tools of Recovery (C.A. Pamphlet)

Before I found the rooms of C.A., I had no real priorities. I wandered aimlessly most of the time, lost in the deep grip of my disease. I had few hopes and even fewer dreams. My addiction ran my life, leading me on a rapid descent downward. I had no hope and found myself a mere shadow with no idea what was next.

I spiraled low enough that when I got here (like a lot of us), I had nowhere else to go. My friends and family were lost to me, my very soul had been abandoned at some dealer's house—honestly, by then, I had no idea what was real or who I was. As a result, I became quite teachable and managed to find a glimmer of hope at the very first meeting I attended. I was beaten up sufficiently to somehow have enough clarity to give recovery a chance.

I did what was suggested, even though it was quite shocking to me. I got a sponsor immediately, started reading the *Big Book*, and caught a meeting almost every day, returning over and over again for a little bit more of the Fellowship's profound experience, strength, and hope. It was mostly hope, more than experience and strength, at that stage; hope kept me captive for quite a while. I heard it said all I have to do is finally be done using and if so, the program will work. I was promised that, at some point, the compulsion to use would be lifted—a promise fulfilled!

I was told early on to make recovery my number one priority every day. As such, each morning, I ask God what His will is for me. Proudly, I now have many hopes and dreams that have come to fruition—even several I never believed would occur, *ever*. In truth, they have surpassed my wildest imaginings. I am exceedingly grateful to the C.A. Fellowship for the gift of hope and showing me how to fill my days with positive action toward the life I desire.

~~~~~

Being an addict, my survival is contingent on staying away from all mind-altering substances. When I do so, great events have come to me as promised. Applying Steps One through Twelve in my life, I can survive anything in my path today. Living drug-free, I can hope to accomplish many things, and I can follow my dreams wherever they lead me.

PAIN BEGETS PAIN

We came into these rooms emotionally, financially, and spiritually bankrupt. We have experienced all sorts of tragedies as a result of cocaine, drugs, and/or alcohol. We have lived many of the same horrors you have, yet today we are happy. We are free from the misery, terror, and pain of drug addiction.

A Higher Power (C.A. Pamphlet)

When I was several years sober and working a strong program, I was involved in a serious car accident. Ultimately no permanent damage was sustained, but my road back to health was quite painful—physically, emotionally, and spiritually. "Why me, why now, why, God?" I asked over and over again. Repeatedly flashing back on other painful times in my life, new and old pain combined to overwhelm and confound me. Why were these former pains coming back? Why did they cut so deep? Where was God in this? How could I combat the triggers urging me to end the pain by picking up?

My sponsor was quick to remind me of the big emotional "thaw" we all experience when we get here. We are learning what it means to feel, perhaps for the first time in our entire lives. I believed this might partially explain things but, as plagued as I felt at every level, I was certain whatever I was going through was much more complicated. While healing began, I sought the reasons (causes and conditions) why this scourge had been so intense—why those old hurts had come to light with such utter depth and intensity. Through inventory, meetings, and Step work, I discovered pain begets pain. The pain unleashed by the accident had triggered every unresolved, festering issue in my brain. Even awful stuff from *before* active addiction kicked in took center stage. Prior to recovery, these pains (all enmeshed in a very sick way) were numbed by drugs and alcohol.

The discovery of this link has been one of my most powerful recovery insights. It's actually a huge relief to understand that pain in my present will inevitably bring up grief from the past. In the midst of this lesson, I also found that God won't give us more than we can handle. When God presents us with something to tackle, the timing and reasons are His to understand, not mine. As everyone always says, more will be revealed.

~~~~~

In recovery, I often get insights linking my life lessons together. I am grateful for the spiritual and emotional awareness to see these connections. Previously, I would have missed them altogether

RE-FOCUS

We will not regret the past nor wish to shut the door on it.
Alcoholics Anonymous, *page 83*

I had been an active addict for over twenty years with intermittent spells of sobriety, followed always by relapse. When I lost my mother, I was three months clean and sober, and no one, including me, thought I'd ever manage to hold it together. Thanks to my C.A. family, I did not go back out. They helped me to focus on how much of a contribution Mom had made in my life and in the lives of my children, rather than sitting on the pity-pot, regretting words unspoken. If only I could have let her know how much I now appreciate all the sacrifices she made for us, raising my kids when I was too busy getting high. I love and miss her so much, but my regrets are fading as I continue working my spiritual program, following the path of sobriety, smiling peacefully along the way.

Gratitude and love abound when I think about Mom these days. I try to share my gratitude with all I meet and thank God for the blessing of self-forgiveness.

~~~~~

Acceptance that my past is and will remain a valuable lesson has been a key point in my recovery. To be able to give back what was freely given, both by the Fellowship of C.A. and family members who loved and cared for me, is the greatest privilege I know.

NEVER UNDERESTIMATE

I know today I can be or do anything I want to in life, as long as I am willing to do the footwork. By working this Program and these Steps in my life, I have learned that I am unlimited; my Higher Power made me that way.

Hope, Faith & Courage, *page 180*

Anytime I travel by air, I always request a window seat because gazing down at our Earth's topography never fails to fascinate me. My mother once said it's like looking at a giant, diversified patchwork quilt. Who can help but marvel upon seeing gargantuan cumulus cloud formations from the top side? What an amazing example of God's majesty!

Recently I had occasion to travel across the country. Although I'm a seasoned traveler, I'd never before taken this particular route. When the foothills of the Rockies appeared in my window, I woke up my husband from his mid-flight snooze so he could have a look, mistakenly believing they were the Rocky Mountain peaks. Much to my surprise, about ten minutes later, we encountered the true rugged, snow-capped cliffs, which continued to unfold beneath me for the next hour, getting increasingly more beautiful with each passing moment.

This experience effectively reminded me how often I underestimate the power and splendor of God's imagination and vast, sweeping presence. The program has taught me that, in keeping Higher Power constantly by my side, life's possibilities are infinite before me. Appreciating the miracle of God's world around me automatically triggers an overwhelming sense of gratitude!

~~~~~

God, help me to remember that Your realm of creative energy reaches far beyond my limited human capacity. Allow me to appreciate the endless beauty of Your ever-evolving masterpiece.

UNITY THROUGH SERVICE

The elder statesman is the one who sees the wisdom of the group's decision, who holds no resentment . . . whose judgment, fortified by considerable experience, is sound. . . .
Twelve Steps and Twelve Traditions, *page 135*

I frequently encounter fellows with a real passion for our C.A. Fellowship, particularly in service work. The C.A. program saved their lives and they are earnest in their efforts to give back as much as possible. Often, these members are not shy about expressing their views on most every issue, generally believing their ideas are correct. Most times, I've found, they are.

Many recovering addicts still rebel against authority figures, no matter who they are, even if they happen to be correct. Some may also resist meetings, workshops, service assemblies, conventions and/or other events, in spite of the fact that they've been organized for the Fellowship's collective well-being. Maybe, I have my own opinions about how these gatherings should have been executed—how I could surely do it better—whether or not the group conscience is being respected!

Coming face-to-face with passionate members who actively possess rebellious character defects is certainly challenging. How can anything constructive ever get accomplished within such a framework? As I studied this dynamic, I had to admit I have surely been one of the non-shy types and definitely belong to the rebellious addict brigade as well. I was gently reminded that trusted servants are all volunteers on God's broad Twelve-Step highway, and they have all earned a seat here, just as I have. Finding a way to stay solution-based and work together to carry the message is our primary purpose. In doing so, I need to remain mindful that just as our experiences are varied, the ways we serve might also be different. There are no wrongs or rights, only impassioned Fellowship members wanting to carry on in the way they think best. If focus remains on our primary purpose and group consciences remain honored, trusted servants will always be protected as they come together to work for our Fellowship.

~~~~

So much potential exists for me to make a real difference in the recovery world, my community, and my own life. All I need to do is work harmoniously together with my fellows in love and service.

FINISHING MY AMENDS

Some of the "not on your life" amends are done, and nearly all have moved up to the willing category. Making amends has allowed me to hold my head high and look people in the eye without fear.
Hope, Faith & Courage Volume II, *page 167*

My experience necessitated several trips through the Steps to finally finish all of the amends on my original Step Eight list. At the time it was written, I honestly thought I would *never* make amends to some of those people, citing a variety of reasons which were misplaced rationalizations at best.

The names and, frankly, my actions continued to haunt me each time I passed them by. I was down to about six entries (my "nevers") when I heard a woman at a meeting share about the complete freedom she experienced by finally finishing her original list. She said her sponsor had asked her how free she wanted to be, and that question was the motivation she needed to finally get the job done. I desired that same freedom; it made complete sense. It seemed so close, but yet so far from my position in the process. I badly wanted to make peace with my list as a next recovery milestone. I could almost taste the freedom of at long last finishing the hardest amends.

I began to pray for the willingness to tackle those last demons once and for all. That is exactly what Step Eight suggests. Those last pesky names, after all, had moved from my "never" category to at least the "maybe" category, which was big progress in my book. Finally, I arrived back at Steps Eight and Nine, and the time had come. I counseled with others, especially my sponsor, and set out toward making my final group of amends. The first three were easier than I thought, which inspired me to carry on. The last three were much more challenging, but I stayed on my side of the street, did not engage, and managed to complete the amends without causing further harm. What a *huge* relief to be done with them once and for all. As promised, a new freedom and a new happiness prevailed.

~~~~~

Finishing my amends was a significant recovery milestone, reaching another goal I never thought attainable. With the help of others in the Fellowship who inspired me, my sponsor and my Higher Power, I am most grateful to have completed this task. Redoubling my efforts as I continue to work the Steps, I'm inspired to share the freedom with the next member down the line.

FAITH, SPIRITUALITY, AND GOD

It is easy to confuse the word spirituality with religion. As it relates to God, Cocaine Anonymous is a spiritual program, not a religious one. In C.A., we believe each individual can choose a Higher Power of his or her own. In short, a God of his or her own understanding.
A Higher Power (C.A. Pamphlet)

Spirituality is a feeling you receive from practicing a spiritual life. It's a connection of mind, body, and soul using a wide variety of exercises. Some believe it is faith in the God of their understanding; some use an altogether different perspective called Higher Power. In my recovery and in the rooms of Cocaine Anonymous, I separate spirituality and faith. I pray to a God of my understanding, and I meditate to gain spirituality. This is my own personal Eleventh-Step exercise.

The *Big Book* tells me the God of my understanding is a personal relationship. To me, that means "between the member and their God." Step Two's simplicity was finding a solution to my addiction with a Higher Power as I chose to believe. That Higher Power does not have to be God. I was told my spiritual connection does not even have to include God.

To me, these concepts (God, faith, and spirituality) can be interpreted in a multitude of personal definitions. Each will create no controversy if I keep it as my own personal belief and involve solely the God of my understanding.

Faith is defined as "confidence or belief in a person or thing." Spirituality can be described as "pertaining to the spirit or soul, as distinguished from the physical nature." God is simply that basic Step Two concept of choosing how to believe in a Higher Power. All are related, but each is uniquely different.

~~~~~

God, please walk with me as I seek to nurture my spiritual understanding and growth. Guide me as I endeavor to enhance my faith and deepen my connection with You.

FORGIVING MY PARENTS

Let's remember that alcoholics are not the only ones bedeviled by sick emotions. Moreover, it is usually a fact that our behavior when drinking has aggravated the defects of others. We've repeatedly strained the patience of our best friends to a snapping point, and have brought out the very worst in those who didn't think much of us to begin with. In many instances we are really dealing with fellow sufferers, people whose woes we have increased. If we are now about to ask forgiveness for ourselves, why shouldn't we start out by forgiving them, one and all?
Twelve Steps and Twelve Traditions, *page 78*

Some addicts have had issues with their parents: how they were raised; whether mom or dad might be alcoholics or addicts passing on their gene; the level of dysfunction in childhood homes. Maybe resentments are still harbored about what was perceived to be a parent's role in addictive behavior. Blame was assigned for hastening a demise into the downward spiral of unmanageability.

Parent issues are demons, rearing their ugly heads in my inventories as I look at my character defects. I am learning to understand my emotions in recovery, which have run the gamut regarding the difference between my parents' part and my own. My job is to forgive my parents, no matter how they showed up in my life. This can be quite a difficult task at many levels. Forgiveness requires the release of blame for their words or actions, or for mine, and a newfound appreciation for whatever positive efforts they were able to make. Forgiveness entails keeping my heart open to my parents, imperfections and all. For me, it's been necessary to acknowledge my hurt and then quit dwelling on it in order to find compassion for them. Ultimately, I need to remember that God didn't give me more than I can handle, even before I got sober. The lessons He wanted me to learn from and through my parents were crucial to my spiritual growth. Seeking recovery, I've found love and a quality life. Recognizing the fact that I made it to the rooms, no matter what my parents' involvement, has permitted me to forgive them in a natural, healthy manner.

It was also suggested that I take the good from my parents, whatever that might be, and leave the rest—a common program tool perfectly applicable to this dynamic. Thus, I set aside the victim role, once and for all. I affirm that their behaviors toward me had little to do with anything I said or did, or could have said or done differently. Although the hurt caused by my parents was very real, I need not engage in their ongoing behavior.

~~~~~

I can forgive my parents as I forgive myself, understanding that they did the best they could with what they had—end of story. With such a perspective, I can find profound empathy for anyone who has hurt me throughout my life, even in the most arduous relationships.

SPIRITUAL CURRENT

Cocaine Anonymous should remain forever nonprofessional, but our service centers may employ special workers.

C.A. Tradition Eight

One addict sharing experience, strength, and hope with another is a sacred and spiritual event. It is the beginning of recovery. When these sacred events are linked together in fellowship, a spiritual current is established. This spiritual current is the binding element in our brotherly and harmonious connection.

Clearly, the one-on-one meeting of addict-to-addict should never be professionalized. But what about the work which paves the way for these sacred events? What about the publication and distribution of literature, the processing of mail and other assorted mundane tasks? Successfully coordinating communication throughout a worldwide Fellowship involves many aspects and reliable, accountable efforts are necessary. Here we find that paid employees have proven to be a necessary, effective, and efficient tool in furthering our primary purpose of carrying the message to the addict who still suffers.

~~~~~

I am grateful for a loving God directing our efforts. I am grateful for the spiritual current which binds us. I am grateful for all the people doing God's will, whether it is a paid employee shipping literature out of a warehouse, or a Fellowship member sharing experience, strength, and hope with a still-suffering addict on the sidewalk.

NO MISTAKES IN GOD'S WORLD

Whatever it was I searching for in all those years of drug abuse had to do with the lack of anything spiritual or beautiful in me or my life.
Hope. Faith & Courage, *page 98*

Step outside and notice how flawlessly God has arranged this planet. A certain beauty and spirituality is present in every moment, in everything and everyone. Perfect order exists at all levels. The longer I am in the program, the more I witness just how interconnected the entire world is, especially we humans.

Before sobriety, I recognized nothing of God's splendor and magnificence. I used to joke about never understanding, or even wanting to spend a moment contemplating what it all meant or how we got here. Even after I found the rooms, this deep sort of inquiry remained outside my realm of thinking for the longest time.

I finally read the chapter in the *Big Book* entitled "We Agnostics" and in my Third Step, I spent a while seriously pondering who I wanted my Higher Power to be. Plainly, the God of my understanding was clearly my own choice. This work solidly launched me on my path to explore how all of this life, nature, and beauty fits together so perfectly at so many levels.

Now, this awareness permits me to see and sense wonders which I totally ignored or took for granted. Today, when I notice them, I smile, filled with appreciation for the marvels surrounding us in everyday living.

~~~~~

In Cocaine Anonymous, I've found people brought together by a common suffering, and yet bound by a shared appreciation for life. May I eternally preserve a keen recognition for all things bright and beautiful, seamlessly entwined in God's world.

CHILDREN OF CHAOS

Over the years every conceivable deviation from our Twelve Steps and Twelve Traditions has been tried. That was sure to be, since we are so largely a band of ego-driven individualists. Children of chaos, we have defiantly played with every brand of fire, only to emerge unharmed and, we think, wiser. These very deviations created a vast process of trial and error which, under the grace of God, has brought us to where we stand today.
Twelve Steps and Twelve Traditions, page 146

My experience has continually confirmed what the *Big Book* expounds, namely, that "We are not saints." Even when I *try* to do the next right thing, I am going to make mistakes in my program, within the Fellowship, in service, as I relate to my Higher Power, and even involving the use and interpretation of the Twelve Traditions. Part of the beauty is how I respond when these mistakes occur, utilizing the Steps and my program to repair any damage. From these mistakes, I often learn more about me, about my disease, and, frankly, how not to repeat the same errors again.

I have heard it said that I am a spiritual being having a human experience. There are going to be times when I am surely wrong, make big mistakes, take a bad turn, and truly exercise my humanness—even when I am quite focused on my recovery. I am not a big fan of when this happens; I don't believe anybody is. However, such errors seem to be well-recognized and accepted at many levels, provided they are not repeated, I ask and pray for the lessons, and I make amends when I have caused harm.

Happily, I do get it right, for the most part, growing and learning as a result, proudly thanking God for wisdom and guidance. Perhaps I might even have been able to place one more solved piece into the recovery puzzle. Further, one of the well-known mantras I heard early and use often is to seek spiritual *progress* versus spiritual *perfection*. This applies to my personal recovery, as well as my varied relationships and how I show up to be of service. *Twelve Steps and Twelve Traditions* (page 149) supports the idea that Groups, from time to time, exercise their right to be wrong and, in so doing, perform a great service to the Fellowship by being humbly willing to apply the resulting lessons learned. This same notion can and does apply to my personal program as well.

~~~~~

I pray my lessons remain gentle. As a child of chaos, may I learn what I am supposed to learn from my mistakes in recovery and in service. I pray, too, for continued perseverance in avoiding making the same error twice. I will neither be paralyzed by my blunders, nor encouraged by my twisted brain to let uncorrected behavior slide when I happen to emerge from the mishap unscathed.

PATHS TOWARD SERVICE

There are so many different ways to be of service. The most obvious way is sponsorship. . . . Another way is by going to meetings. . . . Yet another way is through committee work. . . .
C.A. NewsGram, 4th Quarter 2004

There are many paths one can take toward being of service within the C.A. Fellowship. Sponsorship is perhaps the key position on the service work flow chart. Spiritual experience is meant to be shared. I have heard "I can't keep it unless I give it away." Sponsorship includes guiding others through the Steps and reaching out to the addict or alcoholic who is still suffering.

Going to meetings is service work falling into the responsibility for all who gain recovery. If people stopped going to meetings after a few years sober, who would be there for the newcomer? Today, I want to go to meetings. The deep friendships I've found in C.A. are an integral part of my life, and I never want to give that up.

At a meeting, I can be of service to someone without even realizing it—by sharing a smile, a hug or a kind word. When I share my experience, strength and hope with others, they understand they are not alone. Someone else felt the same and yet found their way to a new freedom and happiness. They begin to believe they, too, can live a life filled with hope, faith, and courage.

Of course, service may also be offered through local District committee work, or even broader at the Area, Regional, or World Service Conference levels. Committee work is probably the least popular of all service work, yet it seems to be the one I like the most. These positions need trusted servants to ensure our Fellowship continues to shine a light when someone is trying to find their way out of the darkness.

~~~~

I will always be mindful just how important service is for me and many others within our Fellowship. I need to take the time to pace myself, and to always make service a true priority no matter what else is going on in my life and program.

I'LL LET HIM!

God, I offer myself to Thee—to build with me and to do with me as Thou wilt. Relieve me of the bondage of self, that I may better do Thy will. Take away my difficulties, that victory over them may bear witness to those I would help of Thy Power, Thy Love, and Thy Way of life. May I do Thy will always.
Alcoholics Anonymous, page 63

"I can't, He can, and I'll let Him!" is a quote I hear regularly in meetings. It simply summarizes Steps One, Two, and Three of our program. When I found the C.A. rooms, this simple equation helped me immensely to develop an initial understanding of what would keep me coming back, one day at a time.

"I can't" refers to my surrender in the admission of powerlessness and unmanageability. I believe "I can't" also refers to my addictive thinking, my need to run my life on self-will.

"He can" refers to my coming to believe that a Power greater than myself could restore me to sanity. Here, I am asked to consider believing in a Higher Power and to have faith another solution is available to replace my previous lifestyle. Step Two lets God in. Step Two acknowledges God can complete His handiwork in and through me.

"I'll let Him" refers to my decision to turn my will and my life over to the care of God as I understand Him. Step Three is about permitting my Higher Power to work with and for me. It is a choice to allow God into my life to care for me as He sees fit. "I'll let Him" represents my willingness to relinquish control with faith in a positive outcome.

~~~~

Today, I am grateful for this simple formula, which reminds me to be centered in the principles contained in these first three Steps. I will remember they need to be a part of my everyday living.

HAPPINESS

Today I know what it is to be happy, joyous, and free. . . .I am a vastly different person than when I got here. Instead of being homeless, unemployable, and destitute, I own my home, have a good job . . . but it's the way I feel inside that's the real miracle. That hole in my soul is gone, hopefully never to return, and I no longer feel alone. The spiritual aspect of this program that I fought so hard in the beginning has become my lifeline. I have absolutely priceless relationships with my friends and family, and with God, and I truly love the person I see in the mirror today. It feels so good to know who I am and to finally be able to be the same person everywhere I go.

Hope, Faith & Courage Volume II, *page 98*

Some special pages I use often in my recovery and with sponsees are those reflecting heavily on happiness and the joy of living. From *Alcoholics Anonymous*, page 133, "We are sure God wants us to be happy, joyous and free." This concept is one of the more celebratory ideas in my program. I have experienced the happiness which results from facing and embracing all my emotions. One of the Promises assures me I "will know a new freedom and a new happiness." (*Alcoholics Anonymous*, page 83.)

The *Twelve Steps and Twelve Traditions* references being happy again and again, especially in its Step Twelve narrative. Admonishing us that we need still more spiritual development, even in working Step Twelve, our chances will be improved "for really happy and useful living" (page 114). This arc is completed several pages later where the *Twelve and Twelve* provides, "Still more wonderful is the feeling that we do not have to be specially distinguished among our fellows in order to be useful and profoundly happy" (page 124).

I have heard being "happy" comes from learning to live recovery in the here and now, always striving to do the next right thing, and, of course, the next right thing after that. Following this suggestion to the best of my ability, I experience heightened senses and a keen feeling of well-being. My life has purpose and meaning well beyond carrying the C.A. message. I am at ease with myself, perhaps for the first time ever, proud and humbled by where I have been. I am satisfied with my current circumstances and quite excited about where I am going. I am right-sized. I now possess some clarity on the nature of my character defects, at the same time embracing my discovered strengths from inventory, prayer, meditation, and conscious contact with a Higher Power.

~~~~~

Recovery is about following a design for living full of lessons, love, vibrancy, humility, and joy. Laughter is also a key. Happiness, spiritual satisfaction and usefulness in my program, to our Fellowship, and to my Higher Power are all found in a life worth living. Recovery has taught me how to love my life.

THE JOY OF LIVING

The joy of living we really have, even under pressure and difficulty. I have seen hundreds of families set their feet in the path that really goes somewhere. . . . There is scarcely any form of trouble and misery which has not been overcome among us.
Alcoholics Anonymous, *page 15*

Sobriety has offered me so many gifts—an abundance of laughter, serenity, friendship, fellowship, and simple moments of plain joy. Healthy joy was a new frontier when I got sober and has been foreign to many of us along our path. *Alcoholics Anonymous* provides the instruction: "We absolutely insist on enjoying life" (page 132). I get joy in helping others help themselves, by being of service anywhere I can pass on the lessons of recovery to a newer member of C.A. Nothing is more enriching than seeing someone grow out of that dark, desolate place full of torment and despair into a vital member of the Fellowship.

The *Twelve Steps and Twelve Traditions* tells us that the joy of living is the theme of Step Twelve and that action is its key word (page 106). This comes on the heels of one Eleventh-Step Prayer which implores us, in pertinent part, that "where there is sadness, I may bring joy" (page 99). For me, joy has been a present theme since I arrived. Even the bad days now (yes, there are still some) are more joy-filled than any before I got sober. The longer I am around the rooms and as I remain in service to my Fellowship, my joy grows continually. Inner joy abounds as I seek to nurture my relationship with my Higher Power and as I am able to sense what is next for me in my life and in my recovery. I got a huge dose of joy when I finally finished my amends, from the standpoint of accomplishment and freedom, and as I work on that life-long process of amends to myself.

I am quite joyous as I repeatedly witness my newfound intuitiveness in knowing how to handle something which would have baffled me previously. I get great joy seeing my sponsees grow, learn, and thrive; and then to be of service themselves, sharing their joy so that the legacy continues. Mostly, I experience joy when I obtain answers to questions that have dogged me, such as how to forgive myself and others; how to affirm myself as I grow and change following God's ideals for me; how to be comfortable now in my "right size"; how to embrace those simple things I missed for years that matter to me now; even how to look forward to my tomorrows, one day at a time.

~~~~~

I vividly remember the first time I went to an H&I panel meeting and heard about the joy in the presenter's life. Long before I understood what that was or how I could ever find such a feeling, I knew I wanted it as a part of my recovery. I am so grateful to have claimed that joy, and I welcome its grace daily.

279

FREEDOM

We are going to know a new freedom and a new happiness.
Alcoholics Anonymous, *page 83*

"Free" is the last of the three concepts culled from the notion of "happy, joyous, and free." Our books and literature often reference "free" and "freedom" in many contexts. C.A.'s trademarked slogan, "We're here and we're free," precisely expresses this key point.

I have finally faced the truth about myself, and it truly has set me free. I realize my choices in my recovery contribute to this freedom and help shape who I am. Today, I am free to choose, no longer a slave to drugs or alcohol. Most of the time, I remain free from fear and the desire to invoke my self-will. I claim responsibility for my choices and actions. Yet, at the same time, I know the results are not in my control but in God's.

I am free from the need to change what I cannot change and free to change what I can. I am free to ask for help and even admit when I don't know the answer. (Believe it or not, this still happens from time to time!) I am free to work the Steps at my own pace. (Based upon my past personal experience, I'd better not move *too* slowly!)

Interestingly, I am free to work my program my way, to go to meetings when and where I desire. The *Big Book* is made up of "suggestions" which I am free to follow or not. The question becomes, then, how "free" do I want, or dare, to be? The answers remain in my heart, between myself and my Higher Power (and, if I'm working a strong program, often with my sponsor as well!). I am able to embrace the wisdom of other Fellowship members as I explore these freedoms, determining where my boundaries lie and how my recovery is shaped by the wide degrees of freedom offered.

~~~~~

Dear God, please guide me in making the right choices in my recovery. I welcome the attendant freedoms, although some still scare me. Help me find the appropriate balance in how much freedom is appropriate and when.

STEP ELEVEN DAILY?

> *The moment we catch even a glimpse of God's will, the moment we begin to see truth, justice, and love as the real and eternal things in life, we are no longer deeply disturbed by all the seeming evidence to the contrary that surrounds us in purely human affairs.*
> Twelve Steps and Twelve Traditions, *page 105*

Step Eleven suggests I seek through prayer and meditation to improve my conscious contact with my God. Daily practice is suggested. Daily? How can I forget God's power has already guided me through the most painful and difficult situations of my life? Could I ever be ungrateful for the positive changes in me as a result of Higher Power's intervention? Human arrogance is a mighty force of its own, and I'm subject to all its consequences, no matter how long I stay sober. Perhaps, then, daily improvement of my spiritual connection isn't such a bad idea after all.

Left without direction from Higher Power, I am like a willful horse. I take the bit in my teeth to run off onto paths leading back to the destructive ends with which I am so familiar. Remember the First Step? It all seemed like such a good idea at the time, until my experience proved that I hit the dead-end brick wall at warp speed. So it is, no matter where I am in the recovery process, or how far in my Step work—no matter how much better or worse my life gets—my connection with my Higher Power is ultimately the solution. Prayer and meditation are the keys to strengthening my connection to God.

Reaching out to my Higher Power takes practice. So every day, I get to practice as I work Step Eleven. Practice on the good days makes it easier to reach out on the bad ones.

~~~~

Ritualize the process if need be. Pray in whatever fashion works to connect you with your Higher Power. Consider God in the quiet moments of your day. If no single quiet moment exists naturally, make one of your own. Is it working? If you connect, it's working. If you can't connect, try something else. When you find a method that works, do it every day. Maybe even more than once.

TRUST AND FOLLOW

We attend meetings to share our experience, strength, and hope with other recovering addicts. What we failed to do alone we can do together.
Tools of Recovery (C.A. Pamphlet)

I was told to look around the rooms and find all the sober people who were working the Steps, and then stick with the winners. In going to the business meetings, doing H&I panels, and being of service, I had unconsciously surrounded myself with winners, people who were serious about the program and who were actively involved in working the Steps. I watched and emulated these people who had the sobriety that I wanted. I got sober and grew with these people.

I think recovery is a lot like elephants. I'm an old stoner, and I like those nature programs. So I think it's like elephants. They line up behind the oldest matriarch, holding onto the tail of the elephant right in front of them. And they follow each other, using the collective wisdom and the old-age experience. I honestly believe that's how this whole thing works, one person following the next. It's a very special, wonderful, beautiful thing. It's truly a blessing in my life. I feel honored and privileged to be a part of it.

I honestly believe that because we can relate to each other, one addict to another, we have the ability to reach out and grab hold of each other and to save each other's lives. Because we can gain each other's trust when nobody else can. Because we can show each other how to do this thing.

~~~~~

I must stick with people who are enthusiastically seeking recovery because they're moving in a positive direction; when I have no direction to go in myself, I adjust to them and keep going.

R-E-C-O-V-E-R-Y

If you're new to recovery, welcome to the party! I want you to know I've been where you've been, I've thought the way you thought, I've felt the way you felt, and I've acted the way you acted. You see, I walked in here a broken-down shell of a man. I rebuilt my life based on the Twelve-Step recovery program of Cocaine Anonymous. Because I jumped into this program with both feet and without reservation, I'm here to tell you that I've got a great life.

Hope, Faith & Courage Volume II, *page 39*

R is for Reason: The reason I came to C.A. was because a couple of good people from another fellowship sent me here. They said, "You keep ranting and raving about cocaine. Go to Cocaine Anonymous." God bless them because I never knew C.A. existed. I came and found my spiritual home.

E is for Everyone: No one can be asked to leave C.A. No matter what your race, religion, gender or sexual orientation. No matter what drugs you used or didn't use; no matter what substance/substances feed your addiction.

C is for Coming Back: I didn't think C.A. and its Twelve-Step program would work for me. The truth is, I had nowhere else to go. C.A. members told me to keep coming back; I did. They told me to get a sponsor; I did. I was helped to gain knowledge of the Steps using the *Big Book*. Then I needed to go and help others as I had been helped.

O is for Obsession: I was taught how an obsession is something so powerful it will make you believe a lie. I understood this because my experience had been devastating. For years, I got no pleasure from drinking or using drugs. The good times were long gone. The obsession would tell me things which simply weren't reality. Due to C.A.'s Twelve Steps, sponsorship, and service, my obsession has been removed. I still have the odd mad thought, it is quickly replaced by the truth.

V is for Vital: I have had something called a vital spiritual experience as a result of following all of C.A.'s Twelve Steps. The obsession has been removed by this experience. I fully understand the vital need for me to work with newcomers to maintain my spiritual growth.

E is for Everything: Everything smashed to pieces in my drinking and using days has been built again, better than it ever was before, my relationships with my spouse and kids and with the rest of my family, as well as my health.

R is for Recovery: All of the above and so much more.

Y is for You: Yes! You, me, and, indeed, anyone can enjoy peace of mind, happiness, and freedom from addiction.

~~~~~

No matter how I spell it or what words I use to describe my gift of recovery on any given day, I am continually reminded just how my life has changed in so many positive ways. I can't do it alone. I must follow the path of those who came before me, while sharing my lessons with those who follow. The obsession has been replaced by hope, faith, and courage.

CLEANING MY SIDE OF THE STREET

Made direct amends to such people wherever possible,
except when to do so would injure them or others.

C.A. Step Nine

Step Nine is often referred to as "cleaning off my side of the street." The process affords me the opportunity to make things right with people and institutions I have harmed. By doing so, I gain the ability to move forward with a great sense of freedom and release from my past.

Making amends is much more than just saying, "I'm sorry." Many of the people to whom amends are owed have already heard this a thousand times, until the words no longer carry any meaning. The term "I'm sorry" also implies that I am seeking some form of sympathy. This is definitely not what Step Nine is about. It involves admitting wrong thoughts and actions and accepting my part in situations. Was I selfish? Inconsiderate? Dishonest? Fearful? I need to let the other person know that I recognize my error and sincerely wish to correct the mistake as best I can. This is the crux of the amends-making process. When done with an open mind, the patterns of maladjusted behavior which resulted from my addiction can clearly be seen.

The very thought of making amends can be terrifying. It is important to remember that I am not alone in this. By the time I have reached Step Nine, I have encountered my Higher Power. I have come to believe this Power can restore me to sanity, and I made a decision to turn my will and my life over to the care of this Power.

In Step Eight, I turned once again to my Higher Power and prayed for the courage to make my amends. I discovered that praying before making amends produces miraculous results. I ask God to grant acceptance of His will for me and the courage to follow through with action. Having prayed about my amends, it is vitally important to make them as soon as I possibly can. When delayed, the amends become increasingly difficult to tackle.

~~~~

Praying for God's guidance as amends are made provides a wonderful bolstering to my resolve. Once my amends list has been made and reviewed with my sponsor, immediate action should follow.

FEELINGS

> *Getting clean and sober can be painful, but with*
> *help, we find our lives get better one day at a time.*
> Hope Faith & Courage Volume II, *page 204*

Somebody once told me that feelings are just feelings. It took me years to understand that concept. What was meant was that feelings don't define who I am. It is all too easy to get stuck in my pain, believing it will never cease or that I somehow deserve to suffer. That intense turmoil always goes away. It may take an hour or a day or even a week, but if I stick it out, it will get better.

As an addict, when I feel pain, I want to escape. It is how I learned to cope at a young age. In sobriety, I retrain myself to stay on the path, even when I am overwhelmed. Part of the process is being aware that my feelings and thoughts may be scrambled sometimes, but I don't have to let them take over. I learn new coping techniques. I talk about what hurts, I do my Step work, I help out at meetings, and I try not to take myself too seriously. Eventually, I realize that emotional pain will not kill me. I will survive, and I can and do heal.

~~~~~

Today, I will not seek an escape for my feelings. Rather than becoming attached to them, I can allow them to come and go.

OCTOBER

DAILY SPIRITUAL CHECK-UP

We went on to Step Ten, and I started working Steps Four through Nine daily. Through this process, I started developing an intuition, a sixth sense about living. My perception is that we are spiritual creatures, born into this world out of love and sent out on this earth to love.

Hope, Faith & Courage Volume II, *page 38*

We have a wonderful Step process known as daily inventory. With Step Ten, we are able to get a check-up every 24 hours (or more often) in order to stay on a spiritual and recovery path. If worked daily and thoroughly, Step Ten will give us a defect list, show us where we've harmed others, remind us to make prompt amends, and even list areas where we have improved—and it's absolutely free. Step Ten requires only a little of our time at the end of the day, or sooner if needed. Although Step Ten somewhat resembles Step Four, the two Steps are very different, in my experience. Step Four calls for a searching and fearless moral inventory of ourselves up to the present. Step Ten calls for a personal inventory. It asks for a daily check on ourselves, on our thoughts and actions. This is how we check the large and small details of our lives *today*. Personally, I like to keep Step Ten simple, uncomplicated, and steady. That works for me.

At night before sleep, I keep a time open before prayer to go over my day. I recall the things I have done, both good and not so good. I review the people I have interacted with and what happened. Sometimes I don't feel comfortable about my actions, and I owe someone an apology. If I am to maintain my spiritual condition, I cannot allow those duties to go unattended. I always say that it's not the big things in life that tear me up as much as all the little things that just don't seem too important at the time. Unattended, they can add up to big problems that are harmful to both my serenity and spiritual condition. This is the reason for Step Ten. If we clean up our side of the street daily, then we can maintain a healthy attitude in our spiritual maintenance and our recovery.

~~~~

My daily Step Ten process is a key part of my program. I do what is suggested and pray, take personal inventory of both the good and the bad, and make things right as soon as I am able. This process continues to give me great relief and provides a constant source of serenity for me.

WATCH, ASK & TURN

> *This thought brings us to Step Ten, which suggests we continue to take personal inventory and continue to set right any new mistakes as we go along. We vigorously commenced this way of living as we cleaned up the past. We have entered the world of the Spirit.*
>
> Alcoholics Anonymous, *page 84*

As we approach the Tenth Step, a powerful promise is awakened within us: we will enter the "world of the Spirit." How fascinating for real addicts to experience! We will certainly want to stay there, and even go much further—but how?

The Tenth Step enables a growing understanding and effectiveness in all of our affairs throughout the day. Learn by using such spiritual practices as *watch, ask,* and *turn.* Today, I will *watch* for character defects like selfishness, dishonesty, resentment, and fear. When I experience one of these, I will recognize it immediately; then I can *ask* God to remove it. By making a proper amends without delay if I have caused harm, I *turn away* from the negative and *turn towards* the positive, which is God and what He would have me be at this exact moment. As I incorporate this into my daily routine, I am granted incredible freedom. No longer stuck, I can *live* the Tenth Step and truly achieve that "position of neutrality" the book *Alcoholics Anonymous* describes on page 85.

~~~~~

In what areas of my life can I apply the principles of the Tenth Step to grow in understanding and effectiveness? Am I willing to "cease fighting" with the help of my Higher Power? The "world of the Spirit" surely beckons me with bright, inviting promises of a better way to live!

MY BACKYARD

The main purpose of Step Ten is to prevent us from being blocked off again from God, whose power ultimately keeps us sober.
A Guide to the 12 Steps (C.A. Pamphlet)

I have learned that working Step Ten on a regular basis keeps the length of my Fourth Steps way down! It also helps keep me *right-sized*. When I continue to see my errors, it's harder for me to think I am "better than" anyone.

I am a far better person today than I ever have been before, but I still have a long journey ahead of me. I sometimes continue to do stupid things—actions that put me in a position where I once again need to make amends.

In addition to doing a Tenth Step every night, I have actually found myself doing this Step continuously throughout the day. As I grow in recovery, I find it easier to promptly make amends when I am wrong. Doing so allows me a clear conscience throughout the day, along with an unfettered night's sleep.

My spiritual 'backyard' needs to be clean and in good order; doing the Tenth Step nightly helps this immensely. As the seasons change, I must adapt, being mindful of the hard work, care and commitment required to maintain continued peace and serenity. Often this care and commitment starts with my daily Tenth Step.

~~~~~

I will keep my own house in order today. I will continue to take a daily check of my spiritual 'backyard,' making sure I stay willing to maintain it as an essential part of my recovery.

₧AIN

The day came when the drugs stopped working.
The emotional pain could no longer be numbed. . . .
Hope, Faith & Courage, *page 152*

Pain is a great motivator. In my experience, change occurs when the pain of staying where I am is greater than the fear of moving past it.

When I was using, pain kept me going to the bar, the liquor store, and the dope house. I didn't know how to feel pain and not use. I didn't know how to feel anything without medicating.

Today I'm so glad to have learned that pain won't kill me. Pain will make me stronger if I allow myself to feel the feelings and walk through them. Strength, wisdom, and sometimes even joy await me on the other side.

~~~~~

I believe my Higher Power sends me lessons. Either I learn what He's trying to teach, or He'll send me the same lesson again. I'm grateful I'm not as hard-headed as I used to be! I am always mindful of the very wise slogan that pain is required, misery is optional.

EXPERIENCE AS A LEARNING TOOL

Along the road there have been pain and difficulties. My father died a few years ago; I have seen my sister in a coma in intensive care; my partner lost his business and with that all our material and financial security. At those times I continued to do what I was shown: trust God, share honestly, and help others. I know, with certainty in my heart, that the program of Cocaine Anonymous works, no matter what life throws at me—the good times, the bad times, all times.

Hope Faith & Courage Volume II, *page 44*

Never having stood by the graveside of a loved one, at nine years clean and sober, it was finally my turn. I lost my sister and my mother-in-law the same year and thought I would lose my mind. I was unable to be a source of strength for my spouse, thinking *my* pain was more important. Forgetting what the program taught me, I fell into a pool of self-pity, but, mind you, I did not use.

A year later, just as I was getting back on my feet emotionally, my own mother passed. This time, I was able to utilize program tools more comprehensively, carrying out funeral plans while comforting the rest of my family and staying connected spiritually. Only months later, my father-in-law died. The program had helped me grow enormously during the previous two years, and I found myself understanding and responding to my spouse's needs quite differently than before. We were, in fact, able to surrender *together* to God's will instead of to our own. The past losses and what I learned from them gave me strength and insight on how to respond in the face of these more recent incidents of severe loss and unexpected crisis. I was able to be supportive to others while staying connected to the Fellowship and my sponsor so I could stay sober myself. For that, I am extremely grateful.

~~~~

Dealing with loss has made very clear the importance of absorbing as much as I can in meeting rooms (whether I think it presently applies to me or not!). I now understand how others' experience, strength and hope provide a valuable source of strength and tools to help me survive life on life's terms.

WOUNDED SELF

It's taken a few years of recovery in Cocaine Anonymous and extensive inventory work to make the shift from being a victim of parents, family, society, jobs, etc., to one of being fully responsible for all facets of my life.
Hope, Faith & Courage, *page 81*

Learning how to take loving care of myself has been a long, difficult task. I was raised by a mother who was unable to take loving care of herself. She shamed and blamed her children for her miserable life. I never understood why she was so angry all the time, but I believed it was my fault. When I came into recovery, I was extremely wounded emotionally. I believed I was unlovable, that something was wrong with me.

Being dependent on others for approval, acceptance, or love kept me feeling alone and afraid. Slowly, I started to mend. I learned that when I'm feeling angry, defensive, or sad, I am acting out of my wounded self. When I'm happy, grateful and full of love, I am acting out of my true self. My true self is the spiritual condition I was meant to live by when I was born into this world.

I have learned to love myself by inviting my Higher Power's spirit into my wounded heart. The healing power of unconditional love has transformed me. I no longer need others to feel good about myself. Trusting in God and knowing He loves and accepts me the way I am, I feel safe and comfortable.

~~~~~

God, help me receive your inspiration in my thinking, in my speech, and in my actions. Please continue to help me heal my wounded heart. I will remember to be loving, not only to myself today, but to extend that love to others all around me.

293

GROWING FAITH

Faith has to work twenty-four hours a day in and through us, or we perish.
Alcoholics Anonymous, *page 16*

Faith cannot be imposed. Think of it as a seed to be cultivated. Seeds planted into the earth produce fruits in time if watered and nourished as needed. With a lot of patience, time accomplishes its creation work. Even a small seed of faith is bound to grow, provided it receives the appropriate nutrients. Our interior garden needs great care to cultivate faith. Faith needs space to grow and can be crowded out by the weeds of fear, doubt, and uncertainty.

Trusting the process of life is a big leap of faith that is sometimes challenging to practice. During difficult moments, faith can falter—I might not feel it, thinking that it has disappeared. Sometimes life's torments can blind me to faith. When this happens, my confidence in universal principles may slip, and my inner peace can be lost. This is when I need to ask a Power greater than myself to intervene. No matter what my concept of God, it can certainly relieve any overwhelming pain or loneliness. Ask for help to restore your faith, unifying your body, soul and spirit.

~~~~~

Living my life can be viewed as an act of faith. Faith is a grace, often initiated through individuals sharing their spiritual journeys.

UNITY OR DISUNITY?

There are different kinds of unity. There is perfect unity. There is unbreakable unity. There is unshakable unity. They all guide us toward permanent unity.
C.A. NewsGram, 2nd Quarter 1997

Unity: (noun) Harmony; the state of being one.

I must always protect and strive for unity. Without it, Cocaine Anonymous may weaken or, worse, perish. If unity does not exist in our home groups or even in my specific home group, it will not exist in our District, Area, or any other functions of C.A.

Unity begins in the home group. A Fellowship is only as strong as its groups' unity. groups are like the spokes of a wheel; if a few spokes are loose, the wheel will wobble. In some Areas, the wheel is wobbling. When a group and its members practice the Traditions, unity is formed. Without unity, there is little hope.

The Traditions have grown out of trial and error to help us with the problems of living and working together. The Traditions also correspond to relating with ourselves, others, and a Higher Power. They measure our progress as individuals, as groups, and at all levels of service.

Continued unity is dependent upon God-consciousness. My personal recovery depends on unity.

~~~~~

Unity permeates all aspects of the C.A. program, especially in Fellowship service work. I will strive to achieve unity in my own program and at all levels of service.

LIVING IN THE SOLUTION

We wish to assure you that there is a solution and that recovery is possible. It begins with abstinence and continues with practicing the Twelve Steps of recovery, one day at a time. Our program, the Twelve Steps of Cocaine Anonymous, is the means by which we move from the problem of drug addiction to the solution of recovery.
We Can Recover (C.A. Meeting Format Reading)

Bit by bit, after working the Steps and staying committed to this way of life, I have handed my life over to God as I understand God. Upon awakening each morning, the first thing I do is ask God for a sober day. I also ask that God's will, not mine, be done. I know what I might want to be doing today, but if God's will is different, I will be doing something else.

I show God I am willing to live this life by my *actions*, not by my *words*. For me, that means having a home group, doing service, praying in the morning, praying at night, writing a gratitude list, phoning newcomers, praying for people's health and happiness when they annoy me, journaling, and reading literature. I am always alert to these actions and do my best to stay rooted in the moment. I am aware of what's happening right now—not in yesterday or next week. I avoid gossip (what he said to them, why she did that)—such a vast change from my old approach.

I stay vigilant, watchful that I am doing the right things. I spend time at night, or whenever needed, to look at where I have been selfish or self-centered, dishonest or arrogant because, believe me, not a day goes by where I could not have done better or I haven't been selfish in some way or another. I know it's okay to make mistakes, provided I learn from them. My aim is to practice the program principles in every aspect of my life, not just in my meetings. Since I am far from perfect at this (just ask my sponsor!), I simply do my best. I take on service work wherever possible, in whatever capacity needed, and I have become a student of the Traditions and Concepts. Sponsoring others when asked, I endeavor to share all I have been taught. This may seem like a tall order, but, truly, it's very simple. Give it a go, start today. A wonderful life is available as a result of the process.

~~~~~

Remember, working this program to the best of my ability by no means resembles perfection. Part of the process entails learning that I will always have more growth and spiritual development ahead.

TARGETING YOUR GOALS

I finally have a goal in life that answers all my questions. I know I don't need to arrive at the goal before I can start living, but I have a direction for every next step I take. The goal in my life today is to be of service to my Higher Power and to others.
Hope, Faith & Courage Volume II, page 25

Being in recovery for a while has taught me the value of setting goals. Certainly, we're told to do this thing one day at a time and live in the present, but that doesn't mean God doesn't want us to dream great dreams, make plans for the future, and aspire to achieve! On the contrary, passively waiting for "the good life" is old behavior. Each day, *this* day, we can set our sights on reaching a goal, and we can take a step or two toward that goal. There is a saying that a journey of a thousand miles begins with a single step. By setting my goals, I have taken that first step toward fulfilling my dreams.

Once you decide to pursue a goal, enthusiasm is released. The word enthusiasm is derived from two Greek words, "en theos," meaning "in God." When a decision and a commitment are made to reach for your goal, the power of God within you is released. The fact is this: the moment one definitely commits oneself, then God moves too. Windows open and events occur that could never be foreseen. Remember to choose your goal based on God's ability rather than just your own!

The most important thing to remember is that reaching a goal is never as important as the progress you make toward it. It's far too easy for most of us to miss the moment's richness because our sights are on a particular journey's end. If the goal you set for yourself evolves into a totally different outcome achieved, just remember, "God's will, not mine, be done."

~~~~

Spend some time today with pen and paper writing down a goals list. Choose one short-term and one long-term goal from your list and make a commitment to pursue them. Invite God to assist in the process.

LEAVING CRIME BEHIND

We were people who took from others and abused friendships all of our lives. We had no concept of doing anything for anyone without the thought of some kind of reward. By the sheer grace of our Higher Powers, we have found several ways of unlearning such behavior in the program.

Being of Service (C.A. Pamphlet)

Very early in my recovery I heard someone say, "If you have any clean time as a result of this Fellowship and you are not giving something back, you are nothing but a thief."

I had spent years stealing from everyone who was ever close to me, so this statement cut straight to the bone. I did not want to be a crook any longer.

I jumped into service at my home group. Making coffee and cleaning up after the meeting enabled me to feel "a part of." From this simple act, I have learned to support and think of other people in all parts of my life, both in and out of C.A.

Today, for me, sponsorship is the most obvious means of contributing. After all, what good is a spiritual experience if I am the only one who benefits from it? The saying "you can't keep it unless you give it away" is 100% true. Sponsorship is simply guiding others through the Steps. I enjoy helping another addict or alcoholic, giving away what was readily given to me.

I love serving my Fellowship at many different levels. More importantly, this gift of service has expanded, and now I take it with me wherever I go, in all parts of my life, on a daily basis.

~~~~~

Now that I've discovered the joy of giving, how many ways can I endeavor to serve my fellow man today—program members and non-program members alike?

A TIME TO INVENTORY

I make sure I do a Step Ten inventory every night. I have found that over the years I have a shorter list all the time. God has removed some of my defects and made me very aware of the others. I take time every morning to thank Him for another day to do His will, and every night I pray for those still suffering that they may find Him, too. I also have a better understanding of others and myself today.
Hope, Faith & Courage Volume II, *page 136*

When I finally made it to Step Ten and started incorporating its practice and wisdom into my program, I was quite unclear about the actual application involved in properly working the Step. I had received ample guidance from my sponsor and others, but I was almost immediately struck by the diverse opinions as to how this Step should be worked.

Some seem to prefer taking this Step each evening, either when they get home from work or just before bed. We are asked to review our conduct during the day to evaluate our progress in recovery. According to most, we also congratulate ourselves on what we did right that day. Included, of course, is recognition of any amends to be made, along with a plan to *promptly* take care of them. This may mean dealing with feelings, being honest with someone, apologizing, or setting right any wrongs. If we are open to God's guidance and honest with ourselves, we will know what to do. We have begun a process we can trust, a process to continually support us in our growth.

Others take Step Ten each morning, perhaps as a part of a daily meditation practice, before the activities, distractions and business of the day take hold. During this time, we are open and receptive to our feelings. We may want to ask: What's going on with me? How should I lovingly and responsibly take care of myself today? Then, we listen for an intuitive thought. Still others share that they are more casual with this Step, trusting their own program and Higher Power enough to know when Step Ten is needed. This could, conceivably, be multiple times throughout the day or evening, or not at all on other days.

I have tried Step Ten many different ways, with varying results. I am clear about the fact that what works for me may not be right for the next person. Personally, I have found great relief in looking at the positive side as well, including my goals regarding Step work, service commitments, and recovery for the immediate future.

~~~~~

Step Ten means taking inventory, admitting when we are wrong, and making amends in order to live a life of the Spirit. The key is to make an effort to do an inventory of some sort at regular intervals, rectifying any harms as best I can.

LITTLE PRAYERS

As we go through the day we pause, when agitated or doubtful, and ask for the right thought or action. We constantly remind ourselves we are no longer running the show, humbly saying to ourselves many times each day "Thy will be done."
Alcoholics Anonymous, *pages 87-88*

We learn how to pray in recovery using lots of different kinds of prayers (Serenity Prayer, Third-Step Prayer, etc.). Meditation is stressed as a means of advancing our spirituality. All are very important and key suggestions on our recovery paths.

However, I've discovered that for me, it's the little prayers that mean the most— living in the present moment and taking time to appreciate what's around me right here and now. One day, I was grumbling to my spouse about having to wait for the light to turn green and what a waste of time it was. She turned to me and said, "Well, instead of complaining about it, why don't you use this time to say a little prayer instead." What a novel idea! These days, I welcome the momentary delays at stoplights and other similar settings to open a line of communication with God.

~~~~~

What other "wasted" minutes during the day can I utilize to pause and connect spiritually? Can I find and then cultivate an ongoing link with the God of my understanding?

THE PROBLEM HAS BEEN REMOVED

That is the miracle of it. We are not fighting it, neither are we avoiding temptation. We feel as though we had been placed in a position of neutrality—safe and protected. We have not even sworn off. Instead, the problem has been removed. It does not exist for us. We are neither cocky nor are we afraid. That is our experience. That is how we react so long as we keep in fit spiritual condition.

Alcoholic Anonymous, *page 85*

I need to always remember that when the *Big Book* tells me the problem (my compulsion to use) has been removed, it does not mean my *disease* has been removed. The disease, although it may be in remission, is still present. From what I have been told, it always will be.

When I have an infection, the doctor gives me a prescription for a ten-day supply of antibiotics. Soon I start feeling better. After six days, I decide to quit taking the prescribed medication because my symptoms have dissipated. Need I wonder why, shortly thereafter, the infection returns, often with a terrible vengeance?

As the result of the recovery process, what I have been given is a daily reprieve from the horrors of my addiction, along with a set of very user-friendly spiritual tools to pick up and employ whenever I need them. If, at any time, I discontinue utilizing my prescription for recovery—the Power I discovered through the Twelve Steps—and choose to ignore program suggestions, I am subject to fall back quickly and deeply into its grip. Just because I am free from mind-altering substances doesn't mean I'm in a state of being recovered. In fact, the only state I am in is a state of grace which God has granted me.

~~~~

God, please help me continue to do whatever is necessary to enjoy recovery from my addictions. May I remember that I cannot remain disease-free and grow without You, the Twelve Steps, and the C.A. Fellowship in my life.

SOMEBODY'S GOT TO DO IT

C.A., as such, ought never be organized; but we may create service boards or committees directly responsible to those they serve.
C.A. Tradition Nine

"Cocaine Anonymous is not organized in the formal or political sense. There are no governing officers, no rules or regulations, no dues or fees. However, the need for services to addicts throughout the world is very important to the Fellowship." (*C.A. World Service Manual*, 2013 Edition, page 11.)

Service boards and committees are necessary in our Fellowship on many different levels. Have you ever wondered who maintains and prints your local meeting lists? Who answers your help line? Someone certainly has to make sure the telephone bill gets paid.

Have you had the opportunity to attend any C.A. conventions or workshops? What about recovery dances or potlucks? Obviously, these things don't just "spring up" of their own accord. A lot of work and planning is involved to bring these events to fruition.

Various jobs need to be performed at the Group, District, Area, Regional, and World levels. Once you have established a firm foundation in your sobriety, learning about C.A.'s service structure is imperative to becoming an involved Fellowship member. Not every person is destined or cut out for every service position that is available, but any responsible addict in our program should at least have an understanding of how the system works. The easiest way to do that is to get involved.

~~~~~

Am I informed about my Group's service structure? Have I participated in either C.A. District or C.A. Area activities? Have I considered how stretching my horizons in service work might help me to grow on a spiritual level? Today let me be open to participating more fully in the functional necessities of carrying our message to the addict who still suffers.

I ASKED

> *I love Steps Ten, Eleven, and Twelve. If I'm watching myself on a daily basis, cleaning up my side immediately and asking God for help, it is absolutely impossible for me not to change.*
>
> Hope, Faith & Courage Volume II, *page 185*

Many times along my recovery path through the Twelve Steps, I have the chance to ask God for help and guidance. In my prayers, as the *Big Book* outlines (especially the Third-Step Prayer and the Seventh-Step Prayer), I ask for God's guidance, wisdom and freedom from the bondage of self.

I have to pose questions to myself in the inventory process as I start looking at my actions and character defects which have been blocking me from God. I again request God's will for me in Step Eleven. Later it is suggested that I petition God in my morning meditation, inquiring what I can do for the still-suffering addict. All these requests to God along my journey through recovery only serve to strengthen my program, my relationship with my Higher Power, and my self-understanding as I trudge the road of happy destiny.

It is amazing to now possess the ability to ask for God's help, knowing in my heart that my requests will not only be heard, but will be acted upon in God's time.

~~~~~

Praying for ability to ask for God's help when needed, especially when I'm unsure of the next right thing to do, should become an automatic reaction. May I step out in faith, knowing that even if I make bad choices, mistakes are a huge opportunity for me to learn and grow.

SPIRITUAL PROGRESS

Cocaine Anonymous is a spiritual program, not a religious one.
We claim spiritual progress rather than spiritual perfection.
Hope, Faith & Courage, *page 209*

I am grateful for my sponsor, who regularly reminds me that the key to my recovery is continued spiritual development. The first time I worked Step Two, I didn't have any problems believing in God. However, I had no clue about how to craft a personal relationship with a God about whom I had no understanding. Step Three opened the door and set me on an exploration, the likes of which I had never dreamed. As promised, by the time I reached Step Twelve, a spiritual awakening had occurred in my life.

Today, not only do I have a relationship with God, my understanding of God and spirituality has changed enormously. Growing and deepening, my spiritual connection evolved with many unexpected twists and turns along the way. Much help ensued from listening to others share about their spiritual journeys. I came to understand and appreciate how each of us navigates a very unique and personal Eleventh-Step process, perfect and beautiful for each individual.

My job lies in the seeking because spiritual progress does not have a finish line. In early sobriety, I couldn't understand it when people would say, "The longer I stay sober, the less I know." It didn't make any sense then, but now I comprehend what it means—the longer I stick around, the more I see how much there is to learn!

~~~~~

No matter what kind of issues life throws at me, my sponsor will always tell me the same thing: "Well, I believe the best solution for you here would be *more spiritual development*." Funny, but the answer always seems to fit!

FELLOWSHIP, RECOVERY, AND SERVICE

The wonderful thing is that for me today, I couldn't think of a better way to live, and I thank God, Cocaine Anonymous, and the wonderful members of our Fellowship—those I know, those I hope to know, and those who came before me—for the opportunity to live life, have a life, and value that life.
Hope, Faith & Courage Volume II, *page 45*

Recently I attended a retreat where the moderator said, "Each of us must find our own means to live life God's way." I am convinced that God's way is the way of service.

I came to Cocaine Anonymous broken, useless, and no longer desiring to live. Through the Fellowship, I discovered spiritual principles which could arrest my addiction. By living these recovery principles, I grasped the true significance of the Cocaine Anonymous Fellowship. This intertwined matrix of Fellowship, recovery, and service is the process by which I can return to the place where I am whole. Then at that very meeting point, recovery and Fellowship intersect. The precise point of intersection is marked by the miracle of service. When one lit candle is used to ignite another candle, both candles burn brighter. A dark room gets lighter.

So it is with our Fellowship. All service work, at every level, facilitates a single greater and higher purpose—to bring one addict together with another to share and carry the C.A. message. Thus, the spiritual sharing of experience, strength, and hope between them brings a new candle to light.

~~~~~

May the Fellowship's glow continue to draw addicts from every dark corner of the world. I pray that the glow of my own miraculous recovery will attract those in need of a similar miracle.

STARTING MEETINGS

Have you ever thought about how a C.A. meeting gets started? . . . In every case, someone made a decision to help Cocaine Anonymous grow by starting a meeting.
Yes, *You* Can Start a C.A. Meeting (C.A. Pamphlet)

Not until I had been sober for several months did it ever occur to me that meetings were started, organized, and then ultimately supported by the very people who attended them. I had naively assumed some master planner was responsible for the operations of C.A. and each of its events/gatherings. Slowly I became aware that a group of committed Fellowship members at each meeting seemed to be responsible.

Shortly thereafter, I was present when our group held elections for a couple of service positions, and I realized I could (and should!) become one of those committed members. My sponsor supported this idea, reminding me that service was one of the key components of our personal recovery, and I had to give back in order to keep what was given to me.

I acquired a service commitment at the meeting and expanded my involvement from simply attending the meeting to helping keep it alive, vibrant, and available to carry the C.A. message to any newcomer who joined us. Gradually, I got to know different members of the group, old and new. At one meeting, an old-timer who returned to celebrate a sobriety milestone, 23 or 24 years sober at the time, spoke about how he was one of the original six group members. He remembered that they were nervous about taking a risk to start a new meeting no one might ever attend—afraid they might offend members of the main C.A. meeting which happened to be on the same night but across town. Since then, this meeting had grown to over a hundred members, making the sobriety celebration especially meaningful.

Not long after that, several of us started another meeting on a different night. That meeting, too, has ripened into a successful, thriving group, from which other meetings have blossomed.

~~~~

Am I aware that God uses people to do His work? May I be a channel for implementing God's will, especially mindful about our legacy of starting meetings, supporting them, and watching them flourish.

APPEARANCES CAN BE DECEIVING

*Could we still say the whole thing was nothing but a mass of electrons, created
out of nothing, meaning nothing, whirling on to a destiny of nothingness?*
Alcoholics Anonymous, *page 54*

One day I was sitting down, drinking bottled water. I started to read the label,
which listed the nutritional value of its contents. As I scrutinized the list, I was
surprised to see every single item showed zero percent. Afterwards, I looked at
that bottle and said to myself, "If I didn't know better, I would think there is
nothing in this bottle and this water has *no* value to me whatsoever."

The truth, as I've learned from the time I was a very young child, is that we all
need water to survive. The composition of the human body itself is mostly water.

This reminded me of my early days in Cocaine Anonymous. I had such a hard time
believing in a Higher Power that I couldn't see, hear, touch, taste or feel. I didn't
know then how gravely I needed Him in my life. But just like that colorless,
odorless, tasteless liquid we so critically need to maintain physical health, my
spiritual well-being depends on God's involvement. Thanks to the program, I've
learned to add this vital ingredient to my life each and every day.

~~~~

God, may I remember to continually nourish myself spiritually on a daily basis, just
as I do physically. In my addiction I was spiritually parched. Help me avail myself of
Your thirst-quenching power.

WORKING STEP TEN DAILY

When mistakes are made, working the Tenth Step affords the opportunity to clean them up right away and to keep clarity of mind.
Hope, Faith & Courage Volume II, *page 106*

Living day-to-day with my traits, good and bad, is God's gift of humanity to me. I am not perfect, will never be perfect, nor will I ever live with others who are perfect. I now understand that God loves us just the way we are: imperfect. A composite of Steps Four through Nine that must be practiced daily, Step Ten is all about minimizing my bad behaviors and nurturing my good ones, taking my imperfect self into the world, and trying to align my actions with God's will for me on a daily basis.

To succeed, I have to exercise humility and restraint in my dealings with others. When agitated, I have to pause and seek guidance. I need to do this as things are happening. Often times, it's not possible for me to seek immediate guidance from my sponsor or another C.A. member; I must do the best I can to invite God into the situation and operate as I believe God would prefer. This is where I grow— performing on-the-spot self-appraisal and trying to act appropriately. Am I being selfish, self-centered, self-righteous, resentful, or dishonest? What am I afraid of? Step Ten is less of a reflective activity for me than it is proactive. In the here-and-now, Step Ten calls me to practice a code of love and tolerance.

Make no mistake, evening reflection is still an important part of Step Ten for me, simply because my on-the-spot practice of self-appraisal is far from automatic. During my evening reflection, I am also able to acknowledge when I've done well. When I have been out of line, I try to correct those things as quickly as possible. Any amends must include a sincere effort to change the offending behavior. More growth for me!

~~~~

God, please help me to watch for selfishness, dishonesty, resentment, and fear. Please help me to direct my thoughts resolutely toward someone I can help. May I remember to practice love and tolerance so that all these things become easier.

PRAYER AND MEDITATION

My belief strengthened as time went by. Through prayer and
meditation, I quietly found a better relationship with my God.
Hope, Faith & Courage Volume II, *page 88*

Prayer and meditation in the most traditional sense have not consistently been a strong part of my program. Because I was told I could have a Higher Power of my own understanding, I had no ritual to follow as a method of prayer and connection. Initially I thought I must be doing Step Eleven wrong. My experience has proven otherwise.

In Step Two, I learned to recognize what I have to be grateful for by doing a gratitude list every day, acknowledging that it all came from my Higher Power. The simple practice of making the list and saying, "Thank you," gave me a new spiritual awareness in my life, even in places I hadn't thought to look. My sponsor called that process prayer, so that's how it started for me. It continued as I talked to God during my normal daily activities. Out loud or silently (it didn't seem to make any difference), my approach provided my conscious attempt to connect. At times, I realized I must look like a crazy person, always talking to myself. My sponsor asked, "Does it work?" It must, because I feel connected to my Higher Power.

I can only come up with three absolutes about my understanding of my Higher Power. What I receive is direction, strength, and comfort. Direction as I seek the path of God's will. Strength to walk forward on that course. Comfort and peace because the direction and strength are constantly revealed to me (if I seek them). My examination of how my Higher Power guides, strengthens, and comforts me gives me the impetus to study prayer and meditation in further detail.

~~~~~

The daily practice of prayer and meditation is vastly beneficial, no matter the means. It opens my connection with my Higher Power, which has evolved over time in the program. I seek to do God's will and ask for continued guidance, strength, and comfort.

TOLERANCE

God has abundantly supplied this world with fine doctors, psychologists, and practitioners of various kinds. Do not hesitate to take your health problems to such persons.
Alcoholics Anonymous, page 133

A large number of addicts also suffer from other mental illness. This illness may take the form of chronic depression, anxiety, or other problems. Many of us seek help outside of the Fellowship for these illnesses, the symptoms of which may impair our ability to function even in recovery. Innumerable C.A. members take medication for various conditions without compromising their sobriety one bit. As Fellowship members, we are not qualified in any way, shape, or form to give medical advice, nor should we pass judgment on what prescription drugs someone else is or should be taking. We leave that to their professionals and remember that God is with them always, just like God is with us always.

The solution that helps us with addiction may not work for other illnesses, so it is vital that we remember to practice tolerance, even if we do not understand issues which may be affecting our program friends. It is not ours to figure out or comment upon. Just as we hoped people would be empathetic of our addiction and its manifestations, there are members among us wishing the same for another condition from which they are trying to recover.

At some level, these other challenges are part of people's anonymity in their own programs. Our place is to honor and respect each individual wherever they are in the process.

~~~~~

Today, I remind myself that love and tolerance of others is essential in my recovery. This attitude is key to my own level of peace and serenity.

RIGHT-SIZED

> In Step Seven, I humbly asked God to remove my shortcomings.
> I found that I could neither wish nor will these things away. I
> had to be willing and follow through with the remaining Steps.
> Hope, Faith & Courage Volume II, page 167

Referenced often in both the *Big Book* and the *Twelve and Twelve*, the notion of humility is a binding thread throughout the Step-taking process. I must admit, early on, humility was a spiritual principle which I didn't readily understand. However, given all the emphasis being placed on this quality, I knew it must rank very highly on the recovery importance scale. I recognized quickly that Fellowship members with any length of clean time all practiced levels of humility foreign to them pre-recovery. As I followed in their footsteps, my experience with humility as a personal trait began to grow.

The *Twelve Steps and Twelve Traditions* (page 58) defines humility as simply a clear recognition of who I really am, followed by a sincere attempt to become what I could be. Some say humility means reaching my own right size. For me, humility exists in the middle ground between two extremes: grandiosity and ego gone wild versus the intense shame and guilt related to the wreckage of my past. I must remember that being humble does not mean being meek and timid. Rather, it means being completely true to myself and my Higher Power.

Thus, in Step Seven, I am required to *humbly* ask *God* to remove my shortcomings. I cannot do this by self-will, as sincere as my determination may be. The Seventh-Step Prayer makes good sense as written in *Alcoholics Anonymous* (page 76): by asking God to have *all* of me, "good *and* bad," I am able to find that mid-point sector leading to my right size.

~~~~~

If I am truly humble, I clearly understand that I am neither *greater* than nor *less* than any other human being.

HAVING HAD A SPIRITUAL AWAKENING

Having had a spiritual awakening as the result of these Steps, we tried to carry this message to addicts, and to practice these principles in all our affairs.
C.A. Step Twelve

Alcoholics Anonymous (page 77) states we should try to fit ourselves to be of maximum service to God and the people around us. The Steps are in order for a reason.

The sunlight of the Spirit was always shining down on me. Trouble was, I couldn't experience it because I spent my whole life building a brick wall around myself. Every time I was dishonest, cheated, stole, or treated someone badly, another brick was added to the wall. The Steps are the tools I use to tear down the wall so that the sunlight can come shining through permanently.

Before I can grow, I have to realize I can't solve my problems alone (Step One). By this admission, I arrive at a place where I can become willing to believe a Higher Power can help (Steps Two and Three). My willingness and belief give me courage and strength to make a moral inventory to share with an understanding person (Steps Four and Five).

My inventory shows me that my troubles are almost always of my own making. I suddenly realize it's me who needs to change, not the world (Steps Six and Seven). I am then able to see value in righting the wrongs I have done to others (Steps Eight and Nine). Formally working Steps One through Nine gives me the experience I need to work all the Steps on a daily basis. I take responsibility for my own actions and no longer blame everyone else for my problems. Turning to my Higher Power each day, asking that *His* will be done, not mine, helps enormously (Steps Ten and Eleven).

At Step Twelve, I have arrived at the place where I can be more useful to God and the people around me, just as the *Big Book* promises.

~~~~~

My spiritual awakening is guaranteed through working the Twelve Steps. As I continue, I learn what it means to have serenity in my life.

BETTER THAN THE NINTH-STEP PROMISES

Continued to take personal inventory and when we were wrong promptly admitted it.
C.A. Step Ten

My problem, as I have learned, is my disease. This problem manifested itself in many ways—addiction, alcoholism, lying, stealing, and trampling on the lives of others—all in self-centered pursuit of immediate gratification. Certain skills were required to maintain this lifestyle—skills considered assets when used under different circumstances.

In the beginning, who among us knew what wonders of sobriety were ahead? After experiencing the reality of the Ninth-Step promises in our lives, who could have guessed recovery's greatest promises were nestled in the Tenth Step? That's right, the Tenth Step. Far from being a "maintenance step," Step Ten is very much about growth. The *Big Book* warns that I must continue to enlarge my spiritual life, and Step Ten is just the tool. It's where I must live day by day. Being prepared to practice Step Ten means I am armed with knowledge concerning my character defects. I am reasonably willing to have them removed. I am familiar with my actions in and reactions to the circumstances surrounding daily life. Having taken the first nine Steps, my side of the street is fairly clean.

In Step Ten, *I really begin emerging as the person God would have me be.* Sure, I did a lot of preparatory work prior to this Step, but Step Ten is the point at which I truly have the opportunity to begin fulfilling God's vision for me. Through the Steps, I identified and learned about the many character traits with which I am equipped, some good, some not so great. After years in recovery, much change in my behavior has occurred. However, I still possess every single one of the character traits in some form or another. Here's the deal. On any given day, a defect can be an asset, and vice versa. By continuing my personal inventory on a daily basis and promptly admitting when I am wrong, these character traits of mine are monitored closely and, for the most part, utilized well.

~~~~~

I believe Step Ten is the gateway to two particularly preeminent program promises: through applying Step Ten's spiritual principles, sanity in my life has returned, *and* the problems related to my addiction have been removed.

A COMMON SOLUTION WHICH BINDS US

Unity is a common bond that transcends all differences. We've discovered no matter how different our circumstances or the paths that brought us here, we all suffer from the same disease: addiction.
Unity (C.A. Pamphlet)

Newcomers arrive at C.A. broken, baffled, sick, and full of despair. Health is precarious, lives are shattered, and once precious relationships seem likely to be permanently ruined. Some of us have had physical problems to complicate recovery, and still others have had mental and psychological troubles, all as a result of our disease. While all of us may have traveled along different paths and through assorted circumstances, addiction finally becomes our master. Many who reach C.A. have some varied state of what the *Big Book* terms "incomprehensible demoralization."

This common reality brings members in the C.A. Fellowship together, providing continued strength as recovery is embraced and as the path through the Steps commences. Unity begins to unfold by the shared suffering that serves as a cornerstone of recovery, and it grows as we collectively find the solution to our drug and alcohol problems.

In the midst of my despair, I have met others who truly understand my pain. These people seem to have experienced something which has graced them with a new life and provided them with continued strength and hope. As they share these lessons with me and I ultimately join them on the path to recovery, I come to a new, profound realization: the promised spiritual awakening found in the Steps, experienced individually and collectively, is ultimately the element which binds us as one.

~~~~~

Let me be grateful today for the Fellowship of Cocaine Anonymous and for the common spiritual solution which binds us. May I consistently appreciate the life I have been given and the privilege it is to be a C.A. member.

DON'T QUIT BEFORE THE MIRACLE

I couldn't for the life of me shut the meeting down when "one" person wanted it. So we carried on.
C.A. NewsGram, 4th Quarter 2003

Earlier this month will mark fifteen years of continued sobriety for me. You all have been a part of that milestone. The meetings here in my small town had fallen off to almost nothing. In fact, only one other person was showing up consistently—a newcomer with eleven months. He is a low-bottom drunk and addict. He surrendered, went to meetings, and ultimately became sold on the contents of the *Big Book*. He had heard many of your stories—either by word of mouth or from my speaker tape library. I did not particularly like him. He irritated me. I became convinced I had done my duty to C.A. by keeping the doors open for this last eleven years here in my town. My mind told me they (the local C.A. Fellowship) didn't want the meeting any longer. I made up my mind to close down our one meeting.

Last night, as I approached the meeting hall, there he sat, in the cold, waiting for me. I noticed another really disheveled looking man standing to the side, but he did not join us in the meeting. After we opened the meeting and shared for about ten minutes, I heard a knock. It was the man from outside. He said that he was "looking for a meeting." He said that it took him that long to get up enough nerve to come and ask us if we could help him, whether he could join us. He worked every day and by the time he got his check, it was already credited out except for fifty dollars, which he smoked up immediately. I told him we had been waiting for him, that we had nearly closed the doors, but God kept the two of us coming so our legacy could carry on and our hope, faith and courage might save another.

~~~~~

Imagine, I almost quit before the miracle. I realize now that everything is a lot bigger than me or my feelings. I have a purpose: whenever anyone reaches out for the hand of C.A., I have a duty to be there.

TERMINAL UNIQUENESS

Though we are different, we are the same.
Regardless of the author, we share the same story.
Unity (C.A. Pamphlet)

When I came into C.A., I had this sense of being dramatically different from the people I met here. It was a classic illustration of the phenomenon I have heard called "terminal uniqueness," a plight suffered by many newcomers. I didn't have tattoos or piercings. I was older than most. I drank and did my drugs differently. I had a higher bottom than some. My addiction lasted a shorter period of time. I never had legal problems or even health issues as a result of my using.

Very early on, I heard that my sense of being different would be the very thing to kill me. I kept asking myself what I could possibly hope to learn from any of the other members. I was warned that unless I could see similarities with these people, I wouldn't be able to see the very truth about the nature of my disease. I would be unable to seek the solution being offered through the C.A. program. I stuck around because I did hear solutions which were attractive enough to consider—perhaps on some future day if I could ever find members more like myself.

Then one day at a speaker meeting, I heard a young, pierced, tattooed lady share her story. I was stunned. Her life had been dramatically different than mine, yet she described exactly how I felt at that moment. The instruction to listen for the similarities and not look for the differences suddenly hit home. The things others had been saying gradually started to make sense, and I no longer felt alone. The crusade of me versus them was over. In fact, much to my surprise, I realized I wanted so much to belong. It was finally time for me to become a member of the Fellowship.

~~~~

May I set aside old ideas so I might have an open mind to experience the newness of this day. I am grateful God has provided the resources for me to recognize how much we are all the same on the inside. Please let me always be mindful of the similarities, not the differences.

LIVING IN THE MOMENT

The thought of making a pledge never to use again can be discouraging. We can stay clean and sober one day at a time and if necessary, one hour or even one minute at a time.

Tools of Recovery (C.A. Pamphlet)

My counselor in a drug treatment facility once told me that I was "future tripping." I had never heard that term before, but I knew exactly what she meant. I was so worried about what my life would be like after my release that I couldn't focus on getting the most out of my treatment—what was in front of me right then.

Our slogan "one day at a time" embodies just that. All we have is this minute. We have all made mistakes in one form or another many times throughout our lives, and chances are we will again. Living in the past or projecting into the future deprives us of the opportunity to experience right now. In this moment, we can choose to stay sober. We can take action to ensure our sobriety. We can enjoy our freedom from addiction and participate in our own lives.

~~~~~

I can focus on the present moment because that is all any of us really have. I am grateful for the choice to stay sober today.

COFFEE ANYONE?

> They told me to make coffee, and I said, "How many pots?" They said, "Chair a meeting!" Well, I was scared, but I was more scared not to, so I did it anyway. They said, "Get a sponsor!" I found a sponsor. . . . They said, "Get involved in service!" and so I did. Most importantly, they said, "Work the Steps," and I started the wonderful, beautiful process of uncovering, discovering, and recovering.
>
> Hope, Faith & Courage Volume II, page 60

What does making coffee have to do with freedom from cocaine and all other mind-altering substances? What does chairing a meeting, getting involved in service, or even working the Steps have to do with that freedom? Everything!

My experience has shown me that the willingness to take directions is a strong indicator of one's willingness to go to any lengths to gain victory over addiction. When I have to ask for help from another who has walked the path before me, and then connect with that person on an intimate level, I begin to let my guard down and become teachable. Later on, I realize that their helping me actually helps them also.

As I take action as suggested to be useful and of service to the Fellowship, I begin to experience a new behavior and a new consciousness developing within me. If I clean house, trust God and help others, I can be certain I am following a proven path to freedom: freedom from my compulsion to drug and drink, freedom from the bondage of myself, freedom from fear, freedom from my past and its wreckage, freedom to select my own Higher Power and then to relate to that Higher Power as I choose.

Such fundamental liberties were inconceivable before I found recovery. And to think that it could all start by simply making a pot of coffee.

~~~~

I appreciate the many freedoms manifested by learning to follow direction. May I always remain willing and teachable to continue dwelling in the free state of recovery.

NOVEMBER

A VISION FOR YOU

Most C.A. members owe their sobriety to the fact that someone else was willing to share a great gift with them.
Choosing Your Sponsor (C.A. Pamphlet)

Our book is meant to be suggestive only. We realize we know only a little. God will constantly disclose more to you and to us. Ask him in your morning meditation what you can do each day for the man who is still sick. The answers will come, if your own house is in order. But obviously you cannot transmit something you haven't got. See to it that your relationship with Him is right, and great events will come to pass for you and countless others. This is the Great Fact for us.

Abandon yourself to God as you understand God. Admit your faults to Him and to your fellows. Clear away the wreckage of your past. Give freely of what you find and join us. We shall be with you in the Fellowship of the Spirit, and you will surely meet some of us as you trudge the Road of Happy Destiny.

May God bless you and keep you—until then. (*Alcoholics Anonymous*, page 164.)

~~~~~

How many times have we heard *A Vision For You* read at a meeting? Do we ever take time to think about what this says and means? Spend a few moments today reading it slowly. Write down your thoughts about how it speaks to you. Share your writing with another program member.

LIVE AND LET LIVE

My sponsor also told me I had to get out of the results business,
that all I had to do was take the Steps and leave the rest to God.
Hope, Faith & Courage Volume II, *page 65*

As I enjoy life today, clean and sober, I am so much more aware of how I want, wish, or hope for a close family member or friend to recover—to be relieved from their hardship like I have been. But one thing I have learned in this program is to remember to ask the question, "What is God's will?" For others, for me, and for us in any situation? We all have our own roads to travel, lessons to learn, lives to touch. To live and let live is allowing those I love to travel their personal pathways, hardships and joys alike.

This doesn't mean I can't share my program with others when appropriate. We are encouraged to *carry* the message. But nowhere does is say we can, or must, *deliver* it. With peace and serenity, I can be a real-life example to those I want to help the most.

~~~~~

God, please show me your will. What is your plan for the journeys of those I love? For my journey? Please allow me to know when to stand back and when to jump in, to know when to live and let live.

NEW FRIENDS

Unity preserves our personal recovery, our reunited families, and our rediscovered dreams.
Unity (C.A. Pamphlet)

Toward the end of my using, the loneliness was overwhelming. This crushing emotion stemmed primarily from innumerable self-centered fears. I had no one close to me. Everyone had been pushed aside by my drug use. Separated from my loved ones, I belonged nowhere. I was bewildered by my inability to stop using and resigned to an isolated life of addiction.

Today things are very different. Having surrendered to the program of Cocaine Anonymous and been guided into good habits by my sponsor, I have a new life! By working the Twelve Steps and making them part of my life, I experience a freedom I never believed was possible. I am surrounded by lots of real friends in my home group and know now what belonging means. Without the need to use drugs, I have a spiritual center in my life.

Many of my friends in C.A. are, perhaps, people with whom I would never have associated. You see, I thought of myself as unique, even special, until I discovered that other addicts shared a similar past as mine. Then I was able to I connect. I began to understand the solution in recovery works for *all* of us.

Today, I am blessed with a changed attitude, allowing me a whole host of new friends. C.A.'s unity transcends any and all of our differences.

~~~~~

I need never feel alone, simply by embracing similarities and striving for Fellowship unity. I pray for continued new friendships, expanding my ability to share program solutions with others I meet on this path.

HAPPINESS, HOPE & HARMONY

> *When I first got there and everybody was laughing and cutting up,*
> *I thought, "What the hell is so funny? If you knew where I just*
> *came from, you wouldn't be laughing." I didn't know that they did*
> *know where I had just come from, that they had been there, too.*
> Hope, Faith & Courage Volume II, *pages 175-176*

In our addiction, we see *the world* as all messed up. Nobody understands, nobody cares or listens to us. It's not *our* fault things are out of whack. That's what we tell everyone. Deep down inside, fear has a grip, but we hide our anxieties, so no one will see them.

Today we can appreciate the world's light and beauty. Recovery has given us a new sense of well-being. Through the self-examination process of working the Steps, we dare to ask the questions we thought we'd never ever want to ask, let alone know the answers to. We listen to our Fellowship, trusting that they do, in fact, understand us. We embrace the concept that we are not unique, and that others like ourselves will always be there for us and have previously walked our path. We breathe a deep sigh of relief in understanding that everything is going to be okay now.

Who would ever have guessed that taking responsibility for our actions and accepting help from a group of strangers would hold the keys to happiness, hope and harmony?

~~~~~

Higher Power, help us experience the healing gifts of recovery. Show us how to listen for Your guidance in the words of another, understanding that we never need to be alone again. Please keep us aware that by accepting help from those in our Fellowship, we will continue to hold the keys to happiness, hope and harmony.

A FRESH BREATH OF RELIEF

. . . I was directed by angels, who appeared as mere mortals, to the Fellowship of Cocaine Anonymous. Attending meetings has become an integral part of my life, as important to my well-being as breathing.
Hope, Faith & Courage, *page 30*

To practice the Eleventh Step, I sit quietly in a chair, close my eyes and breathe deeply. As I breathe in, I imagine that I am drawing new life into my body, soul, and recovery. I breathe in peace, joy, and serenity. As I breathe out, I exhale stress, fear, doubt, and worry.

After five deep, cleansing breaths, I begin a simple mantra: my Higher Power is in me; the Fellowship of Cocaine Anonymous surrounds me. I repeat this for five to ten minutes. Sensing myself surrounded by love and wisdom, I feel safe. With God in me and the Fellowship around me, I can stay clean and sober this day.

I can repeat this meditation anytime, anywhere. If I begin to feel off balance emotionally, I can center myself with the same simple mantra: my Higher Power is in me; the Fellowship of Cocaine Anonymous surrounds me.

If I have God in me and the Fellowship around me, I can make it through anything—sometimes one day at a time, sometimes one minute at a time and sometimes one breath at a time. Relief is never farther away than my breath.

~~~~~

I breathe without having to think about it—my body knows I must have oxygen to stay alive. Can I strive for the same dependence on God and the program, believing completely that without these connections, my soul shall perish? May I always remember to use this meditative tool.

REFLECTION

Prayer is the raising of the heart and mind to God. . . .
Twelve Steps and Twelve Traditions, *page 102*

Take a little time today to reflect on life's ever-changing roles. We are like growing children who need to be ready for anything that comes along. Sometimes, we don't understand the need for these changes, nor do we desire them at all. Eventually, we see how change is often necessary to develop in whatever way our Higher Power sees fit.

God is all there really is—so sweet—amazing grace! I heard the message clearly this morning; I wish it would stay so cloudlessly clean. Bogged down by life, it disappears, then returns, only to be forgotten again. When we connect to the Juice, the Energy, the Power of the God of our understanding, life is bright and warm, a little more rounded, much less sharp at the edges. Change no longer threatens, but beckons us exuberantly.

Allowing for spiritual contemplation whenever possible strengthens the flow; this flow of energy and insight surges through my soul—and it's *all* okay.

~~~~~

A happy day it is! May I see the endless possibilities available through connection with the God of my understanding.

LIFE ON LIFE'S TERMS

> *Our basic troubles are the same as everyone else's, but when an honest effort is made "to practice these principles in all our affairs," well-grounded A.A.'s seem to have the ability, by God's grace, to take these troubles in stride and turn them into demonstrations of faith. We have seen A.A.'s suffer lingering and fatal illnesses with little complaint, and often in good cheer.*
>
> Twelve Steps and Twelve Traditions, *page 114*

One thing I have learned in recovery is that life goes on around us whether we are sober or not. During the past year, I walked through the loss of four family members plus a very dear friend. It has been a privilege to experience these losses clean and sober. Through all of this sadness, sickness, cancer and death, I drew much closer to my Higher Power. All of these matters were out of my control, I learned. Moreover, "why?" and "why now?" are fruitless questions. My prayers became a plea for help in accepting whatever God's plan may be for the ones I love. I prayed that, if it be His will, their pain and suffering be brief, and that they would be given the strength to endure their final days with love and dignity.

Each night, as I closed my eyes to sleep, I prayed for the grace to remain clean and sober in order to be able to show up, not hide, from my loved ones. I asked to be available and present to perhaps meet their needs, no matter what they were on any given day. My dear program friend even showed me it is possible to traverse cancer and death without drinking or drugging.

Knowing that my father was dying, I made sure all of my amends with him were complete so that I would have no regrets after he passed. Doing this made acceptance of what was to come possible. Prayer provided the Power to soothe my soul and I found peace. We will all have these obstacles at one time or another in our recoveries. Using during these trying times will only make things worse. I must suit up, show up, and keep close to my Higher Power to be guided through the tough times.

~~~~~

I can't; God can; I think I'll let Him. I won't give up my sobriety, no matter what! I pray that even in trying times in my recovery I have the strength to stay close to my Higher Power, and that this strength keeps me in the light, clean and sober, and present to support those in need with my love and understanding.

PAUSE FOR PEACE

In all times of emotional disturbance or indecision, we can pause, ask for quiet, and in the stillness simply say: "God grant me the serenity to accept the things I cannot change, courage to change the things I can, and wisdom to know the difference."
Twelve Steps and Twelve Traditions, *page 41*

I came to the Fellowship of Cocaine Anonymous like a child, emotionally stunted from years of drug use. How could I get through a day without using? How could I stop all the consequences of my addiction? How could I survive? Desperate, I found a sponsor, worked through the Twelve Steps, and got involved in the Fellowship and service. Thank God I was beaten down enough to adopt a monkey-see-monkey-do attitude. I watched you all and copied what you were doing. I had no idea what peace was-all I knew was I could no longer endure my life in its then sorry state alone. Gradually, the craziness going on inside my brain subsided. It was replaced with some new, recovery-based insights and tools for survival during trying times.

Today as I look into the eyes of my child, I understand the real essence of peace. I can feel God's peace in my life. Because I'm an addict, I know that this tranquility can leave at any time, often when I least expect it and even when things seem to be going well.

One of the greatest lessons I've been taught is the ability to pause when troubled or fearful. Many times throughout my day, I'll simply stop, quiet myself, and ask God as I understand Him to help and direct me. In this way, my serenity returns, and once again I'm at peace.

~~~~~

Right here, right now, if I am not feeling God's peace, can I *pause* to reconnect? The Serenity Prayer can always bring my priorities and recovery back into focus.

_____

WHO IS THAT ?

> *On awakening, let us think about the twenty-four hours ahead. We consider our plans for the day.*
> Alcoholics Anonymous, *page 86*

I got up this morning, showered, brushed my teeth, and got dressed for work. Now that, in itself, is a miracle—but it gets even better. I spent the next twenty minutes reading some spiritual literature, including *Alcoholics Anonymous*, pages 84-89. This simple discipline set my brain in gear for the day ahead. Was it time to leave the house yet? Not quite. Twenty more minutes in prayer and meditation, raising my consciousness to the realization that God's love fills and surrounds me. God's will for me is always good. I was then able to go to work with assurance that my happiness and serenity today would be a choice, independent from anyone else's influence or behavior.

I'm presently coming to the end of my working day, and guess what? Not once have I thought about using any mind-altering chemicals. I've not wanted to hurt anybody, including myself. I'm actually looking forward to getting home, where I'll cook dinner and open the mail. Afterwards, I'll pop over to one of the local meetings. Before going to bed, I'll review my day objectively, thanking God for seeing me through.

~~~~

Who *is* that grateful recovered addict with God's love and power in their life? That responsible person with serenity in their soul? Believe it or not, it's me!

IT'S A GOD THING

*I didn't know that I was beyond human aid and that I had to find
a God of my own understanding that would solve my problem.*
C.A. NewsGram, 2nd Quarter 1998

At the end of my using, my world came crashing down, and I wanted to die. But God, in His infinite love, had other thoughts. You see, I believe deep down to the very core of my being that God guided me to Cocaine Anonymous so that I might have the opportunity to find Him. And for that, I am forever grateful.

Through cocaine, I lost everything—materially, physically, emotionally, and spiritually. I lost my soul. Through the Twelve Steps of Cocaine Anonymous, I found a God of my understanding, and through His grace, I have been blessed with another day of sobriety. I love being happy, joyous, and free. The journey of sobriety has been one of progress, walked one day at a time, with God and my fellow members of C.A. So if you're having trouble getting sober like I did, the answer just might be the Twelve Steps of Cocaine Anonymous. It's worked for me over many years now—one day at a time.

~~~~~

The blessing of the spiritual awakening, whenever it occurs, no matter how unexpected, is a profound event. The Twelve Steps were the key to my sobriety and have been an enduring part of the changes in my life.

_____

DISCOVERING MY PERSONAL GIFTS

Now and then we may be granted a glimpse of that ultimate reality which is God's kingdom. And we will be comforted and assured that our own destiny in that realm will be secure for so long as we try, however falteringly, to find and do the will of our own Creator.
Twelve Steps and Twelve Traditions, *page 98*

If I really want to live life to the fullest, I must first reach out to God. He wants only the best for me, and He loves me unconditionally. Just as my parents want to see me succeed in life, so does God. He will always respond to my appeals for help by showing me how to be the most excellent human being I can possibly be.

I believe that I have a chosen path, and that I have been equipped with certain gifts that are distinctly unique. By reaching out to the God of my own understanding, in prayer and meditation, I open myself up to His guidance. Thus, I am led to use my personal talents and insights in the way that will most benefit me and those around me. Fulfilling my highest purpose will take a lifetime; however, enjoying the journey is the most essential requirement.

~~~~

God, please open my heart and mind so that I may recognize my special gifts. Please give me the strength and courage I'll need to carry out the plans You have for me. Allow me to be a continued blessing to You, as well as others, during my journey.

DEAL, FEEL, AND HEAL

As I looked around the room, I was amazed at how two or three hundred people who obviously should not belong together could be having so much fun, especially when they all claimed to be clean and sober.
Hope, Faith & Courage Volume II, *page 120*

I would rather deal, feel, and heal today than numb and medicate. When I used drugs or other mind-altering substances, I did not grow, enhance, or develop my life; I just stagnated.

The great escape turned out to be the deceitful thief. Pursuing immediate gratification and avoiding life's tough situations robbed me of the greatest treasures and pleasures, and I can no longer afford it.

I came to C.A. believing I was going to miss the effects produced by drugging my body. Little did I know, the party and fun was just about to begin! By living the C.A. way, I laugh louder, feel more deeply, and enjoy greater relationships. My life has purpose and meaning. I get to actually look forward with humble anticipation to what lies ahead.

~~~~~

Am I letting go of unproductive ideas and attitudes to fully grab onto healthier, more rewarding ones which actually work in my life and my recovery? Today I will choose to grow through life, work the Steps, and enjoy this journey to its fullest.

ANONYMITY ASSURES HUMILITY

Anonymity is the spiritual foundation of all our Traditions,
ever reminding us to place principles before personalities.
C.A. Tradition Twelve

The goal of the Traditions is to safeguard our common welfare through unity. An anonymous organization is one where its members have no interest in receiving personal acknowledgement for the group's efforts. Tradition One states the *goal* of the Traditions (our common welfare) while Tradition Twelve states the *means* (anonymity). The goal of unity is ultimately achieved through the means of anonymity.

Each Tradition is a principle that serves to encourage the member to set aside self-interest in consideration of the group. The individual or group is invited to give up something for C.A.'s general welfare. Anonymity, the spiritual foundation of our unity, is simply the application of the spiritual principles contained in the Twelve Steps in respect to our group life, as well as with respect to society in general.

Finally, this Tradition encourages each member to treat every other member's participation in the Fellowship as sacred. While I can, subject to the provisions of Tradition Eleven, disclose my membership in the C.A. Fellowship, I am never to break another person's anonymity. This truly places "principles before personalities." With anonymity comes an important state of mind, the feeling that "I am one of God's children, *just like the rest of God's children*." Anonymity ensures humility, a fundamental healing tool for the soul-sickness of addiction.

~~~~~

Grant me the courage and wisdom to help others anonymously and to perform service work without seeking recognition. Let me respect the anonymity of the members in my group and of the Fellowship as a whole. May I be grateful that my life today is driven by the practice of spiritual principles in all my affairs.

WILLINGNESS IS THE KEY

Spiritual experiences had happened at other times in my life, but I never used the window of grace to stay in action and seek to improve my connection with God.
C.A. NewsGram, 3rd Quarter 2000

My story of recovery is nothing short of a miracle, which could never have occurred by unaided human will. Of course, somewhere in the world in C.A., this happens every day. No human power could have relieved my suffering. But God could, and did, when sought. I finally took the necessary steps to have a vital spiritual experience.

When I got sober, it was because God gave me willingness to take all necessary action for recovery from a hopeless state of mind and body. I was severely addicted to cocaine and booze and knew that even with faith in God, it would take consistent action on my part to break this hideous cycle. I didn't have time to wait—I was dying fast. I got into service and began to carry the message of the Twelve Steps. Some old C.A. friends stood by me and helped. I was able to get a sponsor who had been involved in a *Big Book*/Step study for many years to guide me through the Steps. He prayed with me right away, and we did a Third Step together.

Most of the time, I live in peace and with serenity. My family, who loves me, is back in my life. I have friends who really care, and I care, too. Frequently, tears of joy flow down my face when I think of the life I've been given. I have the privilege of seeing other folks recover from this fatal disease. Thank you, C.A., for being there for me and countless others in those darkest moments.

~~~~~

No longer do I live in fear on a daily basis. What has happened in my life is truly a miracle! The more I continue to be of service to C.A. and carry the message, the fuller and more enriched my life becomes. No matter how much I give of myself to this Fellowship, it could never equal what I've been given.

BALANCE

I felt as if I were living a dual existence. . . .
Hope, Faith & Courage, *page 53*

When I had my high-powered corporate job, earning lots of money and traveling all over the world, I thought it was a good thing to separate my personal and professional lives. I used to brag about how I could park my car in my company parking spot and envision stepping up onto a big Monopoly board in the game of work, then stepping off that board at night and driving away into my personal world.

I was compartmentalizing my existence and by drawing such deep lines of distinction between "my two lives," I became very skilled at compartmentalizing my emotions and relationships. I grew accustomed to the many masks I found necessary to wear as I played the different roles on the stage that was my life. When tight deadlines at work approached, I became consumed with my business life, completely neglecting my personal life. I was heavily rewarded monetarily on the professional side, but I was completely bankrupt, empty, and broken on the personal side.

Eventually the dual existence produced a fractured reality, and I found myself completely out of balance. When I am out of balance, I make poor behavioral choices and I have no peace and serenity. When I have no peace and serenity, my mind races, sleep is shallow, and I have no energy.

Today in sobriety, I strive to integrate *all* my lives—to incorporate and mingle the personal with the "production"—in order to apply my *full* and well-rounded attention to everything. Living completely in this moment allows me to nurture my awareness of the symmetry in nature, and I feel awake to what's going on around me. Balancing work and play means my days are richer and my sleep is deeper. Being in balance produces harmony in all areas of my life.

~~~~~

As I prepare for this day, let me visualize my life in balance, as a leaf with perfect symmetry. As I go through this day, let me stop and take deep breaths, breathing in and out in synchronized measures as a reminder to be balanced in thought, energy, and action. As I end this day, let me close my eyes in gratitude, reviewing all the aspects of my life and gently letting go to sleep deeply.

LISTENING TO THE SILENCE

When I listen in silence, I hear; and it is in silence that God and I come face to face.
Hope, Faith & Courage Volume II, *page 38*

My sponsor had given me some inspirational tapes to help me with my meditation practice. One was labeled "Silence." Another program friend happened to be at my house and noticed the title. Quizzically, and with a hearty chuckle, he asked, "You have a *recording* of silence?!"

Ironically, we almost do need such a thing. In this day and age where everyone seems to be sporting headphones, how can I unplug and take time each day to get quiet with God? The old cliché "silence is golden" tells me that the importance of quiet space has been recognized for a very long time.

Silence opens my spiritual ear so that I listen with my heart for God's messages. Sometimes the messages come through loud and clear. Other times I'll need to wait, or maybe listen harder.

~~~~~

My silent time is an *intentional* focus inward—minutes carved out of my busy schedule to stop and simply breathe in God.

IMPROVING CONSCIOUS CONTACT

Working Step Eleven has been incredibly rewarding. My conscious contact with God grows stronger all the time. I am learning to trust the process and to listen to my gut without my head intervening.
Hope, Faith & Courage Volume II, *page 96*

Of all the relationships that I am learning to rebuild in my recovery, two remain perpetually in the spotlight: my relationships with myself and with my Higher Power. These two comprise the foundation of every other relationship in my life. An intimate, loving relationship with myself automatically brings me closer to my God. Conversely, my relationship with my God will lead me into a loving, close, spiritually intimate relationship with myself.

Step Eleven shows me how to do both sides of this equation. I pray and meditate to improve my conscious contact with God and with myself. I ask to be shown the best possible course of action for myself each day, as well as the power to do my part while staying just enough out of the way to let God do his part, too.

This Step goes on to focus on the continued need for my praying for the knowledge of God's will and the power to carry that out. Here, we pray and meditate to seek this knowledge. We ask our Higher Power for the right thought, answer, or decision.

Step Eleven specifically instructs us to connect with the God of our understanding by praying, asking our God to reveal His will for us, and to provide the means to carry that out.

~~~~

I pray to continually nurture an intimate, loving relationship with myself and with the God of my understanding. May these connections grow stronger and deeper as I mature in recovery and in life.

A STATE OF GRATITUDE

The central fact of our lives today is the absolute certainty that our Creator has entered our hearts and lives in a way which is indeed miraculous.
Alcoholics Anonymous, *page 25*

Often when I am quietly practicing the Eleventh Step, I'll reflect on the great fortune I have to be experiencing two lives in one lifetime—one before I got to C.A., and another one after. I owe this blessing to the Fellowship of Cocaine Anonymous and to the spiritual program of action I found here. Today is November 18th, the date on which the first meeting of C.A. was held in 1982. Happy birthday, C.A.! I am so full of gratitude for the life given to me as a result of surrender, love and service.

Addiction to cocaine and all other mind-altering substances, in my experience, can be aptly described as the "kingdom of the night." Darkness, confusion, despair, and psychosis are some of the gifts this kingdom has to offer. Emergence from this dark, lonely realm into the sunlight of C.A. fellowship and recovery evokes gratitude. The movement from a state of hopelessness to a state of hope is an infinite leap forward, indicating a Higher Power's presence, which I believe manifests as grace. Gratitude is my response to grace. By God's grace, one day at a time, I practice the principles of recovery in all areas of my life and live free of addiction. Further, daily prayer and meditation keep me aware that my life today is a miracle.

~~~~~

Today, I will acknowledge the founding of the first C.A. meeting held on this day in 1982. I am truly thankful to be able to spend a moment in quiet contemplation about just how grateful I am for the Fellowship's existence and for God's grace in showing us all the light and the path to sobriety. The life I am living today is a pure gift, and recognizing this, I am drawn into a perpetual attitude of gratitude.

PRAYER 101

> *Step Eleven suggests prayer and meditation. We shouldn't be shy on the matter of prayer. Better men than we are using it constantly. It works, if we have the proper attitude and work at it.*
> Alcoholics Anonymous, *pages 85-86*

Prayer is referenced throughout the whole *Big Book* and the Step process. Repeatedly, I am reminded of the need for prayer and how prayer positively affects my program, bringing me closer to God's will. Prayers are integral in the completion of several key Steps.

How I approach praying is not nearly as important as making the effort to actually pray. In my experience, praying is the act of consciously talking to God. A prayer can be a word or a thought. It can be an expression of joy or sorrow, fear or gratitude. A prayer can be something written to God, or something more traditional.

Prayer doesn't need to be complicated. I can simply direct my thoughts toward God, or I can talk aloud, just as I would to a person. I am free to pray any way I choose: standing, sitting, kneeling, eyes closed, eyes open, lying in bed, driving in my car, in the dark, as I meditate, or even, perhaps, walking along a sandy beach at dawn. I can be exactly who I am with God—no pretenses necessary. I can pray whatever I need to pray, whenever I need to pray it.

~~~~~

"We usually conclude the period of meditation with a prayer that we be shown all through the day what our next step is to be, that we be given whatever we need to take care of such problems. We ask especially for freedom from self-will, and are careful to make no request for ourselves only. We may ask for ourselves, however, if others will be helped. We are careful never to pray for our own selfish ends. Many of us have wasted a lot of time doing that and it doesn't work. You can easily see why." (*Alcoholics Anonymous*, page 86.)

MEDITATION 101

> *How do I keep the power? Prayer and meditation. I pray and*
> *ask God for direction, and I meditate to hear the answers.*
> Hope, Faith & Courage Volume II, *page 38*

I was one of those addicts without a spiritual "clue" when I arrived here. I had to be shown everything, even how to pray. Something as simple as learning to ask for help was huge. I was, perhaps, the most challenged in trying to figure out the concept of meditation. After reading and re-reading pages 86-88 of the *Big Book*, along with Step Eleven in the *Twelve and Twelve*, I was still confused about the best way to add prayer and meditation practices to my program.

The beauty (or curse, depending on how you look at it!) is that there are no hard, fast rules for sorting this out. Many practice meditation in a variety of ways—some even using different methods at different times of the day. Similar to the means by which we are able to select our own Higher Powers, prayer and meditative practices are highly personal. We are free to find words and methods uniquely suited to us alone. Usually, these become modified and fine-tuned as we progress along our spiritual path.

Reading a meditation book is one common method, either in the morning or evening. I have employed this practice almost daily since I came into the program. The readings consistently remind me about recovery principles, help me focus on what's in store for the day ahead, or debrief my activities before I retire. Other people listen to songs or sounds to stay relaxed and serene. Still others use prayer, either by itself or in combination with quiet time, to meditate.

Early on, it was explained to me that my goal in meditation, no matter how, where or when I practice it, is to quiet myself and my thoughts, striving to become and remain serene, connected to my Higher Power. I tune into God and myself, focusing on our sacred connection, as well as on the many miracles in my recovery. I seek to improve my conscious contact with God through meditation. Often times, I am pleased to catch a glimpse of the answer, insight, vision, inspiration or healing action I seek.

~~~~~

Early on, I heard it said, quite simply: Praying is how I talk to God. Meditating is how God talks to me.

ALL IS WELL

> . . . *job or no job—wife or no wife—we simply do not stop drinking so long as we place dependence upon other people ahead of dependence on God. Burn the idea into the consciousness of every man that he can get well regardless of anyone. The only condition is that he trust in God and clean house.*
>
> Alcoholics Anonymous, *page 98*

As a newcomer, it seemed my life was in constant turmoil. Dealing with *feelings* that just wouldn't stop didn't help matters. One day I was whining to a program old-timer about how hard it was to deal with life on life's terms. She then quoted a spiritual mystic who said, "All shall be well, and all shall be well; all manner of things shall be well."

She told me this was a line shared with her by her sponsor when she was new and her life felt very similar to what I was going through. "I would say it over and over again, even if I didn't believe it, and it helped me stay sober through some very tough situations. After all these years in recovery, I use it still today,"

What does "all is well" mean when I feel like my world is falling apart? Be still; listen. I will get through this. I am right where I am supposed to be. Go ahead and cry if I need to—the tears will heal me. This too will pass. Trust in my Higher Power with all my heart.

~~~~~

If I can truly believe that I'm going to be okay, *no matter what*, life gets a whole lot easier.

GRATEFUL LIVING

Nevertheless, we find that our thinking will, as time passes, be more and more on the plane of inspiration. We come to rely upon it.
Alcoholics Anonymous, *page 87*

As a result of grateful living, I am increasingly able to live in an inspired fashion. This is one of the Steps' promises for me. The manner in which I live gratefully is to take action in the expression of my gratitude—to actually give my gratitude life. In Cocaine Anonymous, I can do this in a multitude of ways. All these fall under the heading of service. For me, service is inspired living.

No matter how I serve, when I do (which is quite often), I clearly receive gifts. I can't even begin to fathom how powerful and inspiring these gifts will be. I just show up, share the lessons which were given freely to me, exuding hope and strength as best I can. My Higher Power introduced me to the Twelve Steps with the distinct purpose of improving and inspiring my life. The only stipulation attached is that I'm generous enough to give it away.

~~~~~

With a thankful heart, I remain open to the many ways I can try and give back to C.A. what was so freely given to me. As an active member of our beautiful Fellowship, I look forward to every meeting I attend and say yes to service requests when at all possible. Each day, I discover heavenly blessings, simply by being gratefully available.

CONTROL

These were the new attitudes that finally brought many of us an inner strength and peace that could not be deeply shaken by the shortcomings of others or by any calamity not of our own making.
Twelve Steps and Twelve Traditions, *page 116*

Addicts are familiar with losing control over drug use and the feeling of helplessness it brings. A struggle with control may also ensue when it comes to relationships, work, school, or even something as simple as the way other people drive. With few exceptions, I can control what I say and do (so long as I am sober), but not much else. If I have expectations that things need to go my way, I am often going to be disappointed.

Learning to accept people for who they are without feeling the need to judge or control them makes my life flow a lot more smoothly. It keeps me consistently serene. Letting go of control can feel frightening at first, but after a while it becomes very freeing. Part of my path in recovery is understanding what I can control versus what I can't.

~~~~

Trying to control people, places, and things carries a large burden of responsibility and a lot of heartache that I don't need. Today, I can do my best, get out of the way, and leave the rest.

STEP ELEVEN KEPT SIMPLE

> *There are many definitions of prayer and meditation, and a detailed discussion is not practical within the confines of this pamphlet. Some basic suggestions, on pages 86-88 of* Alcoholics Anonymous, *outline a daily and nightly routine we can apply to allow God to monitor and direct our thinking.*
>
> A Guide to the 12 Steps (C.A. Pamphlet)

I am quite thrilled to have made it through the Steps once again to find myself squarely at Step Eleven. This Step reminds me to pray and meditate, seeking to improve my conscious contact with my personal Higher Power, suggesting only that I pray for knowledge of God's will and the power to carry that out.

A bridge connects Step Three to Step Eleven. Step Three references our will and our lives, as contrasted with Step Eleven where I pray for His will for us and the power to carry that out. The process of the Steps in between opens me up to replace my will with God's will.

This quest is often quite difficult because of my tendency to overthink things and because of my ego. Even though my ego has diminished as a result of my Step work, it definitely still exists. My ego makes me think I can ask God for specifics, praying for circumstances to change, life to be easier, feelings to go away or come back, knowledge beyond my capacity. Requests like this assume I know what is best—not a good plan. Step Eleven reminds me to trust my Higher Power with complete abandon, without expectation for any outcome. The instruction to ask only to know God's will for me and have the power to carry it out is quite specific and represents a great starting point for additional spiritual study.

~~~~~

When I work Step Eleven, I keep it simple and try not to overthink the Step's purpose. I pray for continued spiritual enlightenment as the result of my seeking.

ANGER

As the reality of the situation set in, I realized I had a clear choice between anger and acceptance: anger had the power to kill me, whereas acceptance had the power to save me.
Hope, Faith & Courage Volume II, *page 97*

For the longest time in sobriety, I would get mad at a situation or person and not be particularly subtle with my emotions. I was not the yelling type, or the slammer, or even the curser or thrower. I was that intense, seething caldron, just taking it in and sitting with it, but everyone instantly knew I was angry. One of the hardest parts in recovery has been to learn about why I get so infuriated and understand what triggers this reaction. Changing my outrage behavior once and for all certainly seemed a necessary adjustment.

I started by examining my anger before I got sober. This proved of little help since in those days, the fury was immediately numbed with a mind-altering substance. Going back further to pre-addiction, I found nothing on my side of the street but passive behavior as I witnessed both my parents often filled with rage—at each other, at situations, or, sometimes, even at me and my siblings. I didn't piece it together until much later, but their behavior was a textbook example of anger.

Through many inventories, as well as by sharing at countless topic meetings about anger and rage, I finally pieced together some insights. First, I learned that anger is a primary emotion, meaning that another emotion (or two) is always lurking underneath, fueling anger's fire. Often, I realize my anger is masking fear, shame, or both. I have witnessed that with my parents, co-workers, and other program members, the same pattern is prevalent. Second, being angry in recovery from time to time is a piece in my emotional thawing as I continue to experience feelings which are new in my un-numbed life. I have learned to face them all now and attempt to place them in some meaningful perspective. With prayer and a strong daily Tenth Step, this thaw is finally manageable.

I still get upset sometimes, and when I do, I stop to examine whether it's fear, shame, or some other character defect attempting to rear its ugly head at that particular moment. This realization has helped me enormously to remain calm and be slow to anger.

~~~~~

I am grateful for the insight that some other emotion or set of emotions lies underneath my anger. I pray for clarity in understanding the emotions fueling my ire, combined with the ability to implement serenity, and an understanding to arrest this continued pattern.

THE GIFT OF SERVICE

For some unknown reason, service, along with the Steps and a sponsor, and working with folks newer than yourself, forms an almost unbreakable foundation for sobriety.
C.A. NewsGram, 1st Quarter 2002

Service is the greatest gift I've received through this Fellowship. Service has allowed me to discover traits I didn't know I had, like the ability to be a team member within a group context instead of the self-centered, egotistical maniac I used to be. I can view life's actions from the perspective of how this affects our structure as a whole, leaving behind my ever-so-powerful self-inflicting ego. I may not like my own thoughts sometimes, but when I place them on the table for the group to decide which direction we are going, I know God is working through me.

With God in my corner, I can help others recover from this disease. Being involved in service is where I met those people with the gleam in their eyes and a sense of spirituality around them. I call it the "look" of sobriety. It's what I wanted when I got here, so I started following these people around, doing the things they were doing. Miraculously, it happened to me, too. I now possess that light in my eyes, and I feel some of that same sense of spirituality in my heart as well.

~~~~~

Keep doing whatever kinds of service commitments are needed in your local Fellowship. Sooner than later, you will look back and realize you are not only helping the group by being of service, but you are actually enjoying getting out of yourself by helping others.

_____

TAKING A GOOD LOOK

> . . . we examine the wreckage that is accumulating
> from our attempts to run the show and the things
> that have been blocking us from our Higher Power.
> A Guide to the 12 Steps (C.A. Pamphlet)

When I got clean and sober, I had to take a good look at my entire life. I tried to stay objective about what I had become. For the first time, it became quite clear to me that I was an utter, complete, one hundred percent no-good louse! I was so self-centered, so full of my ego, that I had all but destroyed myself and my relationships.

With a new clarity, I saw that God had saved me many times from self-destruction. My new awareness of God's presence in my life made me believe He had spared me for a purpose. I want to express my gratitude to Him and will try to do that by spending the rest of my life helping others discover the solution through the Twelve Steps of recovery. I know that Cocaine Anonymous is where I need to be in order to help myself first and then to show others how to stay clean and sober.

~~~~~

Once we become clean and sober, examining the wake of our destructive behavior can be painful, embarrassing, and filled with remorse. Can I remember to be grateful that today I can feel such feelings?

DOING THE BASICS

If you somehow, some way, get a break from it, get free for a moment with a little clarity, you will know this could be your last chance. You must stop using now, and you are really scared. You want to stay away from cocaine, but you don't know how.
Tools of Recovery (C.A. Pamphlet)

I'm an addict with a long using history. "All other mind-altering substances" was my middle name. In essence, I always wanted to escape, never growing or changing. Feelings were not part of my vocabulary, and I rarely did anything challenging. After many firings, arrests, and hospitalizations, I finally reached the bottom I needed to enter the rooms of C.A. Even then, I suffered relapses regularly during the first six months, but I kept attending meetings. In spite of my struggles and often irrational sharing, people urged me to, "Keep coming back."

The last time I was in the hospital (due to hallucinations), I received a powerful wake-up from doctors telling me I was going to die. By God's grace, things changed after this. I started attending meetings every day. The "basics" became my daily primary purpose. I made coffee, called my sponsor and other program members regularly, and took all the suggestions I was given to stay sober. One day at a time, my life improved in many areas, but I always kept recovery first. For the last two years, being committed to the Fellowship, I have reaped serenity and meaningful spiritual rewards. Trying times have forced me to rely strongly on the God of my understanding. The *Big Book* and the Steps enhance this connection. People in the Fellowship have been helpful and supportive. Today, I am grateful my life is in the care of a loving God. Through program principles, I can keep out of my own head and live in the solution.

~~~~~

I pray to remain aware and grateful for my God and the Fellowship, which has supported me on my path to stay sober. No matter how busy life gets, sobriety will always remain my number one priority. I will always remain mindful of the moment of clarity that led me to realize just how badly I needed this program.

INFORMED GROUP CONSCIENCE

Just prior to the close of this meeting, it was suggested that we take a group conscience to turn this Alcoholics Anonymous meeting into a completely new Twelve-Step program, and call it Cocaine Anonymous. This motion, which sounded like a wonderful idea to me, was quickly voted down.

Hope, Faith & Courage Volume II, *page 3*

C.A. Tradition Two informs and guides the group decision-making process. God is the ultimate authority as expressed through group conscience. Group members can trust that if they make the effort to become fully informed on various issues and then lovingly articulate concerns and thoughts, the group conscience will be expressed collectively.

Freedom is achieved by adhering to this Tradition. No member need feel he or she must carry the heavy responsibility of being the final decision-maker. This burden falls properly on an ultimate authority expressing Himself/Herself/Itself through the group's collective conscience.

groups have sometimes been hopelessly divided on a particular issue—passionate statements are made on both sides of the debate at hand, as are frothy emotional appeals by some of the group's more vocal members. The key is to try to reach a consensus, or to agree to disagree and revisit the issue at a later date as more information is revealed and the group is, perhaps, better informed. Another tool is to really ask, deep inside, what would God do in this instance, at this time. Almost always, with this sincere approach, resolution can be achieved.

~~~~~

Am I an active participant in the decisions made by my group? Can I be open to ideas which conflict with my own? God, help me to participate without resentment, especially when the discussion gets heated. Show me how to channel Your will in the group conscience process.

RECOVERY WITH GOD

> *In my heart, I know recovery is a great change, a*
> *change in myself more than a change in people, places*
> *or things. My life is now centered around my recovery.*
> Hope, Faith & Courage, *page 92*

One of the promises in the *Big Book* Spiritual Experience appendix is that spiritual awakening will bring about a "profound alteration in our reaction to life." Life doesn't change; life is still life. What changes is *how I react* as a result of a relationship with my Higher Power as a cornerstone of my recovery.

I begin to discard my old life because it didn't work. I gave up the failed design for living that had self-reliance as its core. I also discarded old ideals, practices, ways of responding in stressful situations, even not wanting to feel emotions of any type, good or bad. My perspective changed greatly, and the longer I am around, the more I find courage and strength in reliance upon infinite God. I do as I believe my Higher Power would have me do and have faith that I will be given what I need to face the varied issues life presents to me. Staying close to my God and taking the thoughtful actions which are right in front of me, I discover I *can* live a useful and joyous life. As I keep coming back and working the program to the very best of my ability, my God consciousness expands. I see clearly how my recovery ultimately relies on this relationship.

~~~~

I am ever grateful for this new design for living. Let me consistently be aware of how I can be useful to my fellows and to my God. Grant me courage and strength to take the actions I believe God would recommend for each situation I encounter.

DECEMBER

THE LESSONS IN THE STEPS

*Every time I walk through the Steps of this program, I
learn to better understand my place in God's world.*
Hope, Faith & Courage Volume II, *page 108*

The Steps are in order for a reason. Before I can commence to grow, I have to
realize I have a problem, and that alone, I cannot solve it (Step One). This
admission gets me to a place where I can become willing to believe that there just
might be a Higher Power Who can solve my problems (Steps Two-Three). My
belief then gives me the strength and courage I need to take a moral inventory of
myself and share it with another person (Steps Four-Five).

My inventory shows me that my troubles are almost always of my own making,
even if I was simply putting myself between the dog and the fire hydrant. I suddenly
realize it is not the world that needs to change, it is me (Steps Six-Seven). Knowing
this gives me the ability to begin righting the wrongs I have done to others (Steps
Eight-Nine).

Having worked Steps One through Nine gives me the experience I need to work
the Steps on a daily basis by taking responsibility for my own actions and no longer
blaming everyone else for my problems. It helps me turn to my Higher Power each
day, asking that His will be done, not mine (Steps Ten-Eleven). It also allows me
the gift of having had a spiritual experience as "the" result of these Steps (Step
Twelve).

~~~~~

I pray that the lessons in the Steps continue to be revealed to me. I must remain
aware that most of these lessons are about changing my actions and thinking in
positive ways as my Higher Power intended.

SERVICE WORK & WORKING WITH OTHERS—THE HIGHER PURPOSE

We discovered that the best way to serve God was to serve our fellow humans, and we found humility in the process.
Being of Service (C.A. Pamphlet)

I was taught that my abuse of cocaine and other mind-altering substances was merely a symptom of a larger problem. The problem is my disease. At the core of this is the fact that I am a selfish, self-centered individual. Even though I've grown as a result of my recovery in C.A., at times I still suffer from selfish motives and a more narcissistic outlook than appropriate.

Thankfully, I have been taught that when all else fails, there is no better way to get out of my own head and self-misery than to work with another. I've also learned that working with someone does not necessarily mean just with another addict. Service work can take many forms and can include serving C.A., working with a sponsee, helping my children with their homework, or volunteering in my community. Any work I perform that aids another human being takes me out of my own head—the command center of my disease.

Today I have a purpose: to be of maximum service to my Higher Power and my fellow humans. If I practice this purpose on a daily basis, I'm sure to move closer to being the person God would have me be.

~~~~~

I pray that I will be able to join the Fellowship and not attempt recovery alone. May I be continually empowered to take responsibility for whatever life presents. Let me never forget the best way to help myself is by also helping others.

EMOTIONAL SOBRIETY

The joy of living is the theme of A.A.'s Twelfth Step, and action is its key word. . . . Here we begin to practice all Twelve Steps of the program in our daily lives so that we and those about us may find emotional sobriety.
Twelve Steps and Twelve Traditions, *page 106*

When I first crawled into the Fellowship of Cocaine Anonymous, the idea of being able to deal with my changing moods—what some people call "emotional sobriety"—was an alien concept. My sponsor simply told me to work the Steps and things would change. He was right; they did. Very early on, the compulsion to drink or use drugs was totally lifted, and I felt a freedom like never before.

The urge to control everyone and everything around me took a lot longer to be relieved. I discovered that until I could let go of this, I would have no real emotional sobriety (which, by this time, I was beginning to understand). For me, the light came on when I got deeper into my Step work.

Rigorous personal inventory not only improved the way I treated others, it also enriched the way I felt inside. Willingness to change, remaining humble, praying, and meditating, along with the ability to ask for and receive the help of others, have all made a huge difference in my emotional sobriety. Constantly working on my relationship with God, I have been given an inner peace and a level of emotional sobriety I never dreamt possible. This, together with the safety net that is Step Twelve, has ensured my well-being and continued growth.

~~~~~

Once I am clean and sober, the real work begins. I pray that my emotional sobriety will remain strong and grow as I continue to work the Steps and *live* the program, one day at a time.

A FRIEND TO SHOW THE WAY

. . . you will make lifelong friends.
Alcoholics Anonymous, *page 152*

The chairperson of the first meeting I ever attended was to become one of my best program friends. I was too hungover and consumed with self-pity to notice anyone, but he noticed me. Slowly, quietly, and certainly without my cooperation, he became my dearest ally and mentor over the ensuing years.

Despite the numerous occasions I abused this man's kindness and generosity, he was always there waiting for me with a smile, a hug, and a warm greeting. Many times, after a jag and coming back to the rooms, I would fall asleep during the meeting. When anyone would attempt to wake me, my friend would stop them, saying, "Let him be. He is safe now," clearly recognizing his job and leaving the result to God. Eventually I allowed myself to be persuaded to join a particularly strong men's meeting. In spite of my disdain for this pack of disgustingly happy, enthusiastic members, I would go because there always seemed to be someone I could talk out of a few dollars, which I would promptly use to get high again. My friend didn't seem to notice my motive *(or did he?)*; he would simply welcome me with a warm smile and a hug and say, "Don't leave before the miracle." I hadn't a clue what he was talking about!

Such quiet and unassuming actions were a rock solid demonstration of love, patience, sincerity, and humility. There is not a shred of doubt in my mind that I would have been dead long ago if this man with his kind qualities and wise manner had not entered my life when he did and loved me into recovery.

~~~~~

I am so grateful that I did not leave before the miracle and that my friend showed me the true face of God. I am overwhelmed with the amazing life sobriety has created for me. To top it off, I get the gift of countless others who have subsequently allowed me to share my experience with them—priceless!

OPPORTUNITY KNOCKS

> *Instead of feeling like we are missing out on having a good time, we become grateful for the new opportunities we have to celebrate being happy, joyous and free.*
>
> Having Fun in Recovery (C.A. Pamphlet)

So much of life is all about perception. We can choose to see the glass half empty or half full. One of recovery's greatest gifts is the ability to discern an opportunity when it arises.

Throughout each and every 24 hours, we are presented with many kinds of opportunities:

> Opportunities to be of service;
> Opportunities to carry the message;
> Opportunities to practice spiritual principles;
> Opportunities to be closer to employers, family, friends,
>   and even strangers who cross our paths;
> Opportunities to recognize God's loving care and guidance.

While I was still in my active disease, how many opportunities to get clean and sober did I pass by? Now I am grateful for the ability to recognize life's many opportunities as they occur—grateful for the freedom of choice!

~~~~

I wake up every morning with opportunity to see how much I can pack into the stream of life. Today I choose to look for these chances to be helpful to someone, to grow, to be of service, and to carry the message.

GIVING

I want to give all that I can in this life.
Hope, Faith & Courage, *page 179*

What a joy it is to be a recovered addict during the holiday season. Each celebration with friends, family, and Fellowship grows more and more enjoyable. Today the holidays are not the frantic, self-centered excuse for over-indulgence they were when I was using. I remember the festivities being filled with disappointment and high anxiety, trying to do the right thing by my family and failing. I was full of self-centered fear and jealous of those who had more. It seemed as though I had no choice but to disappear to use drugs in secret during the times I felt this way.

I have learned over my years in the program that holiday seasons are a time for thinking of others, of giving, and especially, of recognizing and expressing gratitude. If I consider others more, if I give unconditionally, I feel more whole. When I say "give" more, I don't mean expensive gifts or presents. I mean giving of my time, making that extra call, doing service work, sharing my food, myself, and carrying the message of our program so that those who suffer know there is a solution. My recovery is strengthened when I give to others without expectation of reward or even the notion of one.

~~~~~

I pray that I may find happiness by giving freely of myself to family, friends, and those in the program. May I constantly be reminded that in order to keep it, I *must* give it away.

IT WORKS IF YOU WORK IT

As we recovered, many of us experienced new or reawakened spiritual feelings.
Tools of Recovery (C.A. Pamphlet)

During my first year in the program I experienced a wonderful feeling of awe and peace. It was, in fact, amazing—as if I had become all-connected to the world. Through practicing daily surrender and by working the Steps, it seemed as though a large amount of my life's wreckage was lifted from me. I felt nearer to my Higher Power, while fear and doubt vanished. The Promises literally materialized for me as I quietly spoke the words, "God is doing for us what we could not do for ourselves." (*Alcoholics Anonymous*, page 84.)

Feelings of gratitude and love for others were very new. I had spent so much of life bitter and angry. I remembered what it felt like when I was very young, watching my first sunset, and a powerful Presence awakened within me. With this newfound experience, I began to learn the vital importance of continuing to be honest and open-minded. I started regularly seeking God's will for me and slowly letting go of my need to control things. My spirit had been re-kindled and my life had meaning and importance.

Occasionally, further on in my sobriety, I found myself back in a negative frame of mind. It didn't take long to understand that this was not where I wanted to be anymore. One day, when driving to work, I screamed at God in frustration, "You have it all then!" Guess what? God was listening! Much to my amazement, He took it! That feeling of peace and spiritual connection to the universe flooded over me again. I went to work grateful for having been restored to right thinking.

~~~~~

Today I will continue to practice turning my will (thoughts) and life (actions) over to my Higher Power. I know that doing this works, so I will trust in the process. That process helps me continue to work my program, stay clean, help others, and feel truly a part of the world in which I live.

VANISHING VICTIMHOOD

> *Taking the Twelve Steps prepares us to have a "spiritual awakening" or a "spiritual experience" (page 567 in Alcoholics Anonymous, 4th Edition). These phrases refer to the change in our thinking, attitudes, and outlook that occurs after taking the Steps. This change frees us from active addiction.*
>
> A Guide to the 12 Steps (C.A. Pamphlet)

In early sobriety, I spent a whole lot of time and energy trying to convince everyone I had worked the Steps when, in fact, I hadn't. Little did I know how easy it was for experienced program members to see right through that pretense. I have since realized working the Steps *is* the "easier, softer way."

As with many people, I first thought getting sober only meant no more using. I was not expecting to find the joys of being sober introduced by my Higher Power.

Once I worked the Steps, my whole world changed. I no longer felt worthless or alone. The emptiness inside was slowly being replaced by a vital solid, good feeling—quite a nice feeling, I might add. As a matter of fact, I was practically overflowing with love and gratitude! My "victimhood" was vanishing as I began taking responsibility for the part I played in the many improper actions from my past. This process somehow made me feel wonderful!

~~~~~

By working the Steps with a sponsor and connecting with the God of my understanding, I actually find myself becoming a productive member of our Fellowship and ultimately, society! Who'd ever have guessed that these benefits of recovery would even be possible? I am grateful to receive these benefits as a result of the changes I have made in my life.

TOP TEN

We learned that service is about gratitude and learning
how to contribute to our lives and the lives of others.
Being of Service (C.A. Pamphlet)

In my local Fellowship, it's said that ten percent of the people do ninety percent of the service work in Cocaine Anonymous. I believe this to be correct.

Committee work is perhaps the least desirable of all service work, yet it seems to be the one I like the most. Groups, Districts, Areas, and World Service Conference Committees need members, secretaries, treasurers, chairpersons, etc. How do newcomers discover that you can still have fun and be clean and sober? They go to sober dances, picnics and conventions. Who plans these events? These activities don't happen automatically. Who answers the phone lines? Who orders the chips and pamphlets? Who *writes* the literature? Who brings meetings into the hospitals and institutions where we get our lifeblood of new members and carry our message? Service committees, that's who! These committees are made up of volunteers who are giving back to the Fellowship that which was so freely given to them. No one gets paid for these services, and the work needs to be rotated so that *everyone* gets a chance to pitch in. Many people in our Fellowship swear that being of service is the key component of their continued sobriety.

You know the funniest thing about this kind of work? As much as I often *don't* want to get involved with a service project or event, I *always* end up getting back *way* more than I gave at the service committee level—every time, no exceptions. Amazing!

~~~~

Am I truly willing to go to any lengths for my recovery by volunteering for a service position that requires commitment and effort? Will I have faith that God won't give me more than I can handle but will help me fulfill the service commitments I do make?

A NEW EMPLOYER

We had a new Employer. Being all powerful, He provided what
we needed, if we kept close to Him and performed His work well.
Alcoholics Anonymous, *page 63*

A common definition of insanity is doing the same thing over and over again, expecting different results. Such was my life before recovery, and in the end, it seemed normal. I hoped to die and no longer cared who my death would affect. I was rarely (if ever) sober, whether behind the wheel of a car, at work, or at play.

Then the awful day came when the drugs didn't work anymore. Two stints in treatment centers with no surrender. Insanity prevailed.

In my third rehab, one simple phrase from *Alcoholics Anonymous*, page 63 ("We had a new Employer") changed everything for me. I felt a sliver of hope, a journey beginning. Then action and more action! The simple suggestion from an old-timer to, "Just say *yes*" was finally enough to start me on my path toward sanity and recovery.

Eventually, I made it to Step Twelve. Spiritual awakening had brought me to a realization: my new job was to do my *Higher Power's* work.

~~~~~

One day at a time, I let God know I am ready for whatever task He has for me, large or small. Not only am I ready, but I will tackle the job with gratitude, commitment, and enthusiasm. I pray that I will always remember that a simple phrase about having a new "Employer"—a God of my understanding—was the beginning of my transformation.

FRIENDS IN MANY PLACES

I did what I was told and my life expanded.
Hope, Faith & Courage Volume II, *page 88*

Who knew *committee work* would give me the opportunity to meet people from all over the world? It didn't happen overnight, of course. It started when I was a newcomer and was elected secretary of my home group. That experience gave me the courage to join the entertainment committee, which puts on dances. I would greet people at the door and, as a result, I got to know people from neighboring parts of our Fellowship. Before long, I found myself attending the local C.A. District business meetings. Eventually, I was blessed with the humbling opportunity to serve as a World Service Conference Delegate representing my C.A. Area, which is how I was introduced to people from everywhere. I met fellow addicts in recovery from across the U.S.A., Europe, the U.K., Canada and beyond. How amazing is that? I changed from a relatively shy, introverted girl, to an outgoing, well-liked woman in our C.A. Fellowship.

Sometimes I sit back and marvel, "How can this be my life?" It's as if I have lived two completely different lives. Before I found C.A., I was hopeless, sad, and completely empty inside. I had no real friends—only fellow junkies, all using each other for one wrong destructive purpose or another. And, now? *Worldwide* friendships. Not fly-by-night acquaintances either—real, *true* friends. We care about one another and are willing to help each other whenever needed, no questions asked or judgments passed. I have a good job, a happy family, and I own my own home. I am a productive member of society. Developing these friendships within C.A., both near and far, has been a key factor in making all of these dreams reality in my life. For that, I am quite blessed!

~~~~~

The life I live now is infinitely better than my previous pathetic existence. I am blessed to have made true, life-long Fellowship friends worldwide. What a gift! Real friendships are a priceless asset, much more essential than material wealth.

DODGED THE BULLET

In a crowded room on a Saturday morning, the diligent chairperson of World Services cautiously called to order the first national business meeting. After a passionate exchange of ideas, which set the format for future conferences, the meeting came to a close with a remarkable feeling of optimism.

Hope, Faith & Courage, *pages xxxi-xxxii*

While attending a C.A. World Service Conference, I suddenly experienced a moment of complete awe. I sat back, looked around me. and felt an amazing wave of gratitude that literally engulfed me, filling me up until I almost burst with love for our Fellowship. I looked around at the other members attending the Conference and knew that each of us should be dead, insane, or in prison but had been spared in a profound way for such a higher calling. Collectively and individually, C.A. had been there for us, and we had all dodged the bullet of addiction.

I think about that Conference moment often, especially when in the company of my countless program friends. The sunlight of the Spirit is always shining upon on us. We bask in God's radiance, ever mindful of the miracle each one of us has experienced. We've arrived at a place where we can truly be useful to God and the people around us, and we are immensely grateful to be there together.

~~~~~

C.A. reached out, introducing us to a life we never thought possible. We must never forget the imperative responsibility of demonstrating to newcomers that there is a wonderful, vibrant, purpose-filled life waiting for those who simply seek it. I pray that the special moments in my recovery are long remembered so that they serve as an anchor when I am faced with more trying times throughout the years.

...BUT TRUSTED SERVANTS

I learned that these commitments ensured that I went to a meeting even if I didn't feel like going. They also helped get me out of myself. And before long, I began to notice another benefit of being of service: it helped me in my quest for conscious contact with a Power greater than myself.

C.A. NewsGram, 3rd Quarter 1998

When I started to attend meetings of Cocaine Anonymous, I knew that this program wouldn't work for me. I also realized that in order to prove it didn't work, I had to do everything that was suggested. Otherwise, some sober know-it-all would say, "Well, it would have worked if you'd gone to enough meetings" (or gotten a sponsor, or been of service, or whatever). So I did the drill: I went to meetings every day, read the *Big Book*, called other people in the program, got a sponsor, took service commitments, etc.

I can't tell you how glad I am that I soon realized I was wrong—this program can and does work for me. I started looking around the rooms to see who really seemed to be getting this program. One of the first things I noticed was that the truly happy, joyous, and free people were awfully busy being of service. Yet so many of my friends continued to protest that service committee work was just not their "thing." What I try to explain is that it's not my thing either—that's why I do it!

~~~~~

If you happen to be one of those people who've always thought that service committee work is not for you, maybe you'll consider giving it a try. Chances are you'll find a whole new understanding, appreciation and respect for the Twelve Traditions, feel a little bit closer to your Higher Power, and wake up the next day clean, sober and grateful.

THE SPIRIT OF ROTATION

Rotation helps bring us spiritual rewards far more enduring than a job well done.
C.A. NewsGram, 2nd Quarter 1997

My desire to stop using cocaine and all other mind-altering substances was the driving force for me in early recovery. When told to attend meetings, get a sponsor, adopt a home group, or numerous other suggestions, I followed that direction, looking for any ray of hope as to how I could stop using and stay stopped.

For me, being of service was key. I took on any new job as if my life depended on it, which in reality, it did. I found the best way to show gratitude and add to my recovery was to be of service to the Fellowship of C.A. I also discovered the best way to serve God was to serve my fellow man. I found a feeling of belonging, which had previously been missing in my life. It was the start of replacing self-centered behavior with humility. Service took on a key role, and the Promise that feelings of uselessness and self-pity would disappear soon started to materialize. I wanted so much to give back, to help my fellows.

When the time comes, I rotate out of my service commitment—to give the next person a chance to grow as I did, to feel the power of recovery as I did, to be of service. To step out of a C.A. service position I love can be hard, just as it might have been for the person before me. I was given my chance at growth and involvement, and so should those who come after me. If I have been particularly good at the service position or don't see anyone willing or qualified to do it, moving on is especially tough. Doing so, however, often offers a real spiritual growth opportunity.

~~~~~

Service has been an amazing reward of my recovery and is enhanced by stepping out of the way to allow others the same chance to serve, receiving the same gifts and benefits during their time of service.

THE GIFTS

I have a sense of serenity in my life that I never thought possible. All of these things are wonderful but none of them compare with the greatest gift of all. The Twelve Steps, the love of the people in the Fellowship, my sponsor and sponsees all returned to me the greatest gift of all. They gave me "me."

C.A. NewsGram, 2nd Quarter 1999

I was fortunate enough to find recovery through a treatment center. While there, I was given the first gift on my road to recovery, an introduction to the Twelve Steps of C.A. The Steps have laid the groundwork for all the other miracles that have occurred in my life since then.

The door was opened to the knowledge that my addiction is, in fact, a disease, and so many of the things I had done were done while I was in an altered state. Next came the realization that I was basically a good person. I was not the useless junkie that I perceived myself to be. Instead, I was just another misguided soul, trying to find my way through the world.

From there, I received permission to not be responsible for all the world's problems. I learned that *I was not God*. I only had to worry about my own thoughts and actions.

The miracles continue to explode in my life. Today, my spouse actually treats me like a worthwhile human being (and I work hard at behaving like one). My relationship with my children is the greatest joy in my heart on a daily basis. I now have a sense of serenity that I never thought possible.

~~~~~

The gifts of recovery are plentiful and come at various times as I journey through the program. These gifts take many forms, both internal and external. I realize that having "me" back, or maybe having "me" for the first time, is a huge gift of the program.

ENDLESS POSSIBILITY

Your imagination will be fired. Life will mean something at last. The most satisfactory years of your existence lie ahead.
Alcoholics Anonymous, *page 152*

Recovery is many things. It is having fun, the sound of laughter, the making of mistakes, the experience of pain, the sacrifice of selflessness, the working of Steps, and, still, the desire for additional spiritual and emotional growth as well as serenity. In my disease, the drugs I used were never enough. That desire for "*more*" has been channeled into something healthy, something wonderful in my recovery!

I heard when I came into recovery that at first you work the Steps, and then the Steps start to work you. What was, at first, difficult to understand, let alone to practice, has now become less so. What appeared confusing is clearer to me now. My way of life has been transformed. Answers appear, where before there were only muddled, dark questions.

Having had a spiritual awakening, I am afforded the grace to sit in silence and hear God's words specific to me. If I remain focused on carrying the message while continuing to work the program, I am blessed to share these words with others and to seek to do God's will always. Carrying this message and working with others has become my highest purpose, and for that I am truly grateful and humbled. By maintaining the deep sense of gratitude born from taking the Twelve Steps, I hope to attract many other co-travelers to this incredible way of life.

~~~~~

God constantly reminds me that all is well, and that I can readily accept life as it unfolds. My mind has expanded to explore with eager anticipation the endless possibilities placed in front of me.

THE DAY GOD SHOWED UP

I could no longer look at myself in the mirror because of my self-hatred. Completely demoralized, I knew my only answer was suicide.
Hope, Faith & Courage, pages 11-12

The days when I was still practicing my disease are not so long ago, but it feels like a lifetime from those days to now. There was no hope in my future then, so I decided to just give up on life altogether. Unexpectedly, I found out that I was pregnant. The baby's father, my using partner, was not happy with this news. He thought we should commit suicide and I agreed. In fact, I tried, unsuccessfully, to do so.

We continued to get high and drink. Early one morning, I went to get some more drugs, and I found myself walking down a long alley where I saw an old lady shuffling towards me. As she passed me, she grabbed my arm and said "God has to take life, in order to give life." I was shocked and didn't understand what that meant. I turned to ask her, but she was gone. I searched the alley and around each corner and still could not find her.

I continued with my mission that day and when I got home with the drugs, all of a sudden, my baby began to move. I abruptly realized I didn't want to kill myself anymore. I gave the dope to the baby's father and went to another room, where I prayed for God to remove my desire to use. A short while later, sadly, I discovered my partner dead. He had followed through with our suicide plans.

I know God showed up in my life that day, dressed like an old woman, to save my life and the life of my baby. On the day of the funeral for my baby's father, I started into the program. Ever since then, by God's grace, I have been clean and sober. I am a good mother and eternally grateful to be alive.

~~~~~

One never knows when God is going to show up in human form. I often hear His messages coming out of people's mouths at meetings, but will I recognize Him in the face of a stranger on the street? I pray for the insight to be aware when God is working in my life.

PRIMARY PURPOSE

Each group has but one primary purpose—to carry its message to the addict who still suffers.
C.A. Tradition Five

Step Twelve first acknowledges that we have received something of extreme importance, a "spiritual awakening." The Step then instructs that this gift comes with a profound responsibility to carry this message. No matter our personal concerns, we are bound together by one common responsibility, which is the unifying purpose of our Fellowship.

Some of us are tempted, for numerous reasons, to be so many other things to the newcomer. We'd like to see their marriage put together. We'd like to help some regain jobs or positions of trust with their family. These are all noble endeavors; however, our expertise is that we have recovered from a seemingly hopeless condition. We may be tempted to try to do more than that for which we are qualified. Experience has made clear that only a recovered addict can reach an addict who still suffers. The responsibility to "carry this message" amounts to a sacred trust, and by unifying our Fellowship with this purpose, we honor that trust. Therefore, our primary spiritual intention must remain to simply "carry this message" of hope and recovery to the addict who still suffers.

~~~~~

Let me be aware that a spiritual awakening has profoundly altered my reaction to life, and that I have something to offer to the newcomer. Guide me to be aware of the limitations of C.A. help. Help me to remember that the C.A. message is simple and that I don't need to complicate it. My gratitude today is for a singular purpose unifying the C.A. Fellowship.

USEFUL AND HAPPY

I had never been successful, it seems, at anything until I found the C.A. program. It was as if it were invented for me.
Hope, Faith & Courage, *page 103*

The C.A. program allows me to treat my addiction manifested through three main problem areas in my life. In no particular order, my body, my mind and my spirit are riddled with mayhem. All these problem areas must be zealously and continuously addressed in order for me to recover.

First, I quit using cocaine and all other mind-altering substances. This allows my body to heal from the harmful physical effects produced by ingesting these toxins for so long and in so many different ways. Abstinence also greatly tempers my incessant obsessive thinking. Working the Steps and familiarizing myself with all applicable C.A. literature significantly alleviates the overpowering compulsion to use. Finally, soul healing begins with service to my Higher Power and those around me and continues with doing Step work to the best of my ability, always seeking God's will for my life.

I have found that recovery from my addiction has allowed the God of my understanding to fit me comfortably into the world. While life isn't always simple and pain free, I've increasingly found the ability to maintain a useful and happy demeanor. What a distinct contrast to my previous hopeless condition.

~~~~~

Today, I am grateful for the major healing I've experienced since getting sober in C.A. Let me remember that as long as I am striving to know and do God's will, I will be given whatever I need to overcome all difficulties.

OUR MESSAGE FORWARD AND BACK

Most C.A. members owe their sobriety to the fact that someone else was willing to share a great gift with them. . . . We in Cocaine Anonymous urge you: DO NOT DELAY. We want to share what we have learned with other addicts because experience has taught us that we keep what we have by giving it away. You will likely be helping your sponsor as much as your sponsor is helping you.

Choosing Your Sponsor (C.A. Pamphlet)

The beautiful and wondrous structure of this program has made it uniquely possible for me to hear the C.A. message of hope from another addict who was practicing the Twelfth Step. Today this same structure offers me the spiritually profound opportunity of returning that gift by stepping into the messenger's place.

In our program, we often create interwoven connections as the newcomer reaches forward and those with time reach back to meet and join them on our collective paths of recovery, one day at a time. Each of us then becomes a link reaching out in both directions. Thus, in a continuous relationship of shared experience, one addict to another, bound by a message of hope that we can recover and empowered by our Ultimate Authority, the Fellowship of C.A. is sustained, and the sobriety of each participating individual is ensured for yet another day.

Along this path, and bound by this link, we are blessed to share the little victories over our addiction as well as the more profound victories which are promised as we move through our Step work and continue to be of service to the Fellowship.

~~~~~

I welcome the chance to recognize this link, reaching in both directions, and truly appreciate the special bond produced by sponsorship. I enjoy my sponsorship family, connected by our lineage forward and back.

GIFTS OF SERVICE —
A RETROSPECTIVE

In addition to finding a spiritual way of life, recovery is about changing negative aspects of our personalities into positive ones.
Being of Service (C.A. Pamphlet)

The following was written by a then long-time Chair of the C.A. World Service Office Board, as he rotated out of that position:

> I wanted to communicate a little of what I and others who also serve on the W.S.O. Board of Directors have received as the result of our commitments to service on behalf of Cocaine Anonymous. For some, a chapter of their service life is coming to a close. Three of us will all rotate out at the end of the Conference later this month. Collectively we have served over 15 years on this Board. I know and believe that this effort has changed all of us for the better. Service is not always delightful; we all have to work a strong program to be able to deal with the ups and downs, but it is ever so spiritually rewarding (even when we don't think so). The Fellowship of Cocaine Anonymous will survive if each of us remembers that "personal recovery depends on C.A. unity" (*Tradition One*). It was C.A. that saved my life because there were people willing to take time from their busy schedules to set up a meeting that I could attend. I will always continue to be of service at some level. I owe C.A. *at least* that much.

~~~~

I pray that I may have the chance to serve our C.A. Fellowship in a variety of capacities. Wonderful gifts will come to me as a by-product of service. I can't wait to discover all the spiritual rewards.

HAPPY HOLIDAYS?

In my home we were adept at keeping up appearances, and so long as we dressed well, smiled, and went on the right holidays, everything was fine. Of course, inside our home things were far from all right.
Hope, Faith & Courage Volume II, *page 41*

What is it that makes the holidays especially hard for some? Often it is because family gatherings can breed a negative atmosphere, yet attendance is somehow construed as mandatory or, at the very least, "expected." My being in recovery does not necessarily change my family members. It does, however, give me a choice about voluntarily putting myself in jeopardy. If drunkenness, drugging, fighting, abusive or demeaning behavior exist in my family environment, why bother with it? I can love my family from a distance. The *right* thought or action is to never subject myself to abusive situations. If I do choose to participate, I can shorten my stay or take a recovering friend along for moral support.

Some holiday suggestions which have helped me are to take in some extra meetings or visit a few recovery facilities. Other options include going to a movie with a program friend or volunteering to work my local C.A. helpline. I ask the God of my understanding for direction and inspiration, and then do what feels right.

~~~~~

The key to having a happy holiday season is to treat the holiday like any other day. Do what you need to do to maintain a healthy spiritual condition and to promote serenity and happiness.

SPIRITUAL EXPEDITION

We have found much of heaven and we have been rocketed into a
fourth dimension of existence of which we had not even dreamed.
Alcoholics Anonymous, *page 25*

The Twelve-Step process is a spiritual journey. Step Twelve plainly states, "having had a spiritual awakening as the result of these Steps. . . ."

The bottom line is that each of us will have our own variety of a spiritual experience or awakening. It is by no means an identical course for everyone. I can, however, expect my spiritual awakening to bring about a marked shift in my attitude, thought processes, and conscious connection with my Higher Power. I've come to understand that my spiritual exploration (as outlined in Step Eleven) brings me more joy and serenity than any other aspect of the program. This one facet enables me to handle literally all other areas of my life with grace, dignity and a sense of faith that no matter *what* happens, I'm going to be okay. What a gift! I've also discovered that my spiritual understanding and connection keeps getting broader and deeper the more I delve into Eleventh-Step work.

All of us travel our own spiritual journeys, which come in as many shapes, sizes, and destinations as there are people. I can't tell you which direction yours will take, but I do know that the roadmap begins with the Steps.

~~~~~

Getting clean and sober means nothing without learning how to grow spiritually. Don't cheat yourself out of the best ride in recovery. Hang onto your hat and have an amazing expedition.

THE POWER OF REACHING OUT

. . . what comes to us alone may be garbled by our own rationalization and wishful thinking. . . . While the comment or advice of others may be by no means infallible, it is likely to be far more specific than any direct guidance we may receive while we are still so inexperienced in establishing contact with a Power greater than ourselves.

Twelve Steps and Twelve Traditions, *page 60*

One morning, while sitting at work, I was feeling rather disgusted about doing service work and the program in general. However, through listening and learning, I knew that I'd better share these feelings with someone else who'd understand and give me some much-needed advice. I decided to email a couple of people in my recovery network to ask for help in adjusting my attitude. God truly does work through others—if He is sought!

This is the response that I received, which helped me to start my day over with a smile: "No matter what you do, someone is going to have something negative to say. If we allow negative people to have an impact on something good that we are doing, we will never finish the things we start. There comes a point when we have to brush off those people who comment negatively about our lives, actions or feelings. Those people, regardless of who they are, are not happy."

I must remember, everyone in these rooms is in a different place in their process. They will grow at God's rate of speed and not mine! I simply must pray for God's help in letting the unconstructive comments roll off my back, keep my head high, and walk tall. I need only keep one fact in the forefront of my mind: no matter how large or small the task, we are doing God's work.

~~~~~

How easy it is to reach out to my Fellowship friends when I need an attitude adjustment during the day. The hard part is remembering that I have the option to do so! God, please help me to always make good use of my recovery resources. It's never too late to start my day over.

LOVE AND SERVICE

*The Twelve Steps make me ready for the real solution: to
be of service in a healthy way. Helping others is the way
to both help myself and to grow into another person.*
Hope, Faith & Courage Volume II, *page 26*

Some of the early pioneers of the recovery movement got "it," C.A.'s founders
lived "it," and my old sponsor helped me to comprehend "it" in words that I could
understand. He said, "If you're not giving back to the world around you, you're
letting the best in life pass you by." The world around us today is one of recovery
and gratitude, for a Cocaine Anonymous program showing us how to never have
to use a mind-altering substance again, one day at a time. We've experienced and
learned, through action, love, and service to our fellows, that the peace and
freedom we hear shared in meetings is truly achievable.

In his farewell talk, Dr. Bob said, "Our Twelve Steps, when simmered down to the
last, resolve themselves into the words 'love' and 'service.' We understand what
love is, and we understand what service is. So let's bear those two things in
mind."*

~~~~~

May I reflect on the gift of my recovery, taking a moment to consider how it came
to me and how I can give back to the world around me. No matter how I choose
to give back to Cocaine Anonymous, whether it be great or small, may I know it is
essential to my recovery. May I make a difference in the lives of others, recognizing
that the greatest effect my service has is on my own life.

*July 3, 1950 speech at the First International A.A. Convention in Cleveland, Ohio.

MY JOURNEY

Throughout this journey I have seen miracles. I have seen the desire and obsession to use removed not only in my life but also in the lives of countless others. I have witnessed hopelessness turn to hope and on to joy in the lives of so many of those around me. I know this gift is precious, and keeping it relies on my being of service and continuing to work the Twelfth Step on a daily basis.

Hope, Faith & Courage Volume II, *page 45*

Recovery maps out a spiritual journey, headed away from active addiction. The road travelled is sometimes wide, sometimes narrow, sometimes straight and sometimes meandering. In order to properly enjoy the ride, I don't focus on the journey's destination. I understand the importance of soaking up the details, taking my time to actively move forward. The journey has been wonderfully rich and steady, as well as emotionally, physically and spiritually healing. As healing occurs, love and tolerance of myself and others has been heightened. For the first time, I find meaningful solutions to implement the design for living directly received from working the Steps and from my Higher Power. Choosing a path is paramount, but honoring the sacred expedition itself is imperative.

My journey allows me to witness places, events, and insights I never envisioned or expected. With perfect synchronicity, I meet others who share their experience, strength, and hope with me at just the right moments. Thus, another onion layer peels away, or resolutions manifest to unsolved issues. Along the way, I will be faced with a wide range of challenges. Lessons and solutions will offer themselves just when I need them, as if on cue. The adage "more will be revealed" becomes crystal clear. I will honor the promise found in *Alcoholics Anonymous* (page 164) that God will disclose more to you and to me throughout this journey.

~~~~~

God, please walk with me on my journey in recovery. Please keep me and my co-travelers safe. May our lessons be gentle along the way.

December 27

KEEP COMIN' BACK

We alcoholics are undisciplined. So we let God discipline us. . . .
Alcoholics Anonymous, *page 88*

As I sit here writing this, wondering why after two years of sobriety, I couldn't stay sober for more than sixty-five days at a time, I suddenly realized it's because I quit giving my time to Cocaine Anonymous. I stopped making coffee, giving people rides to meetings, doing service work, sharing my story at meetings, and working the Steps. I also didn't get a sponsor. Most of all, I didn't trust in my Higher Power.

I truly believe I am clean and sober today for one reason only: that God has a job for me to do. That job is to carry the message of recovery to other addicts that still suffer. I also believe that I must place God first, before myself and others. When I live and feel this way, every day, every minute, things seem to work out for the better. Without God, with only *me* trying to run the show, my life was in deep trouble.

With all my heart, I hope you will understand what I have said here. Work the program! It works if you work it. I suggest that if you are feeling down, please talk to someone. Reach out to someone, go to a meeting, pray, and *just keep comin' back!*

~~~~

How easy is it to slack off on your program? Life's going good and complacency sets in: "I can skip my home group tonight, there's a good show on TV." When thoughts like this start creeping in, it's time to *double up* on my recovery efforts.

DESIRE, THE ONLY REQUIREMENT

No matter who you are, no matter how low you've gone, no matter how grave
your emotional complications—even your crimes—we still can't deny you A.A.
Twelve Steps and Twelve Traditions, *page 139*

Do you want to stop? Are you finally tired of the addict lifestyle? Do you have even a little desire to quit cocaine and all other mind-altering substances? If so, you qualify as a C.A. member. It is truly that simple. No matter how much someone might be caught in the disease at any given moment, everyone deserves a chance to recover.

Time after time, seemingly crazy, confused individuals stick around, grow and change into productive members of our Fellowship and society as a whole. Only a Higher Power can know someone's true desire. We are simply carriers of the recovery message. For example, take one of the current members in my local Fellowship. When he first came around, he appeared hopeless and helpless. He would show up for a meeting or two and then would not be seen for months. He would generally be under the influence of some mind-altering substance when he came around and he followed zero suggestions. After years of the same behavior and actions, our members would always welcome him even when it seemed he was lacking the desire to stay sober.

Some four years ago, he reappeared and started to show up regularly. He listened at meetings, participated in fellowship after the meetings, got a sponsor and started working the Twelve Steps. Today he is an active member of C.A. He carries the message to many Hospitals & Institutions panels. He takes part in service work at many levels, freely giving back the gift that was given to him. He is there for his family, friends, and the Fellowship, but most of all, for himself. Had the local members tuned him out or not told him to "keep coming back" each time, he might not be alive today.

~~~~~

C.A.'s doors must always be open for any and all who want a chance at something different—something better than active addiction. It is not my place to judge someone else's desire. Holding out the hand of recovery, without judgment, is my mission. I never know when someone will finally reach out and grab on—for life!

FINE-TUNED STATE OF MIND

We, who prided ourselves on our fine-tuned state of mind! Nothing mattered more to us than the straw, the pipe, the needle. Even if it made us feel miserable, we had to have it.
To the Newcomer (C.A. Pamphlet)

Last night, a friend returned to our meeting. He was coming off a particularly bad run. This man always struck me as being extremely bright, and he shared with us that his way hadn't worked in a long time. Now, he was facing some serious physical manifestations of our disease. The new medical developments scared him enough to make it back sooner than he had planned.

He rambled on about just how bad it was out in the using world, trying to explain and rationalize his confusion about his disease. He spoke of the whirlwind devastation he had caused and, in the same breath, about being baffled over using again. He described crawling around on the floor looking for white specks, which is referenced in our reading, *Who is a Cocaine Addict?* What had become of his fine-tuned state of mind? (*Who is a Cocaine Addict?* C.A. reading)

I could so relate. C.A. offered me a solution to this hopeless state. The Twelve Steps freed me from my self-centered destructive trance, so I could learn to love others and find a way to love myself as well. The solution is readily available to those who seek it.

Frankly, if I am being honest, now that I have some clean and sober days back to back, I forget the little details of what it was really like when I came in. Newcomers and returning members remind me of the horror and hell waiting for me on the other side. I also remember hearing that what addicts do is use drugs, as that is their normal state. In C.A., they have the chance to arrest that normal state by doing what is suggested, one day at a time.

~~~~~

Thank you, Spirit of Intelligence, for freeing me from the ravages of addiction and for bringing me to a life which was beyond my imagination. Let me be a useful agent in bringing about this miracle for others.

IS THIS ALL THERE IS?

> . . . we commence to put our . . . way of living to practical
> use, day by day, in fair weather and foul. Then comes the
> acid test: can we stay sober, keep in emotional balance,
> and live to good purpose under all conditions?
>
> Twelve Steps and Twelve Traditions, page 88

Sometimes in meetings I hear the topic of emotional sobriety discussed. To me, emotional sobriety is what helps me deal with the unpredictable mood swings that hit some of us from time to time, even when sober for a while and still actively working all aspects of the program. I have heard the lows of these emotional fluctuations referred to as the "recovery blahs," where the feeling of discontent and restlessness comes over us, seemingly from nowhere. I do service at many levels, have a sponsor, sponsor others, have both led and participated in Big Book studies and regularly go to meetings. I finished my amends and formally re-work the Steps yearly. Inventory is still a key tool in my recovery, along with active prayer and daily meditation. And yet, sometimes, I still ponder, "Is this all there is? Is this what the rest of my life in recovery is going to look like?"

This "stuck" mood hits me randomly in my recovery, without reason. Those simple gratifications/satisfactions from giving away what I have found or being of service seem temporarily to be for naught. I don't want to drink or use, I just want to be comfortable and confident in my sobriety. The challenge becomes how to achieve and maintain the ongoing emotional sobriety I so earnestly seek, where I embrace and understand what I have versus questioning its very foundation.

How do I move past these recovery blahs back to acceptance? I pray. I continue in service, redoubling my efforts. I work harder on moving past and letting go of my character defects. I practice gratitude. I draw even closer to the Fellowship and my C.A. friends. I remember the grace by which I had that moment of clarity where I became willing to go to any lengths to stay sober. I remind myself recovery is far too precious a gift to ever be taken for granted. I try not to take myself too seriously, practicing Rule #62 (Twelve Steps and Twelve Traditions, page 149). I earnestly try to remain connected, walking sober through these bewildering feelings when they occur. Most of all, I take great satisfaction from my awareness that enduring spiritual progress remains my primary goal, that I had better show up to witness God's miracles every day in my life, that there are no accidents in God's world. When the recovery blahs attack, Step Two is my key defense.

~~~~~

Even when I ponder, "Is this all there is?," I strive to remain content in God's simple graces. I will accept my very humanness and rally using my many program tools. I will remember, "This, too, shall pass."

C·A· FRIENDSHIPS

My father always told me that I'd be lucky to have one good friend who I could count on to tell me the truth no matter what it was, to hold me when times were tough, and to play with when times were good. Today I have more of these friends than I could ever spend time with.

Hope, Faith and Courage Volume II, *page 124*

Most of my life, I was uncomfortable around people. I was afraid of them and unsure of myself. I was resentful and didn't trust anyone. I found great comfort in my lone wolf approach to life. When I came into Cocaine Anonymous, I kept hearing that I should just jump in and thereby become part of the Fellowship. I certainly didn't believe I could do this, especially sober! While I enjoyed meetings, particularly the stories, solutions, laughter and our common bond, I had a hard time connecting with these same people outside the rooms, or even chatting with them before or after the meetings. I still felt hopelessly alone.

Working the Steps and insightful sponsorship changed all this for me. After I completed the Steps once through, I found myself attracted to the Fellowship differently. For perhaps the first time in my entire life, I felt useful. I had developed a deep caring for my sponsor, and my sponsor felt the same about me. We had already trudged quite a bit on my first journey through the Steps. I started to come around more and to chat with fellow members socially. I even started to do things with these people like going for coffee or attending a concert as a group of sober recovering addicts. Close, enduring friendships magically materialized, many of which are still with me, well into my third decade of sobriety. Today, my favorite place in the world is a meeting, convention or gathering of Cocaine Anonymous.

~~~~~

Am I feeling uncomfortable in any area of my life? Today I invite my Higher Power to join me and show me what I need to do to be useful and happy. May I always be the friend to others which I would like them to be to me.

A

TITLE INDEX

389

B

TOPIC INDEX

394

Following Suggestions: See Suggestions

Footwork: Mar 18, Jul 13

Forgiveness: Feb 22, Mar 1, Mar 13, May 7, May 26, Jul 14, Jul 18, Jul 31, Aug 11, Aug 28, Aug 29, Sep 6, Sep 17, Sep 24

Freedom: Jan 26, Mar 10, Mar 28, Mar 29, Apr 19, Apr 23, May 1, May 2, May 9, May 20, May 23, May 28, May 31, Jun 13, Jun 18, Jul 10, Jul 24, Jul 25, Aug 11, Aug 28, Sep 1, Sep 9, Sep 15, Sep 25, Sep 28, Sep 29, Oct 2, Oct 30, Oct 31, Nov 3, Dec 5, Dec 25

Friendship: Apr 3, May 11, May 19, May 20, Jun 18, Nov 3, Dec 4, Dec 11, Dec 31

Frustration: Jul 7

Fun: Feb 24, May 15, Nov 12, Dec 16

Gentle: Aug 2

Gifts Of Recovery: Jan 8, Jan 31, Mar 18, Apr 14, Apr 26, May 1, May 24, May 25, May 28, May 29, Jun 14, Jul 10, Jul 12, Jul 24, Aug 6, Aug 8, Sep 3, Sep 28, Oct 11, Nov 22, Nov 26, Dec 4, Dec 5, Dec 11, Dec 15, Dec 21

Give It Away: See Carrying The Message

Giving: Jul 16, Dec 6

Giving Back: Feb 21, Feb 23, Apr 25, May 9, Jun 20, Jul 19, Jul 24, Sep 8, Sep 12, Sep 21, Oct 11, Oct 28, Nov 22, Dec 9, Dec 14, Dec 25

Goals: Mar 9, Apr 18, Oct 10

God Consciousness: See Conscious Contact

God Reliance: See Reliance

God With Skin: Aug 23, Dec 17

God Within: Feb 3, Feb 8, Mar 16

God's Will: Jan 5, Mar 4, Mar 5, Mar 30, Apr 19, May 3, Jul 5, Jul 29, Aug 15, Aug 21, Aug 24, Aug 29, Sep 22, Sep 26, Oct 9, Oct 21, Oct 22, Oct 26, Nov 2, Nov 17, Nov 19, Nov 24, Dec 7, Dec 16, Dec 19

God's Work: Jun 5, Sep 19, Dec 10, Dec 24

Grace: Jan 19, Jan 24, Jan 26, Mar 2, Apr 4, Apr 19, May 3, Aug 9, Aug 24, Sep 24, Oct 14, Nov 18, Dec 30

Gratitude: Jan 3, Jan 7, Jan 25, Feb 4, Feb 6, Mar 1, Mar 24, Apr 4, Apr 18, Apr 21, Apr 28, May 6, May 14, May 18, May 24, Jun 14, Jun 16, Jun 20, Jul 1, Jul 11, Jul 12, Jul 20, Jul 22, Jul 24, Aug 8, Aug 14, Sep 3, Sep 12, Sep 13, Sep 18, Oct 9, Oct 22, Oct 27, Nov 14, Nov 18, Nov 22, Nov 27, Dec 8, Dec 10, Dec 12, Dec 16

Grief: See Loss

Group: Jan 18, Feb 15, Apr 22, Jun 15, Jul 16, Sep 8, Oct 19, Nov 29

Group Conscience: Feb 15, Jun 15, Jul 26, Sep 14, Nov 29

Group Inventory: Jun 13, Jul 26

Growth: Jan 13, Feb 6, Feb 18, Mar 3, Mar 9, May 18, May 20, May 21, May 24, Jun 7, Jun 25, Jul 2, Jul 4, Jul 28, Aug 18, Sep 20, Oct 2, Oct 5, Oct 9, Oct 16, Oct 21, Nov 12, Dec 1, Dec 14

Guidance: Jan 3, Feb 13, Mar 28, Apr 1, Apr 9, May 27, Jun 24, Aug 18, Aug 21, Oct 16, Oct 21, Oct 22, Nov 4

Guilt: Apr 2, Apr 7, Apr 28, Jul 18, Aug 28, Sep 2, Oct 24

Happiness: Jan 28, Mar 21, May 3, May 6, May 16, May 31, Aug 26, Sep 1, Sep 23, Sep 28, Nov 4, Dec 19

Happy, Joyous And Free: Apr 2, May 4, May 6, May 16, Sep 4, Sep 23, Sep 25, Nov 10, Nov 12, Dec 13

Harmony: Jan 18, Sep 14, Nov 15

Healing: Mar 9, Mar 18, Apr 26, May 7, May 10, May 26, May 30, Jul 20, Aug 4, Aug 20, Sep 11, Sep 30, Oct 6, Nov 4, Nov 12, Dec 19, Dec 26

Helping Others: See Working With Others

Hitting Bottom: Jan 2, Feb 27, Mar 22, Jun 5, Jun 10, Jun 16, Sep 10, Nov 10, Dec 29

Holidays: Dec 6, Dec 22

Home Group: Apr 11, May 20

Honesty: Mar 19, Mar 23, Mar 28, Apr 2, Apr 5, Apr 16, May 1, May 8, Jun 5, Jun 7, Jun 9, Jun 27, Jun 28, Jun 29, Jun 30, Jul 8, Aug 16, Aug 17, Sep 5, Dec 7

Hope: Jan 11, Jan 12, Jan 26, Jan 31, Feb 17, Feb 22, Feb 26, Mar 22, Apr 5, Apr 9, Apr 15, May 25, Jun 1, Jun 10, Jun 16, Jul 12, Jul 17, Jul 24, Aug 7, Aug 14, Sep 5, Sep 6, Sep 10, Nov 4, Dec 10, Dec 18, Dec 20

Hopeless: Jan 12, Feb 17, May 27, Dec 29

Hospitals & Institutions: Jan 26, Jan 31, Feb 17, Feb 23, Mar 26, Jun 20, Jul 12, Aug 20

Hugs: Jan 21, Aug 4

Hurting: May 30, Sep 11, Sep 17

Humility: Jan 3, Jan 24, Mar 23, Apr 25, May 14, May 20, May 28, Jun 4, Jun 28, Jul 1, Jul 8, Jul 24, Aug 25, Sep 2, Oct 21, Oct 24, Nov 13, Dec 3, Dec 14

Identifying: Jan 8, Feb 24, Mar 29, Apr 3, Apr 15, May 2, Jun 20, Jun 25, Aug 14, Aug 19, Sep 7, Sep 27, Oct 29, Nov 4

Impatience: Jun 3

Imperfection: Jul 4, Sep 20, Oct 21

Insanity: Feb 16, May 27, Sep 5, Dec 10

Integrity: May 29

Into Action: Feb 9, May 5, Jul 11, Jul 13, Aug 30, Sep 29, Oct 9, Nov 14

Inventory: Apr 23, May 23, May 24, Jun 13, Jun 19, Jun 28, Sep 17, Oct 1, Oct 3, Oct 12, Oct 16, Oct 21, Dec 3

Inverted Triangle: Feb 23

Isolation: Feb 22, Mar 22, May 13, Aug 18, Dec 31

Journey: Jan 13, Feb 10, Apr 7, May 4, Aug 18, Oct 17, Nov 2, Nov 10, Nov 11, Dec 26, Dec 31

Joy: Feb 24, Mar 19, Apr 18, May 3, May 6, Jun 25, Sep 23, Sep 24, Oct 4, Dec 8, Dec 23

Next Right Thing: Feb 16, Mar 15, May 5, Jun 9, Jul 15

Never Alone: Jan 17, Feb 6, Mar 7, Mar 8, Mar 16, Mar 29, Apr 6, Apr 29, May 11, May 13, May 26, Jun 18, Jul 3, Aug 1, Aug 21

Newcomers: Jan 1, Jan 9, Jan 21, Jan 25, Feb 23, Mar 1, Apr 3, Apr 8, Apr 22, Apr 26, May 12, May 15, May 28, May 29, Jun 22, Jul 12, Aug 19, Oct 28, Dec 18, Dec 28, Dec 29

No Accidents: May 25, Aug 21, Sep 11

No Regrets: Apr 9, Apr 13

Obsession Of The Mind: See Allergy/Obsession

Obstacles: Mar 7, Jun 28, Jul 23, Nov 7

Old-Timers: Feb 23, Apr 8, Jun 22, Aug 8

One Day At A Time: Jan 7, Jan 14, Jan 16, Feb 22, Mar 19, Jun 5, Sep 24, Oct 30, Nov 5, Nov 10

Open-Minded: Mar 19, Apr 27, Jun 4, Jun 7, Jun 27, Jul 5, Aug 16, Aug 31, Sep 5, Dec 7

Opportunity: Jan 31, Mar 10, Jul 25, Dec 5

Outside Issues: Oct 23

Pain: Apr 7, Aug 17, Sep 11, Sep 30, Oct 4

Paranoia: Jan 17

Parenting: Apr 16, Aug 10, Sep 17

Pass It On: See Carrying The Message

Passion: Jan 20, Sep 14

Patience: Jan 25, Feb 22, Mar 28, Apr 9, Jun 3, Jun 28, Aug 13

Peace: Jan 7, Jan 13, Jan 20, Mar 2, Mar 9, Mar 17, Mar 19, Mar 22, Mar 28, May 1, May 3, May 16, Jun 6, Jun 23, Jul 18, Jul 24, Aug 3, Aug 31, Sep 1, Sep 4, Sep 28, Oct 23, Nov 7, Nov 8, Nov 14, Dec 3, Dec 7, Dec 25

People Pleasing: May 21

Perception: Jan 15, Feb 10, Jun 6, Aug 12, Aug 31, Dec 5

Perspective: Mar 17, Apr 11, Apr 28, May 14, Jun 6, Jun 14, Jul 23, Aug 5, Aug 27, Sep 5, Nov 30

Perfectionism: Aug 2

Perseverance: Sep 20, Nov 7

Physical Allergy: See Allergy/Obsession

Physical Recovery: Jul 21

Placing People On Pedestals: Jul 4

Powerlessness: Jan 27, Jan 30, Feb 11, Feb 13, Mar 12, Apr 30, Jun 10, Jun 29, Jul 6, Jul 7, Aug 17

Practicing A Program: Feb 2

Practicing Principles: See Principles

Searching: Feb 3, Feb 11

Self-Discovery: Apr 1, Apr 2, Jul 2, Nov 4, Nov 11

Self-Esteem: Apr 17, Jun 28, Jul 14, Jul 17, Jul 31

Self-Loathing: Mar 18, Apr 2, Apr 14, Jul 31, Aug 4

Self-Love: Mar 13, Mar 18, Apr 2, Jun 21, Jul 5, Jul 21, Jul 31, Aug 2, Oct 6

Self-Pity: Jan 25, Mar 22, Jun 17, Jul 6, Sep 12

Self-Supporting: Jun 26, Sep 8

Self-Will: Jan 5, Mar 2, Mar 30, Apr 19, Jun 2, Jul 1, Jul 7, Aug 15, Sep 22

Self-Worth: See Self Esteem

Selfishness: Mar 24, Jun 3, Aug 15, Oct 21, Dec 2

Serenity: Jan 7, Jan 13, Jan 19, Jan 20, Mar 2, Mar 23, Mar 24, Apr 19, May 3, Jun 2, Jul 7, Jul 18, Jul 24, Jul 30, Aug 13, Aug 26, Sep 1, Sep 4, Oct 1, Oct 23, Oct 25, Nov 8, Nov 14, Nov 28, Dec 15

Serenity Prayer: Aug 5, Nov 8

Service: Jan 21, Feb 23, Mar 21, Mar 26, Apr 3, Apr 8, Apr 11, Apr 13, Apr 18, Apr 25, May 9, May 14, May 20, May 25, May 28, Jun 15, Jun 20, Jun 24, Jul 12, Jul 14, Jul 17, Jul 19, Jul 26, Jul 27, Aug 8, Aug 17, Aug 20, Aug 22, Aug 27, Sep 14, Sep 21, Oct 8, Oct 9, Oct 15, Oct 18, Oct 19, Oct 31, Nov 14, Nov 22, Nov 26, Dec 2, Dec 5, Dec 6, Dec 9, Dec 11, Dec 12, Dec 13, Dec 14, Dec 21, Dec 25, Dec 27, Dec 28

Sex: May 23, Jun 19

Shame: Apr 2, Apr 6, Apr 7, Apr 28, May 26, Jun 19, Jul 18, Aug 28, Sep 2, Sep 5, Oct 6, Nov 25

Sharing: Jan 7, Feb 26, Mar 28, Mar 29, Apr 15, Apr 17, May 12, May 21, May 22, May 25, May 26, Jun 25, Jul 28, Sep 21, Nov 1, Dec 6, Dec 20

Silence: Jun 23, Nov 16

Similarities: Apr 1, Apr 7, Oct 29

Simplicity: Jan 16

Singleness Of Purpose Jul 27, Dec 18

Skepticism: May 5

Slogans: Jan 5, Apr 21

Small-Mindedness: May 4

Sobriety Versus Recovery: Feb 2, Aug 20

Solution: Jan 9, Jan 14, Jan 25, Jan 29, Mar 20, Mar 22, Apr 6, Apr 20, May 1, Jun 17, Jul 6, Aug 20, Sep 14, Oct 27, Oct 29, Nov 27, Nov 28, Dec 29

Special Workers: Sep 18

Spirit Of Rotation: Aug 27, Dec 14, Dec 21

Spiritual Awakening: Feb 4, Feb 8, Feb 11, Feb 12, Feb 25, Mar 2, Mar 18, Mar 24, Apr 17, Apr 25, May 20, Jun 5, Jun 27, Jul 9, Jul 10, Jul 18, Aug 6, Aug 20, Aug 30, Aug 31, Sep 21, Oct 17, Oct 25, Oct 27, Nov 10, Nov 14, Nov 30, Dec 8, Dec 10, Dec 11, Dec 16, Dec 18, Dec 23, Dec 28

Spiritual Connection: Jan 3, Jan 20, Feb 12, Mar 3, Mar 11, Mar 17, Mar 19, Apr 19, May 3, May 13, Jun 6, Jul 5, Sep 19, Sep 26, Oct 13, Oct 17, Oct 20, Oct 22, Nov 11

Spiritual Current: Sep 18

Spiritual Dependence: See Reliance

Spiritual Enrichment: Feb 23, May 21, Nov 6

Spiritual Experience: See Spiritual Awakening

Spiritual Growth: Feb 7, Feb 23, Mar 6, Apr 9, May 21, Jun 27, Jun 28, Jul 2, Aug 5, Aug 24, Sep 17, Sep 23, Oct 15, Oct 17, Oct 26, Dec 14, Dec 23

Spiritual Principles: See Principles

Spirituality: Jan 29, Feb 8, Feb 10, Mar 1, Mar 5, Mar 16, Mar 19, Jun 4, Jun 6, Jun 27, Jul 14, Aug 3, Aug 17, Sep 11, Sep 16, Oct 17, Nov 6, Nov 26, Dec 12

Sponsorship: Jan 7, Jan 16, Feb 21, Feb 25, Apr 1, Apr 10, Apr 28, May 8, May 20, May 21, May 23, May 24, May 28, Jun 19, Jun 22, Jun 24, Jul 4, Jul 9, Jul 28, Aug 1, Aug 22, Sep 15, Sep 21, Sep 24, Oct 9, Oct 11, Oct 31, Dec 20, Dec 31

Step One: Jan 2, Jan 4, Jan 8, Jan 10, Jan 27, Jan 29, Jan 30, Feb 3, Feb 28, Jun 10, Jun 29, Aug 16, Aug 30, Sep 22, Oct 25, Dec 1

Step Two: Feb 8, Feb 20, Feb 28, Feb 29, Mar 2, Mar 12, May 27, Aug 30, Sep 16, Sep 22, Oct 17, Oct 25, Dec 1, Dec 30

Step Three: Feb 5, Feb 9, Mar 2, Mar 4, Mar 5, Mar 14, Mar 15, Mar 27, Mar 30, Mar 31, Apr 19, Apr 30, Jun 17, Aug 3, Aug 15, Aug 30, Sep 22, Oct 9, Oct 17, Oct 25, Nov 14, Nov 24, Dec 1, Dec 7

Step Four: Mar 25, Apr 2, Apr 14, Apr 23, Apr 28, May 23, May 24, May 26, Jun 19, Jun 25, Jun 28, Jul 11, Oct 1, Oct 25, Nov 27, Dec 1

Step Five: Mar 24, Apr 16, Apr 28, May 2, May 8, May 23, May 26, Jun 25, Jun 28, Jul 11, Oct 25, Dec 1

Step Six: May 26, Jun 7, Jun 8, Jun 28, Jul 3, Jul 5, Jul 11, Jul 14, Oct 25, Dec 1

Step Seven: Mar 5, May 26, Jul 3, Jul 9, Jul 11, Jul 13, Jul 14, Oct 16, Oct 24, Oct 25, Dec 1

Step Eight: May 26, Jul 13, Aug 11, Sep 6, Sep 9, Sep 15, Sep 29, Oct 25, Dec 1

Step Nine: May 26, Jul 13, Jul 18, Jul 25, Aug 28, Sep 9, Sep 15, Sep 29, Oct 25, Dec 1

Step Ten: May 26, Jul 13, Oct 1, Oct 2, Oct 3, Oct 9, Oct 12, Oct 21, Oct 25, Oct 26, Nov 9, Nov 25, Dec 1

Step Eleven: Feb 8, Apr 19, Jun 6, Jul 13, Aug 3, Aug 10, Aug 15, Sep 16, Sep 24, Sep 26, Oct 16, Oct 17, Oct 22, Oct 25, Nov 5, Nov 9, Nov 17, Nov 18, Nov 19, Nov 20, Nov 24, Dec 1, Dec 23

Step Twelve: Feb 1, Mar 1, Apr 18, Aug 30, Oct 11, Oct 17, Oct 25, Dec 1, Dec 3, Dec 9, Dec 10, Dec 12, Dec 18, Dec 23

Stick With The Winners: Feb 16, May 15, May 22, Sep 27

Stinking Thinking: May 17, Jul 10, Dec 7

Struggle: Feb 28, Feb 29, Mar 2, Mar 24, Jul 11

Stuck: Aug 21, Dec 30

Success: May 22

Suggestions: Jan 16, Feb 8, Feb 25, Apr 27, May 9, May 20, Jun 1, Jun 5, Jun 30, Jul 8, Aug 6, Aug 17, Sep 10, Sep 25, Oct 31, Nov 8, Nov 28, Dec 13, Dec 22

Suicide: Jun 30, Dec 17

Sunlight Of The Spirit: Mar 24, Apr 27, Jun 28, Oct 25, Dec 12

Surrender: Jan 4, Jan 5, Jan 30, Feb 5, Feb 16, Feb 17, Feb 19, Feb 26, Feb 28, Mar 2, Mar 23, Mar 28, Apr 18, Apr 27, May 10, May 20, Jun 2, Jun 10, Jun 29, Jun 30, Aug 3, Aug 16, Aug 24, Oct 29, Nov 21, Dec 7, Dec 10, Dec 28

Synchronicity: Mar 16, Mar 26, Apr 21, Dec 26

Teachable: Feb 6, Mar 22, May 20, May 22, Jun 10, Jul 8, Sep 27

Telephone: Jan 7, Feb 21, Apr 10, May 13, May 19

Temptation: Feb 16, Mar 10

Terminal Uniqueness: Oct 29

Thinking: Jan 15, Apr 10, Dec 7

Third Step Prayer: Mar 14, Mar 30, Jun 23, Oct 16

This Too Shall Pass: Dec 30

Tolerance: Jan 8, Jan 23, Feb 22, Apr 8, Apr 9, Apr 12, May 4, Jun 4, Jun 12, Jul 27, Oct 21, Oct 23, Dec 26

Tools Of Recovery: Jan 16, Feb 16, Apr 5, Apr 10, Apr 28, May 7, May 16, May 17, Jun 8, Jun 27, Jul 7, Jul 15, Jul 22, Aug 23, Oct 5, Oct 9, Oct 14, Dec 30

Tradition One: Jan 18, May 4, Jun 24, Oct 8, Nov 3, Nov 13, Dec 21

Tradition Two: Feb 15, Jun 21, Jul 26, Nov 29

Tradition Three: Jan 10, Jan 23, Jan 29, Sep 7, Dec 28

Tradition Four: Jun 13

Tradition Five: Jan 10, May 29, Aug 19, Dec 18

Tradition Six: Apr 22

Tradition Seven: Jun 26, Jul 16, Sep 8

Tradition Eight: Sep 18

Tradition Nine: Oct 15

Tradition Ten: Apr 12

Tradition Eleven: Aug 9

Tradition Twelve: Nov 13

Transformation: Jan 15, Mar 13, May 2, May 18, Jul 3, Jul 9, Aug 6, Oct 2, Nov 9, Nov 10, Dec 16, Dec 17

Travel: Aug 14

Triggers: Sep 11

Trust: Jan 17, Mar 7, Mar 17, Mar 31, Apr 14, Apr 27, May 10, May 21, May 26, Aug 12, Aug 21, Aug 31, Sep 27, Oct 6, Nov 21

Trusted Servant: Feb 21, Feb 23, Apr 25, Jun 15, Jun 24, Jul 26, Sep 14, Sep 21

Truth: Feb 11, Apr 16, May 8, Jul 5, Jul 15, Aug 17, Sep 25

C

TWELVE STEPS OF COCAINE ANONYMOUS

1. We admitted we were powerless over cocaine and all other mind-altering substances—that our lives had become unmanageable.

2. Came to believe that a Power greater than ourselves could restore us to sanity.

3. Made a decision to turn our will and our lives over to the care of God *as we understood Him.*

4. Made a searching and fearless moral inventory of ourselves.

5. Admitted to God, to ourselves, and to another human being the exact nature of our wrongs.

6. Were entirely ready to have God remove all these defects of character.

7. Humbly asked Him to remove our shortcomings.

8. Made a list of all persons we had harmed, and became willing to make amends to them all.

9. Made direct amends to such people wherever possible, except when to do so would injure them or others.

10. Continued to take personal inventory and when we were wrong promptly admitted it.

11. Sought through prayer and meditation to improve our conscious contact with God *as we understood Him,* praying only for knowledge of His will for us and the power to carry that out.

12. Having had a spiritual awakening as the result of these Steps, we tried to carry this message to addicts, and to practice these principles in all our affairs.

THE TWELVE STEPS OF ALCOHOLICS ANONYMOUS: 1. We admitted we were powerless over alcohol—that our lives had become unmanageable. 2. Came to believe that a Power greater than ourselves could restore us to sanity. 3. Made a decision to turn our will and our lives over to the care of God *as we understood Him*. 4. Made a searching and fearless moral inventory of ourselves. 5. Admitted to God, to ourselves, and to another human being the exact nature of our wrongs. 6. Were entirely ready to have God remove all these defects of character. 7. Humbly asked Him to remove our shortcomings. 8. Made a list of all persons we had harmed, and became willing to make amends to them all. 9. Made direct amends to such people wherever possible, except when to do so would injure them or others. 10. Continued to take personal inventory and when we were wrong promptly admitted it. 11. Sought through prayer and meditation to improve our conscious contact with God *as we understood Him*, praying only for knowledge of His will for us and the power to carry that out. 12. Having had a spiritual awakening as the result of these steps, we tried to carry this message to alcoholics, and to practice these principles in all our affairs.

D

TWELVE TRADITIONS OF COCAINE ANONYMOUS

1. Our common welfare should come first; personal recovery depends upon C.A. unity.

2. For our group purpose there is but one ultimate authority—a loving God as He may express Himself in our group conscience. Our leaders are but trusted servants; they do not govern.

3. The only requirement for membership is a desire to stop using cocaine and all other mind-altering substances.

4. Each group should be autonomous except in matters affecting other groups or C.A. as a whole.

5. Each group has but one primary purpose—to carry its message to the addict who still suffers.

6. A C.A. group ought never endorse, finance, or lend the C.A. name to any related facility or outside enterprise, lest problems of money, property and prestige divert us from our primary purpose.

7. Every C.A. group ought to be fully self-supporting, declining outside contributions.

8. Cocaine Anonymous should remain forever nonprofessional, but our service centers may employ special workers.

9. C.A., as such, ought never be organized, but we may create service boards or committees directly responsible to those they serve.

10. Cocaine Anonymous has no opinion on outside issues; hence the C.A. name ought never be drawn into public controversy.

11. Our public relations policy is based on attraction rather than promotion; we need always maintain personal anonymity at the level of press, radio, television and films.

12. Anonymity is the spiritual foundation of all our Traditions, ever reminding us to place principles before personalities.

The Twelve Traditions are reprinted with permission of Alcoholics Anonymous World Services, Inc. Permission to reprint and adapt the Twelve Traditions does not mean A.A. is affiliated with this program. A.A. is a program of recovery from alcoholism. Use of the Traditions in connection with programs and activities which are patterned after A.A. but which address other problems does not imply otherwise.

THE TWELVE TRADITIONS OF ALCOHOLICS ANONYMOUS: 1. Our common welfare should come first; personal recovery depends upon A.A. unity. 2. For our group purpose there is but one ultimate authority—a loving God as He may express Himself in our group conscience. Our leaders are but trusted servants; they do not govern. 3. The only requirement for A.A. membership is a desire to stop drinking. 4. Each group should be autonomous except in matters affecting other groups or A.A. as a whole. 5. Each group has but one primary purpose—to carry its message to the alcoholic who still suffers. 6. An A.A. group ought never endorse, finance or lend the A.A. name to any related facility or outside enterprise, lest problems of money, property, and prestige divert us from our primary purpose. 7. Every A.A. group ought to be fully self-supporting, declining outside contributions. 8. Alcoholics Anonymous should remain forever nonprofessional, but our service centers may employ special workers. 9. A.A., as such, ought never be organized; but we may create service boards or committees directly responsible to those they serve. 10. Alcoholics Anonymous has no opinion on outside issues; hence the A.A. name ought never be drawn into public controversy. 11. Our public relations policy is based on attraction rather than promotion; we need always maintain personal anonymity at the level of press, radio and films. 12. Anonymity is the spiritual foundation of all our Traditions, ever reminding us to place principles before personalities.

E

TWELVE CONCEPTS OF COCAINE ANONYMOUS

1. The final responsibility and the ultimate authority for C.A. World Services should always reside in the collective conscience of our whole Fellowship.

2. The C.A. Groups delegate to the World Service Conference the complete authority for the active maintenance of our world services and thereby make the Conference—excepting for any change in the Twelve Traditions—the actual voice and the effective conscience for our whole Fellowship.

3. As a traditional means of creating and maintaining a clearly defined working relation between the Groups, the Conference, the World Service Board of Trustees and its service corporation, staffs, and committees, and of thus insuring their effective leadership, it is here suggested that we endow each of these elements of World Service with a traditional "Right of Decision."

4. Throughout our Conference structure, we ought to maintain at all responsible levels a traditional "Right of Participation," taking care that each classification or group of our world servants shall be allowed a voting representation in reasonable proportion to the responsibility that each must discharge.

5. Throughout our World Service structure, a traditional "Right of Appeal" ought to prevail, thus assuring us that minority opinion will be heard and that petitions for the redress of personal grievances will be carefully considered.

6. On behalf of C.A. as a whole, our World Service Conference has the principal responsibility for the maintenance of our world services, and it traditionally has the final decision respecting large matters of general policy and finance. But the Conference also recognizes that the chief initiative and the active responsibility in most of these matters should be exercised primarily by the Trustee members of the Conference when they act among themselves as the World Service Board of Cocaine Anonymous.

7. The Conference recognizes that the Charter and the Bylaws of the World Service Board are legal instruments; that the Trustees are thereby fully empowered to manage and conduct all of the world service affairs of Cocaine Anonymous. It is further understood that the Conference Charter itself is not a legal document; that it relies instead upon the force of tradition and the power of the C.A. purse for its final effectiveness.

8. The Trustees of the World Service Board act in two primary capacities: (a) With respect to the larger matters of overall policy and finance, they are the principal planners and administrators. They and their primary committees

directly manage these affairs. (b) But with respect to our separately incorporated and constantly active services, the relation of the Trustees is mainly that of custodial oversight which they exercise through their ability to elect all Directors of these entities.

9. Good service leaders, together with sound and appropriate methods of choosing them are at all levels indispensable for our future functioning and safety.

10. Every service responsibility should be matched by an equal service authority—the scope of such authority to be always well-defined, whether by tradition, by resolution, by specific job description or by appropriate charters and bylaws.

11. While the Trustees hold final responsibility for C.A.'s world service administration, they should always have the assistance of the best possible standing committees and service boards, staffs and consultants. Therefore the composition of these underlying committees and service boards, the personal qualifications of their members, the manner of their induction into service, the system of their rotation, the way in which they are related to each other, the special rights and duties of our staffs and consultants, together with a proper basis for the financial compensation of these special workers will always be matters for serious care and concern.

12. General Warranties of the Conference: In all its proceedings, the World Service Conference shall observe the spirit of the C.A. Tradition, taking great care that the Conference never becomes the seat of perilous wealth or power; that sufficient operating funds, plus an ample reserve, be its prudent financial principle; that none of the Conference members shall ever be placed in a position of unqualified authority over any of the others; that all important decisions be reached by discussion, vote, and whenever possible, by substantial unanimity; that no Conference action ever be personally punitive or an incitement to public controversy; that though the Conference may act for the service of Cocaine Anonymous, it shall never perform any acts of government; and that, like the Fellowship of Cocaine Anonymous which it serves, the Conference itself will always remain democratic in thought and action.

THE TWELVE CONCEPTS OF ALCOHOLICS ANONYMOUS: 1. Final responsibility and ultimate authority for A.A. world services shall always reside in the collective conscience of our whole Fellowship. 2. The General Service Conference of A.A. has become, for nearly every practical purpose, the active voice and the effective conscience for our whole Society in its world affairs. 3. To insure effective leadership, we should endow each element of A.A.—the Conference, the General Service Board and its service corporation, staffs, committees, and executives—with a traditional "Right of Decision." 4. At all responsible levels, we ought to maintain a traditional "Right of Participation," allowing a voting representation in reasonable proportion to the responsibility that each must discharge. 5. Throughout our structure, a traditional "Right of Appeal" ought to prevail, so that minority opinion will be heard and personal grievances receive careful consideration. 6. The Conference recognizes that the chief initiative and active responsibility in most world service matters should be exercised primarily by the trustee members of the Conference acting as the General Service Board. 7. The Charter and Bylaws of the General Service Board are legal instruments, empowering the trustees to manage and conduct all of the world service affairs. The Conference Charter is not a legal document; it relies upon tradition and the A.A. purse for final effectiveness. 8. The trustees are the principal planners and administrators of overall policy and finance. They have custodial oversight of the separately incorporated and constantly active services, exercising this through their ability to elect all the directors of these entities. 9. Good service leadership at all levels is indispensable for our future functioning and safety. Primary world service leadership, once exercised by the founders, must necessarily be assumed by the trustee. 10. Every service responsibility should be matched by an equal service authority, with the scope of such authority well defined. 11. The Trustees should always have the best possible committees, corporate service directors, executives, staffs and consultants. Composition, qualifications, induction procedures, and rights and duties will always be matters of serious concern. 12. The Conference shall observe the spirit of the A.A. tradition, taking care that it never becomes the seat of perilous wealth or power; that sufficient operating funds and reserve be its prudent financial principle; that it place none of its members in a position of unqualified authority over others; that it reach all important decisions by discussion, vote, and whenever possible, by substantial unanimity; that its actions never be personally punitive nor an incitement to public controversy; that it never perform acts of government, and that, like the Society it serves, it will always remain democratic in thought and action.

F

MORE ABOUT COCAINE ANONYMOUS

Cocaine Anonymous is a Fellowship of recovering addicts throughout the world whose members meet in local Groups, as well as on the Internet. The following definition of "Cocaine Anonymous" is found in our Fellowship's literature and is often read at meetings of C.A.:

> Cocaine Anonymous is a Fellowship of men and women who share their experience, strength and hope with each other, that they may solve their common problem and help others to recover from their addiction. The only requirement for membership is a desire to stop using cocaine and all other mind-altering substances. There are no dues or fees for membership; we are fully self-supporting through our own contributions. We are not allied with any sect, denomination, politics, organization or institution. We do not wish to engage in any controversy and we neither endorse nor oppose any causes. Our primary purpose is to stay free from cocaine and all other mind-altering substances, and to help others achieve the same freedom.*

C.A. is concerned solely with the personal recovery and continued sobriety of individual addicts who turn to the Fellowship for help. Cocaine Anonymous does not engage in the fields of drug addiction research, medical or psychiatric treatment, drug education, or propaganda in any form—although our members may participate in such activities as individuals.

The maintenance of our recovery depends upon the sharing of our experience, strength and hope with each other, thus helping us to identify and understand the nature of our disease. As the Twelve Steps are our guide to recovery, the Twelve Traditions are our guide to Group unity, growth and discipline. The Twelve Concepts are our guide to Fellowship service structure.

412

For more information about Cocaine Anonymous, please visit our website at www.ca.org or contact us at one of the addresses below:

Cocaine Anonymous World Service Office
P. O. Box 492000
Los Angeles, CA 90049-8000
310-559-5833 Office
800-347-8998 C.A. International Referral Line
e-mail: cawso@ca.org

*Adapted with permission of the A.A. Grapevine, Inc.

G

WORKS CITED

C.A. Books

Hope, Faith & Courage:
Stories from the Fellowship of Cocaine Anonymous

Hope, Faith & Courage Volume II:
Stories and Literature from the Fellowship of Cocaine Anonymous

C.A. Pamphlets

. . . And All Other Mind-Altering Substances
A Guide to the 12 Steps
A Higher Power
A New High from H&I
Being of Service
Choosing Your Sponsor
Crack
Having Fun in Recovery
Newcomer Booklet
Cocaine Anonymous Self-Test
The First 30 Days
The Home Group
Tips for Staying Clean & Sober
To the Newcomer
Tools of Recovery
Unity
What is C.A.?
Yes, *You* Can Start a C.A. Meeting

Other C.A. Materials

C.A. Meeting Format
C.A. NewsGram
C.A. World Service Manual

Other Books

Alcoholics Anonymous, 4th Edition (sometimes referred to herein as the "*Big Book*")

Twelve Steps and Twelve Traditions of Alcoholics Anonymous (sometimes referred to herein as the "*Twelve and Twelve*")

The excerpts from *Alcoholics Anonymous* are reprinted with permission of Alcoholics Anonymous World Services, Inc. ("AAWS"). Permission to reprint these excerpts does not mean that AAWS has reviewed or approved the contents of this publication, or that AAWS necessarily agrees with the views expressed herein. A.A. is a program of recovery from alcoholism *only*—use of these excerpts in connection with programs and activities which are patterned after A.A., but which address other problems, or in any other non-A.A. context, does not imply otherwise.

NOTES